301.43
R896
Rubin

SLC

51348

Mother Butler Library
Marymount Manhattan College
221 East 71st Street, N. Y. 21

A million candles have burned
themselves out. Still I read on.
—Montresor.

D1213099

A Publication of the

CENTER FOR EDUCATION IN LATIN AMERICA

INSTITUTE OF INTERNATIONAL STUDIES

Teachers College, Columbia University

Lambros Comitas, Editor

HQ
199
T7
R82

We Wish
To Be
Looked Upon

*A Study of the Aspirations
of Youth in a Developing Society*

VERA RUBIN

MARISA ZAVALLONI

Center for Education in Latin America
Institute of International Studies
Teachers College, Columbia University

TEACHERS COLLEGE PRESS

Teachers College, Columbia University
New York, New York

COPYRIGHT © 1969 BY TEACHERS COLLEGE, COLUMBIA UNIVERSITY
LIBRARY OF CONGRESS CATALOG CARD NUMBER: 69–19415

SW50/400/4/9/20

MANUFACTURED IN THE UNITED STATES OF AMERICA

Editor's Note

We Wish To Be Looked Upon is the first publication of a series on educational issues sponsored by the Center for Education in Latin America. The series focuses on those political units, those nations, territories, and colonies, commonly referred to as Latin America and the Caribbean. Within this vast area, the constituent societies form a complex and heterogeneous sphere, which, with considerable theoretical difficulty, has been ordered by some social scientists into three culturally distinctive segments.

Putting aside taxonomic arguments, this three-part scheme illuminates the complexity of the area. One subdivision includes the territories and countries of the Antilles and the Circum-Caribbean. Characteristically, these societies contain institutions that bear the imprint of a long colonial heritage and a social legacy from forced connection with the metropoles of Western Europe. Their populations have been derived primarily from Africa, but they also include socially important pockets of people with origins in Europe, China, and the Middle East. This first volume provides an example of one such society, the newly independent country of Trinidad and Tobago. A second subdivision includes those countries, most often located in the highlands of South and Central America, which contain large, culturally viable populations of Amerindians and in which the process of social and cultural integration of native peoples has dramatically influenced the course and form of nation-building. The third subdivision encompasses the societies of the southern, temperate zones of the Western Hemisphere, which demographically and culturally are dominated by the descendants of migrants from Europe.

Within each of these subdivisions of America south of the Rio Grande, the distinctiveness of historical events, the particular patterns of economic exploitation, and the size and complexity of the indigenous population have led to structurally similar forms of social organization and articulation. Social institutions in each of these areas, including those related to education, have taken distinctive forms and carry specific social significance. Consequently, from a substantive point of view, this series attempts not only to bring forth the specifics of formal education, but also to provide materials and analyses that place the educational process in a meaningful context. From this perspective, *We Wish To Be Looked Upon*, an anthropological and social psychological study of one West Indian society, fulfills these objectives with clarity and skill.

Lambros Comitas

Preface

This fine book on the young people of Trinidad—their attitudes, their concerns, their aspirations—needs no introduction from me or anyone else. It speaks for itself, clearly and effectively. The young Trinidadians, too, speak for themselves, giving eloquent testimony about the world in which they live, and the world in which they would like to live.

The fact remains that I was delighted to be asked to write a few introductory words. For one thing, the authors and I have been friends for many years, and although that fact is irrelevant to the content and quality of their work, it adds to my satisfaction at having this opportunity to recommend their work to others.

I can easily—and with some justification—be accused of bias in their favor. The reader will have to decide whether my bias is justified in this case. I found the book not only interesting, but sound and constructive in its methodology; combining a meticulous concern for data with breadth of interpretation. A psychological technique, the autobiography of the future, is subjected to careful content analysis, and the results are presented both clinically and statistically, with the interpretation seen against a background of ethnological information. This appears to me to represent a true interdisciplinary approach, made all the more effective because both authors, the ethnologist and the social psychologist, had considerable knowledge and experience of the other's discipline.

As far as the specific content is concerned, I shall single out only two points for comment. Programs of technical assistance (now more euphemistically called "technical cooperation") have not always been based on an adequate acquaintance with the wishes and values of those who live in a "developing" country. To the extent that educational reforms are to be introduced in Trinidad, either from within or through external aid, or both, the detailed knowledge this book gives us as to what the young people themselves want, should be of the greatest practical value.

Such knowledge leaves us, however, with some complicated, as yet unanswered, questions. One of the most striking findings in this study is the frequency with which young people from relatively underprivileged backgrounds, particularly East Indian and Negro, see their future in terms of grandiose achievement. They hope to become great inventors, winners of the Nobel Prize, leaders of their country. Unfortunately but obviously, most of these hopes will not be realized. What happens then? What will be the consequences of disillusionment? Even if it is true that a man's reach should exceed his grasp, is it psychologically healthy to have such great discrepancy between dreams and possible achievements?

The book discusses these and related problems, but the issues are important enough to deserve further study. I for one am grateful to the authors for drawing our attention to these questions, and for at least showing us the direction in which we may find the answers.

Otto Klineberg

Acknowledgements

We wish to acknowledge the cooperation of the government officials of Trinidad and Tobago in the Ministry of Education who facilitated the research and assisted with the arrangements for administering the 1957 survey. We are most indebted to the principals and teachers at each participating school who arranged for both surveys to be carried out and provided background information for the study. The Central Statistical Office was especially cooperative in providing census data and information on socioeconomic classifications. Intensive discussions were held with people at all levels of public and private life to check various points of information. We cannot acknowledge them all individually here, but we wish to express our deep gratitude for their interest in the research, their constant cooperation, and their generous hospitality to the researchers.

The survey was undertaken as part of a program of Caribbean research launched by the Research Institute for the Study of Man, affiliated at that time with the Department of Anthropology, Columbia University. The major survey instruments were adopted from the international study by Gillespie and Allport of aspirations and attitudes of youth (*Youth's Outlook on the Future*; Doubleday, 1955). The survey in Trinidad was undertaken as an exploration of multi-disciplinary techniques and teamwork, as well as an exploration of various social science hypotheses about social and cultural pluralism. Field work for the first survey was carried out by Ira Greiff, a social psychologist, and by the senior author. Mr. Greiff was responsible for carrying out the sampling procedure and participated in the initial analysis of the data. Major analysis of the data and interpretation of the findings was carried out by the present authors. Analysis of the data and preparation of the manuscript was completed during the tenure of the senior author as Associate in the Center for Education in Latin America, Teachers College, Columbia University. Research and technical assistance have been provided by Donald Dunkenberg, Pina Moneta, Mary Beckwith, Alain Finalteri, Urd Duquesnes, Halle Sissman, and June Murray. Miss Candace Rogers has been extremely helpful in editing the tabulations and providing general editorial suggestions. Joan Geismar served as editorial consultant. At various stages the manuscript has been read by Lloyd Braithwaite, Wilfred Cartey, Lambros Comitas, and Carl Withers, and we are grateful for their comments, but must absolve them of any responsibility for the content or conclusions.

Finally, and foremost, we wish to acknowledge the participation of the students in Trinidad, whose willingness and interest made this study possible. The study is dedicated to them.

Vera Rubin
Marisa Zavalloni

Contents

I

Introduction

For centuries, the Caribbean has played an important part in world history. An unexpected product of the Voyages of Discovery, it became the much-coveted prize of European rivalries for the expansion of colonial empires, the scene of large-scale development of slave-manned sugar plantations, a source of capital for the Industrial Revolution(1), a meeting ground for many races and cultures, and the setting for unprecedented race mixture and transculturation(2). With the decline of the old plantation system in the nineteenth century, world interest in the Caribbean area diminished. In the twentieth century, however, the mechanization of sugar production, new technologies for the refining of minerals, and above all, new political alignments and the rise of nationalism in former colonial areas have once more brought the Caribbean into a larger geopolitical realm.

A fascinating diversity exists within the unity of the Caribbean as a result of differences in metropolitan settlement patterns and economic and political strategy, in the background and composition of New World populations, in the development of island social structures, and in culture contact and the formation

1. See Eric Williams, *Capitalism and Slavery* (Chapel Hill, N.C.: University of North Carolina Press, 1944).

2. Magnus Mörner notes in *Race Mixture in the History of Latin America* (Boston: Little, Brown, 1967) that "No part of the world has ever witnessed such a gigantic mixing of races as the one that has been taking place in Latin America and the Caribbean since 1492" (p. 1). For historical reasons "the Americas became the principal scene of the biological process [of race mixture] " (p. 4); and he adds, "In Latin America miscegenation became an important vehicle in acculturation and very often race mixture and culture mixture coincided" (p. 5).

1

of "Creole cultures"(3). In addition to their intrinsic interest for comparative studies, the small island societies provide a feasible framework for research on linkages between community and national levels of integration and have attracted an increasing number of researchers in recent decades(4).

Trinidad, one of the most ethnically diversified of Caribbean societies, has relatively recently changed from a plantation-based British Crown Colony to an independent nation. Economic development since World War II and the advent of political independence have rapidly modified the social structure, with new statuses emerging for the multi-ethnic population originally derived from many Old World societies. A number of studies have focused on particular segments of the population, emphasizing either cultural retentions and conservatism or cultural assimilation(5). Research on retentions has been undertaken in specific villages, generally based on information from older members of the community, and until recently there has been little documented research from other communities on which to base comparisons(6). The research strategy, used in this study, of an extensive survey among secondary school students provides cross-sectional samples of the population, whose values and attitudes could be studied comparatively.

Studies of the attitudes and aspirations of youth provide a broad perspective on currents of continuity and change; young people reflect both the traditional and the transitional, the established ways of life and the emerging values of the society. In new nations where high goals have been set for social development and broad participation in national life, individual aspirations as well as potentials for achievement are heightened. Ascriptive barriers of class and color are lowered as the social structure is modified and the traditional elite are replaced; levels of living are expected to rise, and aspirations for social mobility permeate all sections of the population. But it is essentially the youth who

3. Vera Rubin (ed.), *Caribbean Studies: A Symposium,* 3rd ed., American Ethnological Society Monograph No. 34 (Seattle: University of Washington Press, 1966).

4. See Vera Rubin and Lambros Comitas, "The Caribbean as an Ethnographic Region; Theories and Methodologies for the Study of Complex Societies" (VII International Congress of Anthropology and Ethnology, Moscow, 1964; mimeographed); and Lambros Comitas, *Caribbeana 1900–1965, A Topical Bibliography* (Seattle: University of Washington Press, 1968).

5. Frances and Melville J. Herskovits, *Trinidad Village* (New York: Alfred A. Knopf, Inc., 1947); Morton Klass, *East Indians in Trinidad: A Study in Cultural Persistence* (New York: Columbia University Press, 1961); Daniel J. Crowley, "Plural and Differential Acculturation in Trinidad," *American Anthropologist, 59* (October 1957), 817–824.

6. Colin Clarke, "Caste among Hindus in a Town in Trinidad: San Fernando"; Barton M. Schwartz, "The Failure of Caste in Trinidad"; and Arthur Niehoff, "The Function of Caste among the Indians of the Oropuche Lagoon, Trinidad," in Barton M. Schwartz (ed.), *Caste in Overseas Indian Communities* (San Francisco: Chandler, 1967).

anticipate the fulfillment of the social promise and bring into focus the range of value systems of the society.

This study(7) is based on two successive surveys of the aspirations of youth which were undertaken in Trinidad and Tobago on the eve of major changes in the sociopolitical situation. The first survey was carried out in 1957, on a representative sample of students in the fifth and sixth forms of thirty schools, including all government and government-assisted secondary schools and several registered private ones(8). One-third of the students in these forms, approximately nine hundred, participated in the first survey(9).

THE RESEARCH INSTRUMENTS

The survey instruments consist of two protocols: (a) the autobiography of the future, in which the respondents are asked, under conditions of anonymity, to write freely about their hopes, plans, and expectations up to the year 2000; and (b) a self-administered questionnaire covering the same dimensions through open-ended and multiple-choice questions. (See Appendix D.) Both protocols were developed by Gillespie and Allport(10) for cross-national studies of values and aspirations of youth, as a method of investigating national similarities and differences in value-orientations as reflected in self-perception and perception of the future.

Between 1949 and 1951, Gillespie and Allport carried out studies of

7. The study was undertaken as part of a program of research and training in the Caribbean, established in 1956 under the auspices of the Research Institute for the Study of Man.

8. Permission to carry out the survey was secured from the Ministry of Education, and an invitation was extended to the secondary schools to participate. Administration of the study was made possible through the courtesy and cooperation of the local school officials. At the time of the first survey there were twenty government and government-assisted secondary schools and twenty-one registered private schools. The survey was administered only in the schools with upper forms. (See Appendix A for a list of schools in the surveys.)

9. Additional data were collected among several hundred students at two training colleges for teachers, an orphanage, and an industrial school in Port of Spain. This data is not included in the present study.

10. Certain modifications were made in administration of the survey in Trinidad and Tobago. Gillespie and Allport allotted approximately one hour for writing the autobiography, but a pilot study in Trinidad indicated that one hour would not be sufficient, and the students were given the entire day to complete both sections. The morning period was devoted to the essay and the afternoon to the questionnaire and a sentence-completion test. The sentence-completion test was devised for the survey, but the data are not included in this analysis. A code number was assigned to each student to match protocols and to check on background data.

university students in ten countries(11). Significant patterns of orientation in these countries were determined by the relative frequency of selected variables. The instrument has since been used by Stoetzel in a survey of Japanese youth(12), by Hyman among Turkish university students(13), by Danziger among South African university students(14), and by Segall among Ugandan high school students(15). Veness independently used an autobiography of the future to assess the aspirations of secondary school leavers in England(16). Cross-national data on students' attitudes is consequently available, adding to the comparative interest of the present findings.

For the second survey the instruments used were basically the same, but a number of questions were omitted, other standardized survey questions were added(17), and several were developed specifically for the Trinidad study in order to clarify some of the results obtained in 1957. (See Appendix D.)

THE SAMPLE

The sampling procedure for the first survey was as follows: alphabetical lists of all the students in each form had been prepared in advance by the staff of each school; on the day of the study, every third name was selected from the school list by the research staff, starting with the first name. In cases of absences, the succeeding name on the list was selected. The students whose names had been drawn were assembled in a separate classroom, and the entire day was set aside for the project(18). At the end of the day, group interviews

11. James M. Gillespie and Gordon W. Allport, *Youth's Outlook on the Future: A Cross National Study* (New York: Doubleday, 1955).

12. Jean Stoetzel, *Without the Chrysanthemum and the Sword* (New York: Columbia University Press/UNESCO, 1955).

13. Herbert H. Hyman, A. Payaslioğlu, and F. W. Frey, "The Values of Turkish College Youth," *Public Opinion Quarterly, 22* (1958), 275–291.

14. Kurt Danziger, "Psychological Future of an Oppressed Group" *Social Forces, 42* (1963), 31–40.

15. Unpublished study.

16. Thelma Veness, *School Leavers: Their Aspirations and Expectations* (London: Methuen, 1962).

17. Rose K. Goldsen, Morris Rosenberg, Robin M. Williams, Jr., and Edward A. Suchman, *What College Students Think* (Princeton, N.J.: Van Nostrand, 1960).

18. The students had never previously taken part in attitude surveys, and in this regard they represent an "unsophisticated" population.

were held with the students, and their views on themes in the study were elicited. Interviews with individual students were also carried out during the course of the study.

The students themselves provided background information on their social class, ethnic reference group, and denominational affiliation. In the first survey each student was asked to state the occupation of his father or the head of the household, and also to specify the degree of his father's or father surrogate's managerial responsibility, the size of business or farm where appropriate, and the monthly income of the family. (See Appendix C.)

The research staff independently classified students on the basis of phenotypic criteria (color of skin, form of features, and hair type) to determine the ethnic membership group, as recognized by the society, rather than racial categories. Ethnic classifications and social class data were checked by the research staff in consultation with the school principal or the faculty member most familiar with the students. In order to delineate ethnic categories as clearly as possible, for comparative purposes, only the essays of students in four major subgroups — colored(19), East Indian, Negro, and white — have been included in this analysis.

In the Caribbean, as in other plantation societies, status has historically been determined by the ascriptive criterion of color as well as by ethnicity. Ethnic classification was consequently used primarily as an indicator of social position, conditioning the similarities of life chances based on ascriptive status. Similarly, social class criteria were used in the Weberian sense as groupings of persons of like life chances. These criteria have been used as independent variables to determine the interaction of group membership, self-identity, and social change, and the ways in which youth in a changing social framework may incorporate or revise traditional patterns in their pictures of themselves and of their place in the society.

The sample in the first survey, used for the present analysis, represents four major ethnic groups(20) — colored, East Indian, Negro, and white — and consists of 725 respondents in the upper forms of the secondary schools, aged sixteen to

19. The category of "colored" is here used to indicate only white-Negro mixtures; other "colored" students — Chinese-Negro, Negro-East Indian, East Indian-white, or other of the mixtures which occur in Trinidad — were eliminated. Cases of "very dark colored students" were also eliminated, as the ethnic membership group could not be clearly established. Chinese students were also eliminated from the final analysis due to the small size of the sample. The census uses the term "mixed" as well as "coloured" to combine all categories of ethnic mixtures. The term "colored" is used here, as in popular usage, to denote the specific Negro-white group.

20. Ethnic groups are listed alphabetically in all tables.

Table 1. Ethnic Composition of First Survey Sample

	Colored	East Indian	Negro	White	Totals
Boys	83	207	139	40	469
Girls	52	72	115	17	256

Table 2. Religious Denomination of First Survey Sample,
by Sex and Ethnicity

Denominations	Colored		East Indian		Negro		White	
	Boys	Girls	Boys	Girls	Boys	Girls	Boys	Girls
Catholic	50	24	26	4	60	34	26	12
Protestant	21	27	62	33	66	79	8	2
Hindu	–	–	71	23	–	–	–	–
Moslem	–	–	43	12	–	–	–	–
Other	–	–	–	–	–	–	–	2
No Answer	12	1	5	–	13	2	4	3
Totals	83	52	207	72	139	115	40	17

Table 3. Socioeconomic Status (SES) Distribution of First Survey
Sample, by Sex and Ethnicity
(in percentage)

Socioeconomic Class(a)	Colored		East Indian		Negro		White	
	Boys (83)	Girls (52)	Boys (207)	Girls (72)	Boys (139)	Girls (115)	Boys (40)	Girls (17)
Class I (Upper SES)	31	33	14	33	15	10	55	82
Class II (Middle SES)	31	22	30	22	22	21	28	–
Class III (Lower SES)	37	45	49	45	54	63	8	–
Not Ascertainable	1	–	7	–	9	6	9	18

a. See Appendix C for construction of the socioeconomic index.

Table 4. Ethnic Composition of Private and Government
School Sample (Boys – First Survey)
(in percentage)

Ethnic Groups	Private	Government and Government-Assisted	
	Form 5 (104)	Form 5 (276)	Form 6 (89)
Colored	9	20	21
East Indian	48	41	26
Negro	41	26	34
White	2	13	19

Table 5. Ethnic Distribution of Boys at Private and Government Schools
(First Survey)
(in percentage)

Schools	Colored (83)	East Indian (207)	Negro (139)	White (40)
Private				
Form 5	10	27	25	2
Government and Government-Assisted				
Form 5	68	59	51	75
Government and Government-Assisted				
Form 6	22	14	24	23

twenty years(21). (See Table 1.) Denominational affiliations, by ethnicity, are presented in Table 2, and the socioeconomic status (SES) distribution of the students, based primarily on the father's occupation, is presented in Table 3.

Type of School Attended

The best educational facilities in Trinidad are provided by government and government-assisted schools. The private schools generally accommodate pupils who could not gain admission to the preferred schools. (See Chapter III.) Both the ethnic composition of the schools and the ethnic distribution of the students at each type of school provide interesting information on the social structure of the island. The boys' sample in the first survey includes 104 fifth-form students in private schools and 276 fifth-form and 89 sixth-form students in government schools. Table 4 gives the ethnic composition of the sample in both types of boys' schools.

Negroes and East Indians, who comprise the majority of the island population(22), represent the largest proportion of students in both types of schools. But they make up almost the entire enrollment in the private schools, while white and colored boys are found mainly in the preferred government and government-assisted schools. The ethnic distribution of the boys at both types of schools may be seen in Table 5.

21. This group corresponds to college freshmen in the United States, which was the sample used in the Gillespie and Allport study. The *Draft Plan for Educational Development in Trinidad and Tobago 1968-1983* (Port of Spain: Government Printery, 1968), hereafter called the Draft Plan, notes that the University of the West Indies is leaning "towards taking on the responsibility for the 6th form work....However, the 6th form course has two advantages which all poor countries should bear in mind − it is cheaper than the University alternative, and it has the merit of selecting those most likely to succeed on a University degree course" (p. 36).

22. See Appendix B for population statistics.

Table 6. Ethnic Composition of Private and Government School Sample
(Girls — First Survey)
(in percentage)

| Ethnic Groups | Private Form 5 (84) | Government and Government-Assisted | |
		Form 5 (119)	Form 6 (53)
Colored	18	23	18
East Indian	18	31	38
Negro	62	36	38
White	2	10	6

Table 7. Ethnic Distribution of Girls at Private and
Government Schools (First Survey)
(in percentage)

Schools	Colored (52)	East Indian (72)	Negro (115)	White (17)
Private Form 5	29	21	46	12
Government and Government-Assisted Form 5	52	51	37	71
Government and Government-Assisted Form 6	19	28	17	17

The proportions attending both types of school are somewhat different for the girls. (See Table 6.) Negro and East Indian girls comprise the majority of the students in the sample, consonant with their proportion of the general population. Negro girls, however, constitute the majority of students in private schools, while white girls, like white boys, make up only 2 per cent of the private school sample. As seen in Table 7, the majority of East Indian girls in the sample are in Form 5 of government-assisted schools, and the majority of Negro girls are in private schools.

THE SECOND SURVEY

One of the unresolved questions of social science research is to what extent expressed attitudes reflect temporary social moods and situations or more persistent characteristics of the sample populations. The question may be resolved through the perspective gained by trend research, collecting information

Table 8. Ethnic Distribution of the Second Survey Sample(a) at
St. Mary's College and Presentation College

	Colored	East Indian(b)	Negro	White
St. Mary's College	19	21	69	25
Presentation College	2	83	13	3
Totals	21	104	82	28

a. Students in other ethnic categories are not included, for comparability with first survey.

b. Religious denominations of East Indian students are as follows: 44 Hindu, 29 Moslem, and 28 Christian.

repeatedly on equivalent samples(23). Although trend studies cannot explain *how* changing social situations may modify attitudes, they can provide information about the effects of change.

It would not have been possible, given the limited resources available, to fully duplicate the survey undertaken in 1957, collecting another representative sample of students in the fifth and sixth forms of thirty schools. It was felt, however, that even a limited sample would provide useful information about attitude trends. Consequently, a second survey was conducted four years later, in 1961, on the eve of Independence, to examine the possibility that shifts in orientation had occurred during this period. This survey was carried out at two boys' schools, St. Mary's College in Port of Spain and Presentation College in San Fernando, which draws on rural areas. Consequently, unlike the sample in the first survey, the sample in the second survey cannot be considered representative of the island-wide student population in Forms 5 and 6. The total sample in the second survey included 353 students, all male; 235 students were classified in the four major ethnic subgroups as in the previous survey and constitute the sample on which the present analysis is based. Their ethnic distribution is shown in Table 8. As may be seen, the majority of colored, Negro, and white students in this sample are from St. Mary's College, while the majority of East Indian students are from Presentation College in San Fernando(24). The sample at St. Mary's College is all from Form 6, and that at Presentation College from Form 5, the highest form at that school.

Socioeconomic stratification of the students in the second survey, presented

23. See Charles Y. Glock (ed.), *Survey Research in the Social Sciences* (New York: Russell Sage Foundation, 1967).

24. Of the 21 East Indian students in the sample at St. Mary's College, 15 are Christian, and 6 are Moslem or Hindu. Of the East Indian students at Presentation College, 67 are Hindu or Moslem and 13 are Christian.

Table 9. Socioeconomic Status (SES) Distribution of
Second Survey Sample, by Ethnicity(a)
(in percentage)

Socioeconomic Class	Colored (21)	East Indian (104)	Negro (82)	White (28)
Class I (Upper SES)	28	5	17	71
Class II (Middle SES)	48	30	55	29
Class III (Lower SES)	19	65	27	–
Not Ascertainable	5	–	–	–

a. Based on the respondents' description of their fathers' occupation.

in Table 9, reveals the same general polarities by ethnic grouping as in the first sample. The majority of white students, 71 per cent, fall in the upper SES and comprise by far the highest percentage of students in Class I. Again, as in the first survey, there are no white students in the lower SES. The majority of East Indian students (especially Hindu and Moslem) are ranked in the lower SES; there is an inverse ratio in class rankings between these groups in both samples(25). The majority of Negro students in the second sample fall in the middle rather than the lower SES. The Negro students, however, still constitute a higher proportion of Class III than the colored students.

In the second survey the questionnaires were administered by local school personnel, which required some modification of the 1957 research procedure: first, the questionnaires were administered to the entire student body in each form instead of to every third student; second, ethnic affiliation of the respondents was obtained through self-classification; third, father's occupation and social class placement were also determined solely through self-rating. As we shall see, despite these differences in sampling and administration, and despite intervening changes in the society as a whole, the findings of the two studies are very consistent.

ANALYSIS OF THE DATA

In their pioneering study, Gillespie and Allport based the analysis of their data primarily on comparison of multiple-choice questions, and only a limited number of variables were derived from the open-ended questions and essays. In the present study a coding system was developed to include as many categories as possible based on the essays and open-ended questions as well as the multiple

25. As has been noted, the second survey was limited to two schools, St. Mary's in Port of Spain and Presentation College in San Fernando. The majority of East Indian students in the sample attend Presentation College and come from rural areas, while the majority of the Negro students attend St. Mary's, the urban school.

choices. For the coding of essays and open-ended questions, reliability was established on the basis of independent coding by three judges. Each category of response (essay, multiple-choice questions, and open-ended questions) thus becomes a dependent variable. Different techniques of statistical analysis were used: comparison of frequencies(26), index construction, factor analysis, and analysis of variance. (See Appendix F.) These different methods were used for multiple analysis of certain variables in order to explore their meaning as fully as possible. Those variables which were not used to establish frequencies were all included in the factor analysis.

The present analysis is based on the protocols of 960 students in both surveys. There was initially some concern that the students might be reluctant to write about themselves and to answer questions freely, but they all responded fully to the questionnaires and the majority wrote profusely about many facets of their lives, present and anticipated. In fact, a number of students expressed their gratification for the chance to write their autobiographies. The opportunity to discuss themselves on the threshold of movement into a new era seemed to open psychological floodgates. As one boy wrote, "In this very eventful era of the 20th century, we face more problems than has ever confronted children of similar ages in previous centuries. All the advantages of the modern world and also more difficulties."

The importance of education to the developing society has been publicly recognized and administratively supported by the present government of Trinidad and Tobago. Various studies of the educational system and of educational needs have been carried out both by UNESCO, at the invitation of the government, and by national committees. The Draft Plan for educational development for the fifteen-year period from 1968 to 1983 observes:

> What are we educating for? We are supposed to produce citizens who are intellectually, morally and emotionally fitted to respond adequately and productively to the varied challenges of life in a multi-racial developing country and to the changes which are being brought about rapidly in the economic foundations of civilization, particularly the challenges of Science and Technology. And we are supposed to anticipate and cater for such inevitable situations such as the disappearance of the totally unskilled labourer, the rapid increase in the body of highly specialized knowledge upon which the world society progresses (in other words the barest educational demands of effective citizenship will be increasing rapidly as well), and the rapid increase in population which will mean (in addition to other influences working towards the same end) and a greater degree of urbanisation of life in the country(27).

26. To test the significance of differences obtained in frequency distributions, chi squares were computed. Differences in frequency distribution indicated in the text are always significant with respect to this measure, at at least .05.

27. Draft Plan, p. 5.

National problems of development and of reorganization of secondary school education, in particular, are viewed in relation to social change:

A secondary system which was born in an era of exclusivism and privilege has been changing rapidly to fit into a system of career open to the talented and of accountability to the public(28).

The meaning of rapid social change to the students, and their definition of the situation, need to be examined against the background of the social history and of the traditional educational institutions of Trinidad and Tobago. The following chapters present the social context, past and present, in which the existential attitudes and projected views of the students may be examined.

28. *Ibid.,* p. 37.

II

Historical Background

On August 31, 1962, the British territory of Trinidad and Tobago became an independent nation. Trinidad, with a population of approximately a million in 1966, and a diversified economy based on sugar, oil refining, and light industry, is the major island of the two and one of the leading countries of the former British West Indies. Similar in certain ways to other Caribbean countries, Trinidad is nevertheless unique in many characteristics and has a distinctive national culture forged by its particular history of settlement and the cultural diversity of its multi-ethnic population.

The social and cultural complexity of contemporary Trinidad developed within the framework of the colonial expansion and plantation systems that mark the history of the region. From its discovery until modern times, the Caribbean has been the scene of international rivalries, of multiple settlements by metropolitan powers, and of intensive migrations. While sharing many features of the historical, social, and economic backgrounds which characterize the area, the complex fabric of Trinidad society was conditioned by its comparatively late development in the colonial period. Discovered by Columbus in 1498 on his third voyage to the West Indies, Trinidad remained for three centuries essentially a colonial outpost under Spanish rule. The conquistadores had come to the New World in search of El Dorado — "not to till the earth like peasants" — but they found no gold in the Trinidad hills. By the sixteenth century, the lure of mineral wealth in Mexico and the discovery of the fabulous silver mines of Alto Peru turned the tide of post-conquest settlement toward the Spanish mainland, and Trinidad became a military garrison to protect imperial interests against rival metropolitan powers. Even if Spanish mercantile policy had favored the internal development of colonies, the heavy forest cover and

13

limited technology in Trinidad discouraged agricultural production; there was no incentive for increasing the small population of Spanish settlers(1).

Given the lack of mineral wealth and disinterest in the development of the agricultural potential, no imperative existed for the expansion of the labor force. The first colonial labor force was recruited primarily from the aboriginal Amerindian population. As elsewhere in the West Indies, the Amerindians were rapidly decimated through exposure to diseases introduced by the settlers(2), through the collision of cultures, and through their harsh treatment under the system of enforced labor. The first instances of slavery in the New World stem from the Spanish-Amerindian contact(3).

The coming of the Spanish was the first trickle of an Old World migration that was to create a remarkable cultural crossroads in the New World. By 1797 only some 1,080 Amerindians remained in Trinidad(4), but a new series of migrations had started. The motivating force for settlement had shifted throughout the Caribbean to the development of crops for the European market — tobacco, cocoa, spices — and, ultimately, to the intensive cultivation of sugar. As it turned out, the cultivation of sugarcane, which Columbus had introduced in Hispaniola, was to have a far greater impact on both the Old and New Worlds than the search for gold. Sugar determined the course of West

1. It is conjectured that about 300,000 Spanish arrived in Spanish America in the sixteenth century. See Magnus Mörner, "The History of Race Relations in Latin America: Some Comments on the State of Research," *Latin American Research Review, 1* (Summer 1966), 19. There were only 326 Spaniards in the capital city of Trinidad in 1772. See Eric Williams, *History of the People of Trinidad and Tobago* (London: Deutsch, 1964), p. 28.

2. "The mortality was most striking and drastic with the densely settled population of the Greater Antilles when the Spanish first landed." See Philip Curtin, "Epidemiology and the Slave Trade," *Political Science Quarterly, 83* (1968), 200, for a discussion of epidemiology and demography in the colonization of the New World.

3. The first philosophical concern with the implications of slavery came from the writings and mission activities of Bartolemé de las Casas, a Dominican friar and Protector of the Indians, who argued that "the Indians were truly men capable of becoming Christians." See Lewis Hanke, "The Dawn of Conscience in America: Spanish Experiments and Experiences with Indians in the New World," *Proceedings of the American Philosophical Society, 107* (April 1963), 90.

4. Eric Williams, *History of the People of Trinidad and Tobago,* p. 47. James Millette reports that there were 2,082 Indians in 1781 ("The Founding of a New Society — Trinidad 1783-1810" [typescript, 1966], p. 15). See also Irving Rouse, "The Arawak," in Julian H. Steward, *Handbook of South American Indians,* Smithsonian Institution, Bureau of American Ethnology Bulletin 143 (Washington, D.C.: Government Printing Office, 1948) *4,* 518–519.

Indian history and conditioned the development of Creole(5) institutions, as it also conditioned the course of European capitalism and colonialism(6).

With the ascendancy of rival metropolitan powers – especially Britain – in the Caribbean, the Spanish foothold in Trinidad was threatened. In 1783, in a belated effort to secure the area and establish a colony of permanent settlers, incentives for colonization were offered to French planters from neighboring islands seeking a political haven. The first French immigrants to Trinidad had arrived from St. Lucia in 1777 with African slave labor to set up small estates for the cultivation of sugar, coffee, cotton, and cocoa. The first sugar factory was established in 1787; by 1789 the population had increased to approximately eighteen thousand(7). The French settlement consisted of planters, technicians, and slaves who provided both field labor for the estates(8) and domestic service for the great houses. Given the sociopolitical vacuum in the colony, the effect of the new settlement was to set up "a French State within a Spanish State"(9). The social structure of the small estates made possible closer personal contacts between masters and slaves than on the larger overseer-managed plantations later established by the British. French cultural influence in Trinidad, starting in this period, has been much greater than the actual numbers of settlers would indicate.

The sweep of British colonial expansion in the Caribbean did not reach Trinidad until 1797, when the British seized the island from the Spanish without a battle. Formal acquisition took place in 1802, under the Treaty of Amiens, just five years before the abolition of the slave trade. At the time of the British conquest, only one twenty-fifth of the island (approximately 36,000 acres) was under cultivation, and the labor force was correspondingly small, consisting of

5. "Creole" literally signifies anything native to the area, and by extension to populations born in the New World. The term is generally applied to Negroes in the West Indies. When it is applied to native-born Europeans, it is generally hyphenated, as in "French-Creole." The term, however, is never applied to native-born East Indians.

6. Williams, *Capitalism and Slavery.*

7. 2,151 whites, 4,467 free colored, 2,200 Indians, and 10,000 slaves (Millette, p. 29).

8. In 1797 there were 159 sugar estates producing 7,800 hogsheads of sugar (Williams, *History of the People of Trinidad and Tobago,* p. 47). By 1807 there were about 300 sugar factories operated by mule, wind, or water power.

9. *Ibid.,* p. 40.

10,009 Negro slaves out of a population of 17,718(10), a labor force far smaller than in many other islands(11). As Spanish policy had not been geared to internal development, and French interests in the brief period of settlement had been oriented toward the development of the small estate, Trinidad was not yet a plantation society. The British, however, were concerned with the expansion of monocrop production of sugar as the basis of wealth from the colonies and undertook the intensive exploitation of land under the plantation system. Consequently, with the abolition of the slave trade in 1807, a severe labor shortage occurred. There had been active intervention to forestall or modify this legislation, but, "Frantic efforts by the British planting and mercantile interests connected with the Island to show that Trinidad because of the recency of its plantation development would be peculiarly and disastrously affected by the proposed abolition had failed" (12).

As a result of Britain's late acquisition of Trinidad — on the eve of the abolition movement — a new system for recruiting plantation labor had to be devised. After the abolition of the slave trade in 1807, various attempts were made to recruit labor, both legally and extralegally, but without much success. Several thousand slaves were brought in from other islands, supposedly as domestic servants, and other illicit means of securing slave labor for the plantations were attempted. As the emancipation movement was gaining momentum, schemes were tried to recruit a labor force among Portuguese, free Africans, and Amerindians from other areas, and in 1806 and 1807 several hundred Chinese were imported as contract workers. For a variety of reasons, none of these migrants proved suitable for plantation requirements. Some returned to their homeland; some remained, turned to other pursuits, and became permanent settlers, contributing to the heterogeneity of the population but not to the ranks of the plantation labor force. It had been estimated that some 250,000 slaves would be required to place all the arable land of the island

10. A British survey printed on a map titled "Plan of the Isle of Trinidad from actual surveys made in the year 1797" (London: Robert Laurie and James Whittle, 1800) lists the population as follows:

	Whites	Colored	Slaves	Indians	Totals
Men	994	1,196	4,164	305	6,659
Women	590	1,624	3,505	401	6,120
Boys	301	898	1,232	190	2,621
Girls	266	758	1,108	186	2,318
TOTALS	2,151	4,476	10,009	1,082	17,718

11. Curtin points out that the "fundamental development of plantation slavery in the Americas took place . . . in Tropical America" ("Epidemiology and the Slave Trade," p. 191). See also Rubin, *Caribbean Studies*.

12. Millette, p. 351.

under cultivation; however, in 1808 there were only 21,895 slaves out of a total population of 31,478. After the Act of Emancipation in 1833, it was evident that "Trinidad contained a potential planters' frontier at the time of emancipation, but it could only move forward with a large supply of imported labor" (13).

During the parliamentary debates in London on the slave trade in Trinidad, various settlement schemes were proposed to solve the labor problem. George Canning, an abolitionist, saw the abolition of the slave trade "as a first step towards the construction of a society based not on coercion and cruelty, but on freedom and liberty." To offset slave labor, he urged

> the encouragement of new classes of settlers to cultivate Trinidad; peons from the South American mainland, free blacks and creoles from the other islands and an intelligent encouragement of the labour and industry of Trinidad's native Indians and soldiers of regiments stationed in the West Indies, irrespective of whether they were British or foreign; it mattered only that they were free(14).

The idea of recruiting settlers from India, again primarily as small peasant cultivators, had been suggested as early as 1814. The scheme for small settlers reflected the original colonization scheme which Cromwell had envisaged in the "Western Design" in the mid-seventeenth century. Small-scale cultivation in Trinidad, however — as elsewhere in the British Caribbean — was to be superseded by plantation cultivation, which offered the inducement of large profits as sugar became a lucrative commodity on the world market. This development was forseen as early as 1799:

> Trinidad should be regarded as a sugar Colony, the lands being generally more favourable to the production of Cane, than of Coffee or Cotton. The quantity of land to be granted should certainly depend upon the means of cultivation, but everything considered the smallest class of sugar plantation cannot consist of less than 200 acres of good land, of which 100 acres for cane, 50 for pasture, and 50 for Negro grounds, establishments and Casualties. A plantation of this class carried on with the greatest economy will require a capital of about £8,000 sterling(15).

The small cultivator obviously did not have the means to fulfill such requirements, and, furthermore, post-Emancipation legislation was designed to

---

13. Philip D. Curtin, *The Image of Africa* (Madison: University of Wisconsin Press, 1964), pp. 439–440.

14. Quoted in Millette, p. 136.

15. Dispatch from Colonel Pictin, first Governor of Trinidad, to the Secretary of State on July 30, 1799, quoted in Williams, *History of the People of Trinidad and Tobago*, p. 74.

discourage the development of a class of small cultivators and peasants(16). Political as well as economic considerations undoubtedly came to the fore as the new British colony found itself with a population predominantly "foreign" in origin in that the French, Spanish, Corsican, and free colored outnumbered the British(17). The Haitian revolution had stirred the planters' latent fears about slave revolts, and not only the slaves but also the free colored population and some of the French settlers were seen as potential threats to the British plantocracy(18). Consequently, the encouragement of a small, self-sufficient peasantry might be a threat to the political order in addition to creating serious competition for scarce labor resources.

The planters were to prevail in their search for a suitable large-scale labor force. Trinidad's requirements for plantation labor coincided with severe economic problems in India, and a system of indentured Indian immigration was established in 1844. It was recorded that "East Indians first set foot in the country on Friday, 10th May 1845" (19). That was the beginning of an Indian migration to Trinidad which was to continue until 1917. Spurred by recruitment drives, the early trickle of immigration became a rapid stream within a few decades.

Under the indenture system, the Caribbean received about a half-million Indian laborers, of whom approximately 143,000 came to Trinidad in due

16. "Burnley tells how, in Trinidad, squatters had been encouraged before emancipation to settle on Crown lands, but immediately after emancipation the planters tried to eject the squatters in order 'to condense and keep together the population in such a manner that it may always contain a due proportion of labourers;' and the government itself collaborated in this policy 'by diminishing the facilities of obtaining land . . . by fixing the price of fresh land so high as to place it above the reach of the poorest class of settlers' " (John Horace Parry and Philip M. Sherlock, *A Short History of the West Indies* [New York: St. Martin's Press, 1956], p. 238).

17. The heterogeneous character of the population initially had been set when the British declared Port of Spain a free port in 1797. French settlement, the lure of the new colony for settlers from other islands, especially the free colored, had further diversified the population. (See Williams, *History of the People of Trinidad and Tobago*, pp. 67ff.) Millette points out that during the early period of settlement, "legal sanction was given to non-white planters as a property owning class." He states that "the security and scope which Trinidad offered to the non-white property owners was unrivalled" (Millette, pp. 307 and 32).

18. Millette, *passim.*

19. Carlton Robert Ottley, *The Story of Port of Spain* (Trinidad: The Author, 1962), p. 69. Judith Ann Weller cites May 30, 1845 as the first day of arrival in "A Study of the Regulation of the East Indian Incentive System in Trinidad, 1845-1917" (Doctoral dissertation, Columbia University, 1965), p. 46.

course(20). By 1883 they constituted one-third of the population(21) and were engaged almost entirely as estate laborers. In 1960, East Indians constituted 37.9 per cent of the population(22), and it has been estimated that by 1975 they will constitute one-half of the population(23).

THE SOCIAL STRUCTURE OF THE COLONIAL SOCIETY

At the time of Emancipation in 1833, as Williams points out, Trinidad was not yet a plantation society(24). The large-scale introduction of indentured workers from India made possible the development of the plantation system which dominated the economic and social organization of the territory. Political controls were maintained under the Crown Colony system, which reserved all essential powers to the British government. The Crown Colony had been established in 1810 on the premise that the territory was incapable of self-government, since the majority of the freeborn population was nonwhite, and less than half of the whites were British(25).

The question of constitutional development of the colony was considered in the light of metropolitan interests, continued international rivalries, and British cultural exclusiveness. In relatively mild language, it was stated that "An Assembly was inadmissable in a Community such as Trinidad where the numbers

20. G. W. Roberts and J. Byrne list 143,939 migrants from India in the period from 1845-1918 in "Summary Statistics on Indenture and Associated Migration Affecting the West Indies, 1834–1918," *Population Studies, 20* (July 1966), 127. Weller lists 141,615 in the period from 1845 to 1917 (p. 239).

21. Parry and Sherlock, p. 237.

22. *Eastern Caribbean Population Census, 1960: Trinidad and Tobago* (Port of Spain: Central Statistical Office, 1963). East Indians constitute 36.5 per cent of the total population of Trinidad and Tobago, but there are only 437 East Indians in Tobago; the percentage is given for Trinidad alone. See also George W. Roberts, "Populations of the Non-Spanish-Speaking Caribbean," in *Pan-American Assembly on Population* (Cali, Colombia, 1965), *Population Dilemma in Latin America* (Washington, D.C.: Potomac Books, 1966), pp. 61-85.

23. See Selwyn Douglas Ryan, "Decolonization in a Multiracial Society: A Case Study of Trinidad and Tobago" (Doctoral dissertation, York University, Toronto, 1967), p. 485.

24. The slave population consisted of 17,439 individuals; the average of only seven slaves per slave owner is indicative of small holdings in comparison with the other islands in the area (Williams, *History of the People of Trinidad and Tobago,* pp. 84 ff).

25. See Parry and Sherlock, p. 211, for a discussion of the view that it would be "easier to protect the people of colour" and enforce the abolition of the slave trade under the Crown Colony system.

of white foreigners were substantially larger than those of British descent" (26). A more impassioned position held that the population was composed of a "motley and pyebald crew of English, French, Spanish, Italians, Genoese and Corsicians, needy adventurers, men of desperate fortune and uncultivated intellects" (27). The British were clearly in a minority and the political philosophy of the times reflected this: "because of the differences in language, customs and heritage, representative government was unthinkable" (28). Cultural differences were used to buttress the case for central colonial controls in the initial stages of constitutional development.

Aside from the implications of political control from abroad, Crown Colony government meant that most positions in government and civil service were held by English expatriates rather than by the native population; the development of a politically effective Creole middle class was inhibited. Britain was the mother country; the local governing group was made up of British nationals, and the influential planters and commercial interests were British. The British were the power elites, and the British model became the normative pattern for the society, especially for the status-conscious free coloreds.

In the plantation society based on sugar and slavery, one out of every ten slaves was a domestic slave (a much higher ratio than on the other sugar islands) and thus had the possibility of closer proximity to the styles of life of the master. House slaves were generally in closer contact with the masters and the culture of the masters than the field slaves. They received a modicum of education and some were manumitted before passage of the Act of Emancipation; they constituted a slave elite. Close contiguity also engendered race mixtures and the formation of new racial types. Planters and overseers commonly took female house slaves as their concubines or mistresses(29), and their offspring created a new social as well as racial group(30). These "free men of color" were predominantly offspring of Spanish or French fathers and Negro slave mothers. Although the British were reputedly more aloof in their relations

26. Millette, p. 307.

27. *Ibid.*, p. 308. In 1802 the population consisted of 1,166 Indians, 19,709 slaves, 5,275 free colored, and 2,261 whites. Of the latter, 663 were British, while 1,598 were of "foreign" origin. The free colored population was also predominantly foreign in origin; 599 were British, 1,751 Spanish, and 2,925 French (Millette, p. 184).

28. *Ibid.*, p. 182.

29. Mörner maintains that sexual exploitation was one of the two main functions of slavery. A significant demographic and economic factor must be added; the slave population was not self-sustaining, partly due to sex imbalance; there was also an imbalance in the sex ratio of the European population (*Race Mixture in the History of Latin America*).

30. When Britain acquired Trinidad in 1797, there were 4,476 "free people of color" in the colony (Williams, *History of the People of Trinidad and Tobago*, p. 47). By 1808, the number had increased to 5,450, while the white population comprised only 2,476 persons.

with female slaves than the Spanish or French, they nevertheless also fathered the progeny of slave women and frequently provided for their racially mixed offspring.

Metropolitan concepts of individual achievement may have become social goals superseding ascriptive values for the emerging class of ex-slaves, but attainment was limited to the few. In the flood of proposals following the abolition of the slave trade, the idea was put forth that "the condition of the free people of colour should be improved, their privileges should be increased and their education facilitated since 'it is considered that upon the felicity and attachment of this class of Inhabitants the Security and Prosperity of the West India Islands may hereafter greatly depend' "(31). By the mid-nineteenth century there had emerged a small but well-defined colored middle class that was set apart from the lower class of Negroes socially and culturally as well as phenotypically(32). And while following the life styles and cultural norms of the dominant whites, they were nevertheless also set apart from them. They were a definable group which performed needed services in the society, but as elsewhere in the British Caribbean status was determined by the ascriptive values of color:

> The influence of these ascriptive values made it impossible for the small intermediate group of people of mixed blood to bridge the social distance between the classes above and below them, because they were too alienated, both from the blacks and from the whites, by the inescapable significance attached to colour in the communal life of the slave society(33).

The social structure had assumed a pyramidal form, with a very small white upper class at the top, a small middle group comprising the colored as well as the "second rank of whites"(34), and a broad lower-class base of the black population(35). The upper class consisted of the large-scale planters and proprietors, members of the major commercial and managerial groups, and those who occupied high government posts. The "second rank of whites" comprised overseers, lower officials in government and commerce, small planters, and the

31. Millette, p. 372. Regarding this and the general liberalization called for in the proposals, Millette notes that nothing was done by way of implementation: "Metropolitan indifferences and colonial dissension had once again been the death of good intentions" (p. 373).

32. "Peau noir, masque blanc, a black skin, a white mask, a European culture in a Afro-Asian environment" (Williams, *History of the People of Trinidad and Tobago*, p. 41).

33. Elsa V. Goveia, *Slave Society in the British Leeward Islands at the End of the Eighteenth Century* (New Haven: Yale University Press, 1965), p. 323.

34. Goveia, p. 314.

35. Lloyd Braithwaite, "Social Stratification in Trinidad," *Social and Economic Studies*, 2, 2–3 (1953), 44 and *passim*.

51348

like. The colored middle-class group included some small landholders and those for whom light color and education had opened channels for social mobility; they shunned manual labor yet were circumscribed in their range of achievement. They were generally employed in white-collar and professional occupations — teaching, minor civil service posts, commercial clerkships and the like, and, eventually, in medicine and law. There were few, if any, independent colored entrepreneurs. The absence of entrepreneurial interests and skills in the colored middle class is one of the footnotes of colonial history that would make an interesting comparative study. Apparently planters in all metropolitan groups were reluctant to impart entrepreneurial skills to their mixed progeny. The colonies needed teachers, clerks, doctors, lawyers, and some civil servants which the mother country could not provide, but large-scale business enterprise was presumably to be undertaken only by expatriates. The values of the "Protestant Ethic" to be imparted to the slave and ex-slave population were honesty, loyalty, and industry, not thrift or capital accumulation for independent enterprise. The influence of the missionaries in this respect is noteworthy: they were able to foster in their converts "the practice of Christian virtues, such as diligence, honesty, obedience and fidelity, which would make the converted Negro a better slave"(36). Evidently, other attributes of the "Protestant Ethic" theoretically linked with the development of capitalism, such as austerity for the sake of ultimate accumulation of wealth for investment, were not inculcated in either the slave or free population presumably because this would not have been advantageous for the planter class. Limited interest in entrepreneurship is historically evident in many former colonies. Small capitalistic enterprises in Trinidad were introduced by outsiders — Syrians, Lebanese, and Chinese, and eventually by the East Indians.

After Emancipation, the Negro lower class consisted of unskilled and semiskilled laborers, rural and urban, peasants and proletarians. Lamming has said that "to be black in the West Indies is to be poor"(37). To be black in the West Indies also meant to be disenfranchised, to be cut off from existing channels of mobility, and to be at a disadvantage psychologically. The concept of the "white man's burden," which provided a psychological as well as ideological underpinning for the colonial system, became imbedded in pseudo-scientific concepts of racial superiority. By the early nineteenth century, the reciprocal concept of Negro inferiority was firmly entrenched among most Europeans, and "a heavy emphasis on racial particularism characterized the entire social order"(38). A "pigmentocracy"(39) had undoubtedly existed since

36. Goveia, p. 324.

37. George Lamming, *The Pleasures of Exile* (London: Michael Joseph, 1960), p. 53.

38. Goveia, p. 312.

39. Some historians (Tannenbaum, Elkins, Freyre) have developed an idealization of Latin American slavery *vis à vis* Anglo-Saxon slavery on the grounds that (a) the Iberians

the Spanish colonial period, and the plantation-slavery system created binding color-class correlations. Although, with the rise of the colored middle class, cultural and social characteristics became status symbols almost as significant as phenotype, historical factors had "favored the general acceptance of race as a determinant of both individual and group status"(40).

The feeling of insecurity was perhaps greatest among the colored groups insofar as they had no economic or political power as a social class, although they were in favored positions individually. Furthermore, they were separated from both the blacks and the whites, socially and psychologically; relationships with lower-class blacks seemed unthinkable, and actual equality with upper-class white Europeans was unattainable. Lines of social stratification are not so rigid in real life as they appear to be in social analysis since some individuals are always able to straddle the barriers. Nevertheless, in the context of the sugar society of Trinidad, whiteness generally placed the individual at the top of the social order and blackness at the bottom(41), and white Europeans set the "somatic norm-image" for the society(42). By the mid-nineteenth century, Trinidad, with its heterogeneous population, had assumed the social class configuration of the classic plantation society(43).

East Indian migrants were thus introduced into a social order based on traditional Caribbean color class ascriptions, where achievement was highly circumscribed. At the outset of the immigration, status ascription for East Indians was determined by the indenture system. In fact, they were regarded as

---

were already experienced with Moors and had no color prejudice, and that (b) Catholicism was essentially more humanistic than Protestantism. There is now conflicting evidence with regard to the application of the "humanistic" Spanish slave code, which inspired Tannenbaum's thesis. Essentially differences in slave-master relations were conditioned by ecological factors in the plantation society (see Mörner, "The History of Race Relations in Latin America," p. 30 and *passim,* and Williams, *History of the People of Trinidad and Tobago*). Moreover, it has been demonstrated that the Spanish colonial situation and relations with the existing subordinated groups gave rise to a "pigmentocracy" (see Alejandro Lipschütz, *El Indoamericanismo y el Problema racial en las Américas,* 2nd ed. [Santiago de Chile: Nascimento, 1944]).

40. Goveia, p. 314.

41. Braithwaite, "Social Stratification in Trinidad," p. 46.

42. Harry Hoetink, " 'Colonial Psychology' and Race," *Journal of Economic History, 21* (1961), 629–640.

43. Vera Rubin (ed.), *Plantation Systems of the New World* (Washington, D.C.: Pan American Union and Research Institute for the Study of Man, 1959). Curtin refers to the plantation "complex of commerce and production" as the "South Atlantic System" ("Epidemiology and the Slave Trade," p. 191).

being outside of the social system(44). Called "East Indians," presumably to distinguish them from Amerindians, they were thus also distinguished from West Indians. They were "coolie"(45) laborers doing work previously done by slaves, and their status was not very much higher than that of slaves. The long, arduous voyage around the Cape of Good Hope, the conditions of the passage overseas(46) – *kalapani*, the "dark waters" – the substandard barracks life on the estates, and the rigorous conditions of indenture are still compared to the Middle Passage and to slavery by descendants of the immigrants.

The original indenture ordinance had guaranteed free return passage to India after the five-year period of indenture was served. Although many immigrants enlisted for a second term on the plantation, many initially availed themselves of the opportunity to return(47). However, as a result of changing conditions in the colony, and probably also because of the relaxation of caste orthodoxy in Trinidad, the number returning to India steadily decreased, and by 1902 "only about one in five persons completing indenture chose to return"(48). Those who chose permanent settlement outnumbered those who sought repatriation. In fact, "many returned to Trinidad a second and third time," including "some who had originally been indentured elsewhere in the Caribbean – and the number who re-emigrated from India steadily increased"(49).

Public opposition to the free return passages had mounted during the 1850's, both for financial reasons and because of continuing labor requirements. To mitigate the situation, some planters reluctantly permitted Indian laborers to buy small plots of land in exchange for the return passage to India. In 1878 the Trinidad Planters' Association was protesting the settlement of East Indians on the land, but the vacillation of the sugar economy created new social trends. Declining prices of sugarcane on the world market in the late nineteenth century, resulting from competition with beet sugar, led to the decline of the indenture system. To offset the consequences of the depression in the sugar market and the great expenditure which repatriation would entail, the West

44. Braithwaite, "Social Stratification in Trinidad," p. 49.

45. "The term coolie appears to have been borrowed from Tamil: Kuli equals a porter, laborer. Said to have been first used by Dr. Pritchard to designate persons of the laboring class." See Dwarka Nath, *A History of Indians in British Guiana* (London and New York: Thomas Nelson and Sons, 1950), p. 10.

46. Despite regulations to check the health of emigrants at the depots and on shipboard, there was a high mortality rate on the ships (Weller, *passim*).

47. Roberts and Byrne, p. 132.

48. Weller, p. 186.

49. *Ibid.*, pp. 195–196. Weller also notes: "it must have been hard for those persons to assume these traditionally subordinate positions in a village in India – after life and work in an island where the chance to better themselves was more easily attainable" (pp. 197–198).

Indian Commission of 1897 advocated the transfer of land to individual cane growers. The Trinidad Workingman's Association opposed the continuation of the indenture system on the grounds that there was a sufficient labor force in the country, and by the turn of the century opposition to the indenture system began to mount in India and England as well as in Trinidad. Indenture became an outworn policy in the economic and social climate of the period(50). A class of small East Indian proprietors was formed; cultivating cane on the "gayap"(51) system they could sell their crop below estate prices and acquire cash while also cultivating rice and other subsistence crops.

The East Indian migrants to Trinidad had come mainly from Bengal, the United Provinces, and Madras. Lower-caste "coolies" were considered the most desirable for plantation work and were consequently recruited more frequently(52); however, there were members of all the varnas among the migrants. The emigrants had little idea of the physical or social or cultural conditions they would find in Trinidad. The colony was also unprepared to receive the Indian immigrants; little was known of their languages or customs, and there was no compulsion to ease the culture shock which they must have experienced: "it was almost as though, in the British mind, the fact that both India and Trinidad were part of the Empire, reduced the Indians' problems merely to that of accommodating themselves to a new environment"(53).

Restrictive laws had militated against the rise of a peasantry in order to ensure a plantation labor force, but they became increasingly difficult to enforce. By the end of the century, many had succeeded in becoming free peasants. East Indians, however, whether peasants or plantation workers, were still considered socially "outcaste," a subordinate minority group, partly because they could not attain the middle-class requirements of education. While much of the lack of integrative social legislation in Trinidad has, for over a century, been attributed to cultural diversity – the "motley and pyebald crew" has repeatedly been invoked as a rationale – the very absence of integrative institutions has provided the base for a "self-fulfilling prophecy." It has been postulated that minorities "are differentiated from the majority by unequal access to social resources"(54), and this is substantiated in the history of ethnic groups in Trinidad as social rather than numerical "minorities." During the nineteenth

50. *Ibid.*, p. 199, note.

51. *Gayap* is the Creole term for cooperative work group.

52. Weller states that "it is obvious that the majority of those who came to Trinidad were 'Sudra' " (p. 225).

53. *Ibid.*, p. 137.

54. Eric Wolf, Review of Emerich Francis, *Ethnos und Demos: Soziologische Beiträge zur Volkstheorie, American Anthropologist, 68* (October 1966), 1258–1259.

century East Indians had been effectively cut off from the possibility of achieving status through education, thus fulfilling the lower status "prophecy"; but as they achieved their first freedom from the indenture system by establishing themselves as a peasantry, the "coolies," like the Creoles, began to seek educational avenues of achievement for their children. The spread of East Indians through the social and occupational strata of Trinidad society was to take almost a century.

Early relations between lower-class East Indians and Negroes were conditioned by the structure of the society(55). The availability of a large, low-paid labor force through the indenture system effectively discouraged a Negro labor force on the plantations and generally threatened the wage structure for unskilled and semiskilled labor(56). Legislative restrictions had discouraged the cultivation of cash crops and the development of a Negro peasantry; however, small plots for cocoa cultivation were probably sold more readily to East Indians in order to offset commitments for return passages to India. While Negroes shunned the plantations, the East Indian small holder would still remain a seasonal plantation worker. Furthermore, relations between Negroes and East Indians were adversely affected by the fact that a third of the cost of return passages was to come from public funds, in addition to the expenses of administering the indenture system(57).

The existence of real economic grievances, even though displaced onto ethnic group stereotypes, is documented in various Royal Commission Reports at the end of the century(58). These reports also document the social distance and the cultural cleavages engendered by the plantation society. "Coolie culture," as in British Guiana, "became a mark of low status in the eyes of the white upper status group, as well as of the coloured and black lower status groups"(59).

55. Williams notes that "the Caribbean was historically the first area in the world which saw the emergence of the modern problem of race relations – the pattern of race relations was worked out in the context of a system of unfree labour" (*The Historical Background of Race Relations in the Caribbean* [Port of Spain: The Author, 1955], p. 3.)

56. Gordon Lewis observes that "the harsh servitude of the indenture system, at once technologically inefficient and socially degrading . . . operated as a cheap labour-recruiting scheme" which created racial separatism and proletarian disunity (*The Growth of the Modern West Indies* [New York: Monthly Review Press, 1968]), pp. 200–201.

57. As Williams points out, indenture "was financed . . . part by the taxes of the very emancipated slaves with whom the new workers were to compete" (*History of the People of Trinidad and Tobago*, p. 101).

58. Vera Rubin, "Culture, Politics and Race Relations," *Social and Economic Studies, 11* (1962), 433–455.

59. Chandra Jayawardena, *Conflict and Solidarity in a Guianese Plantation* (London: Athlone Press, 1963), p. 17.

Isolated in barracks communities(60), with substandard styles of life and low levels of health, uncertain themselves whether settlement would be temporary or permanent, with no stake in the greater society, considered aliens and disdained by the enclaving society, they constituted a marginal immigrant group, which had to develop its own mechanisms of adaptation.

Both slavery and the indenture system had uprooted vast populations from their traditional societies; however, the acculturation of Africans and of Indians differed with the different structural and historical requirements of each system. While "all these, Africans and Indians, were men who had lost a country"(61), the East Indians were able to retain their cultural identity as an ethnic group, the family system tended to remain intact, and their marginal position fostered cultural cohesion. Although caste lines had been blurred by immigration and indenture, they found themselves in the position of outcastes in the new society and, "Isolation of the coolies during the indenture period helped to form Indian group consciousness"(62). The temporary character of initial immigration was an important factor in limiting levels of integration(63).

Slavery as a social institution had systematically undermined the African culture heritage by mixing individual slaves from different tribal and linguistic groups in order to offset the possibility of revolts. Related slaves were systematically separated, and, since marriage was not permitted, there was little possibility for the development of extended family loyalties. In order to be made tractable for plantation work, slaves had to undergo a three-year period of "seasoning" for acculturation to the new society(64). The language of the masters became the new lingua franca, and the manners of the masters became the ideal pattern of behavior. The structure of the slave society permitted few traditional elements of culture to be retained other than those which seemed to hold no inherent threat to the institution of slavery. Slavery was a swift, if

60. Jayawardena remarks that "the complete isolation of the plantation and the coolies was indeed the most striking feature of the social system of the plantation system during and even after the indenture period" (p. 16).

61. Philip M. Sherlock, "Prospects in the Caribbean," *Foreign Affairs, 41* (1963), 745.

62. Jayawardena, p. 27.

63. As Hart noted in 1866, in commenting on the difference in acculturation between Chinese and Indian immigrants: "The Indians have an idea 'of returning' to their native land [which] causes them to stand aloof from all Christian influences. The Chinese who has no such prospect before him, more readily falls into the ways of the country, more easily learns the language, and is altogether more amenable to Christian instruction" (Quoted in Arthur and Juanita Niehoff, *East Indians in the West Indies* [Milwaukee: Milwaukee Public Museum Publications in Anthropology, 1960], p. 16).

64. Seasoning included survival of "seasoning sickness" (Curtin, "Epidemiology and the Slave Trade," p. 211).

brutal, medium of acculturation, and acculturation to the plantation society was reinforced by internally induced change. New Creole forms, forms indigenous to the area, were developed, and in time the consciousness of African tribal identity faded as identity as Creoles, Trinidadians, West Indians developed(65).

Neither the religious nor educational institutions of the nineteenth century fostered integration of the major ethnic groups of the society, and social and cultural barriers persisted as the channels of mobility were effectively closed. These patterns of racial cleavage were carried over to the twentieth century as "the ethnic factor was the main status giving factor" in the social stratification of Trinidad(66).

After Emancipation curtailed the Negro labor force on the plantation Trollope had written in his imperious style, "Give me my heart's desire in Coolies, and I will make you a million hogsheads of sugar without stirring from the Colony"(67). Sugar outputs were increased by "coolie" labor, but as they became a permanent population, their occupational and social horizons expanded. By 1925 East Indians were plantation workers and peasant proprietors of 100,000 acres of land. They also became, in due course, small shopkeepers and large merchants, oil workers and technicians, taxi drivers and trucking contractors, teachers and clerks, politicians and priests, doctors and lawyers. In fact, with the exception of the police force and the civil service(68), by the time Independence was attained, East Indians had entered all the occupational strata of society(69).

This occupational diversity denotes both acculturating mechanisms and acculturative processes. A number of recent studies point to the breakdown of the caste system in Trinidad regarding occupational specialization and segregation and to the shift from caste to social class as the criterion of status. Plantation labor was not conducive to caste segregation; it served rather as an

65. The liberated Africans, members of various tribes, Ibo, Congo, Mandingo, Ashanti, Fulani, and Yoruba, and others who arrived after Emancipation tended to form their own squatter villages once they left the estates. In the mid-nineteenth century, several African settlements were formed in the Belmont Valley. Almost a century later, Carr reported a number of cultural retentions, particularly in ritual, in a community established in 1868 by Radas from Dahomey. See Andrew Carr, "The Rada Community in Trinidad," *Caribbean Quarterly, 3* (1953), 36–54. African retentions are still manifest in the Shango cult and in rituals surrounding death in rural areas. Elements of African culture have been incorporated into dance, art, and music in the new esthetics of nationalism.

66. Braithwaite, "Social Stratification in Trinidad," p. 169.

67. Quoted in Nath, p. 161.

68. Ryan, p. 398.

69. "Our people have permeated every cell of business life in this Colony" (*Indian Centenary Review: 100 Years of Progress, 1845-1945, Trinidad, B.W.I.* [Port of Spain: Indian Centenary Review Committee, n.d.], p. 103).

equalizing mechanism. As economic and occupational alternatives became available, individual achievement values superseded ascriptive caste boundaries(70), and the East Indians sought and achieved new statuses. The East Indian's accommodation to the larger society of Trinidad needs to be examined within the framework of economic, social, and political events of twentieth century Trinidad.

THE MODERN PERIOD

The discovery of oil in Trinidad in 1910 marked a major break not only in the limited-crop economy but in plantation psychology as well. The classic economic picture of the sugar islands was modified by the development of oil production and refining, and in succeeding decades the oil industry became the chief source of national income. Reliance on export crops already linked local crops to the world market and the national economy to the world economy. It has been said that in the nineteenth century "the world price of sugar was the barometer of West Indian prosperity." Although the resource base has shifted, the oil economy is also necessarily dependent on external factors, for portions of Trinidad's oil industry are tied up with the vicissitudes of the world market, perhaps to a greater extent than with most other oil producers since local production is geared to the refining of oil(71). Nevertheless, oil revenues have helped to make incomes in Trinidad the highest in the West Indies, recently almost 50 per cent higher than in the other islands(72). Equally important, the development of the oil industry helped to diversify the island economy and occupational structure and to create a base for further industrialization(73); it also provided the impetus for the rise of the modern trade union movement and the growth of working-class political parties.

Labor unrest, which developed in the oil areas in 1937, stimulated both colonial constitutional reforms and internal movements for self-government. The emergent nationalism of the West Indies, further stimulated by the world movement for self-determination following World War II, broadened the base of political participation. The Second World War also introduced a new element

70. See Schwartz (ed.), *Caste in Overseas Indian Communities*, especially Clarke, "Caste among Hindus in a Town in Trinidad: San Fernando," pp. 165–199.

71. *West Indian Economist, 2* (February 1960). By 1936 Trinidad became the leading oil producer in the British Empire, but produced only .92 per cent of the total world output (see Ryan, p. 538).

72. A World Bank Report noted that "with a per capita income of about $500 (US) (in 1960) the people of Trinidad enjoy one of the highest standards of living in any Afro-Asian community. Trinidad is one of the most prosperous areas in Central and South America" (*The Nation* [Port of Spain: PNM Publishing Co., January 15, 1962], p. 4).

73. Oil and sugar, nevertheless, constitute 90 per cent of exports.

into the complex society through the Churchill-Roosevelt agreement for American occupation of bases in the Caribbean. American occupation of Chagaramas, the base established in Trinidad, lasted from 1941 to 1967. Carrington states that "It had a tremendous and enduring influence on the country's political and economic structure and on its values and view of the world"(74). The growing demands for self-government were channeled by a new political party which arose in 1956 under the leadership of Dr. Eric Williams, The People's National Movement (PNM)(75). Self-determination had been the goal of both the imperial power and the colonies, and Independence in Trinidad was achieved constitutionally and cast in the framework of British constitutional democracy(76). Recognizing that economic viability was an essential ingredient of Independence, the new government, under Dr. Williams' leadership, undertook an intensive program of internal development. The new party had captured the national imagination(77). Nevertheless, the new society was still saddled with many old problems: economic and social disparity, educational inequality, limited experience in political participation, the heritage of race, class, and ethnic divisions, and the enervating psychological attitudes stemming from ambivalence about personal and national identity. To a certain extent, ethnic polarization and latent subgroup conflicts were intensified during the period before Independence as old fears of domination were inflamed. Although the PNM Manifesto of 1961 pointed out that "a national revolution cannot be expected, in a mere five years, to correct the neglect and deficiencies of centuries"(78), the old ascriptive correlations of color and class were crumbling; "Hold up your heads high, all of you, the disinherited and dispossessed, brought here in the lowest states of degradation to work on a sugar plantation or a cocoa estate for Massa"(79). Dr. Williams declared, "Massa Day Done connotes a

74. Edwin Carrington, "The Post-War Political Economy of Trinidad and Tobago – I," *New World Quarterly*, 4, 1 (1967), 46.

75. For a detailed account of the rise of nationalist sentiment and political movements preceding the PNM, see Ryan. The PNM established the "first genuinely successful mass nationalist movement, under the leadership of Dr. Eric Williams" (Ryan, p. 4).

76. Vera Rubin, "Colonialism, Nationalism and Parochialism in the West Indies" (Paper read at the American Association for the Advancement of Science Symposium on the Development of New Nations, New York, December 1960), p. 19.

77. It was the first time that a political party had won the majority of the elective seats in the Legislative Council (Ryan, p. 198).

78. Ryan, p. 345.

79. Eric Williams, in a speech at Nariva during the 1961 campaign, undated, quoted in Ryan, p. 354.

political awakening and a social revolution"(80). A new opportunity structure was opening, and a new nation brought with it the promise of new life chances. Free universal education, one of the major goals of the new government, was put into effect in 1962. The role of education, especially, was to spread the universalistic and achievement norms which had been blocked throughout the society.

80. "Not all Massas were white, nor were all whites Massas. Massa is the symbol of a by gone age" (Williams, *Massa Day Done* [Port of Spain: PNM Publication Co., 1961], p. 2).

III

Educational Background

If it is true that "division is the heritage of the Caribbean"(1), this is perhaps nowhere more striking than in the multiple educational systems of Trinidad which developed over a century and a half of diverse metropolitan, social, and religious influences and laissez-faire government policies. The development of educational institutions in Trinidad, as elsewhere in the West Indies, reflects the changing requirements and philosophy of different historical periods. No formal education system had been established under Spanish administration, and in the early years of British administration the social climate was not favorable to popular education, let alone the education of the slaves. The educational work carried out by Wesleyans and other missionaries in the British colonies was as yet quite limited and: "On any count popular education had not begun under slavery, despite the praiseworthy striving of the missionaries"(2).

Rising interest in educational systems in England and the abolitionists' concern for education of the slaves slowly began to be reflected in the colonies. The first national school was established in Port of Spain in 1823 for "twelve freeborn boys" in order "to afford to the male children of the poorer classes, white and coloured inhabitants of the island, the desirable advantages of religion and useful instructions, and with a view also to ensuring a more general use of the English language"(3). In 1826 a second school was established, for "twelve freeborn girls."

1. Sherlock, "Prospects in the Caribbean," p. 744.

2. Shirley C. Gordon, *A Century of West Indian Education* (London: Longmans, 1963), p. 14.

3. Ottley, p. 57.

In the first attempts to create a national culture, a primary and continuing concern of the multicultural society was the standardization of English as the national language. The "freeborn" requirement in itself seriously limited enrollment in the national schools, and it continued for a long period as the society debated its course of development. Education of slaves was carried out primarily through the process of "seasoning," although some were given instruction in the paternalistic manorial pattern. Governor Woodford had proposed in 1827 that slave children should be permitted to attend the national school, but the School Board did not regard the suggestion as "palatable"(4). Under ordinances passed in the Crown Colonies of Trinidad and British Guiana, "slave schools were started in Port of Spain and Georgetown"; however, "It is doubtful whether much instruction took place on the estates where the majority of the slave children were"(5). Despite the general opposition of the planters in the colony, the abolitionists were developing plans for post-emancipation education of the former slaves, and in 1833 a ten-year plan for universal education was introduced into the Act of Emancipation.

The British public education movement had received its impetus in the early nineteenth century; however, equivocal ideological and economic considerations were involved in the spread of education to plantation societies, both under slavery and later under the indenture system. The moral ambivalence underlying slavery and the ambivalent legal status of the slave – whether he was a person or a thing – had led to rationalizations about the spiritual capacity of the slave to be Christianized. A Christian should not be enslaved, and the rationale for limiting the education of slaves was bolstered by the fact that education was administered principally by Christian missions. Education might inculcate the slaves with Christian concepts of freedom and Western ideas of individual achievement(6). The spread of education would have been a threat to both the

4. *Ibid.,* p. 60.

5. Gordon, p. 12.

6. "One of the difficulties which faced the British government in its efforts to improve the condition of the slaves before emancipation was the fact that many of the officials in the colonies were themselves slave-owners. The Attorney-General of Trinidad in 1829 was 'a considerable slave owner and proprietor of three sugar estates,' and it was suggested that this caused him to ignore gross violations of the law. The Protector of Slaves was another slave-owner, while the Customs Officers were accused of corruption in allowing slaves to be imported into Trinidad from other British colonies under the pretence that they were domestics accompanying their masters. Some of the Governors sympathised with the slave-owners and thought that the insistence of the British Government on the necessity for amending the slave laws would lead to trouble. Some were themselves slave-owners and in 1826 a general directive was issued forbidding the ownership of slaves by Governors and Lieutenant-Governors. One of the most determined opponents of too rapid reform was Governor Sir Ralph Woodford of Trinidad, who shared the general antipathy felt by the white community towards the missionaries. When he was instructed in 1818 to permit them

ideological and the economic underpinnings of the institution of slavery. After Emancipation it became clear that extensive education was equally incompatible with the indenture system. The plantation, whether under slavery or indenture, required a large, stable, and cheap labor force. Education of the workmen and their children was not consonant with this fundamental requirement. There were, of course, some outstanding individual exceptions of planters who provided domestic slaves with education and permitted their conversion to Christianity, but the mass of slaves remained illiterate, as did the mass of indentured laborers who followed them.

The abolitionists had recognized that, after Emancipation, with the new social requirements for the absorption of slaves into a free society and the emergence of free wage labor, popular education would become a necessity. Provision for the support of popular education for the coming decade had been built into the Act of Emancipation under the Negro Education Grant(7). The main achievement of the Negro Education Grant was that the idea of popular education had been "established for good in the West Indies; no responsible person queried whether schools should be maintained after the Grant was finally withdrawn by the British government in 1845"(8).

There were special problems of implementation in Trinidad, however. Education was still largely the province of Protestant missions(9), but differences in religious, as well as cultural, backgrounds threatened to create denominational schisms in the predominantly Catholic population. Crown Colony government had been maintained presumably because of the preponderance of "foreign" elements in the population and the lack of a common language and of common denominators of culture. The urgent need for the development of a system of universal education in Trinidad was recognized by Governor MacLeod, who delineated the argument in a proposal for government schools sent to the Secretary of State for the Colonies in 1841:

> There is perhaps no British Colony, where, from the mixed nature of its inhabitants . . . the necessity of some general plan of Education is more required than in Trinidad. The number of Immigrants we are receiving

---

to administer the Sacraments to the Negroes he argued that they were 'not persons of responsibility, that such a power might be very much abused by them in baptizing without proper authority the children of negroes as free' " (Sir Alan Burns, *History of the British West Indies* [London: Allen & Unwin, 1954] , p. 639).

7. The first grant allocation made in Trinidad, in 1835, provided £800 sterling for the education of Negro ex-slaves. Responsibility for the funds for public education was to be assumed locally by the end of the decade.

8. Gordon, p. 43.

9. With the exception of the Mico Charity, which was nondenominational (Parry and Sherlock, p. 248).

renders the demand of an extension of the means of Education of greater consequence. . . .(10)

In reply to this despatch, the Secretary of State, Lord Stanley, cited "the peculiar difficulties" surrounding the question of education in Trinidad, with "the majority of the population being foreign in language and Roman Catholic in religion, the bulk of property being English and Protestant"(11). Multiple conflicts of interest thus posed a problem for a "general plan of education" in the colony, and Governor MacLeod stressed the need for free secular education as a solution(12). The argument that had beclouded the constitutional issue in 1810, that foreigners had a greater proportion of the landed property and would be favored by a franchise based on property holdings, was now turned about. MacLeod's proposal was not implemented, but the seeds had been sown, and principles for a free secular school system were laid down by Lord Harris, the succeeding governor, in a proposal to the Legislative Council in 1851. To counter religious criticism, the proposal included setting aside a period of time for private religious instruction. Free primary ward schools were established under Lord Harris' scheme in 1852, and within the decade there were thirty such schools in the territory, in addition to about forty denominational schools. The principle of denominational control of educational facilities was entrenched, however, and the clergy took an uncompromising attitude toward the development of secular schools. The most significant departure from this pattern was the establishment by the government of The Queen's Collegiate School in 1859, a secular secondary school, later named The Queen's Royal College(13).

Wealthy planters had customarily sent their children abroad to the metropolitan capitals for secondary education, but, with the vicissitudes of the sugar economy, "the Catholics started secondary schools to meet the crisis faced by the changed economic position of the planters"(14). Political and cultural as well as economic and religious considerations undoubtedly motivated the establishment of Catholic secondary schools. The French feared breaking cultural ties with France and the spread of anglicization as much as they feared political and economic discrimination. Denominational control of the schools

10. Governor MacLeod to the Secretary of State for the Colonies, 1841, quoted in Gordon, p. 47.

11. Williams, *History of the People of Trinidad and Tobago*, p. 197.

12. In a resolution to the Secretary of State, April 15, 1846 (Gordon, pp. 46,47).

13. St. Joseph's Convent, a secondary school for girls, had been started in 1836, and the following year St. George's College (later St. Mary's College) was established in Port of Spain.

14. Lloyd Braithwaite, "The Development of Higher Education in the West Indies," *Social and Economic Studies*, 7 (1958), 14.

assured French-Creole control of education, but the schools were the arena for conflicting national, as well as denominational, interests(15).

By 1870 a dual system of government secular schools and government-assisted denominational schools had been established; however, the expectation that The Queen's Collegiate School would lift the "moral" tone and would do much to nationalize the society was to be fulfilled only by a select few(16). Lord Harris' plan to broaden the base for education(17) was hedged by the entrance requirement that all pupils be legitimate. The requirement of legitimacy was an overt discriminatory practice, effectively excluding the children of former slaves as well as many of the freeborn and insuring education exclusively for the "legitimate," which meant the privileged classes of the society. The broad concept of "facilitating education" which had been set forth in the proposals for the abolition of the slave trade had not yet been realized, even for the "free people of color."

The classical education provided by the secondary schools was also essentially a class prerogative. The report made by the Inspector of Schools in 1861 speaks of "the morbid sensitiveness that shews itself at times against what is considered an over-educating of the minds of persons in the humbler walks of life, whose career it is thought had better be confined to mechanical or manual occupations than those requiring an exercise of the more elevated powers of the mind." He went on to reassure his readers:

A distinction will always, however, be maintained in the social scale by means of the superior classical education afforded at The Queen's Collegiate School. And had it not been for the establishment of this important institution, there seemed a likelihood of the "toe of the peasant coming so near the heel of the courtier as to gall his kibe," for those born

15. The Queen's Collegiate School was planned, consequently, to counteract French-Creole Catholic influence in secondary education, as much as to meet educational needs. Governor Keate pointed out in his proposals to the Secretary of State for the establishment of a secular secondary school: "the Roman Catholic college is at present the only establishment which affords classical and general instruction to the children of parents in the upper ranks of life." He went on to say: "I think that if a good government high school or college were established . . . a great impetus would be given to the progress of education generally throughout the colony and that numbers of children who are now debarred from a participation in the benefits intended to be offered to all by Lord Harris's scheme would be brought within its range, and that a higher tone would gradually be imparted to the moral and social life of the community" (Quoted in Gordon, p. 75.)

16. Gordon, p. 237.

17. Lord Harris' plan had called for the "establishment of a college, to which those scholars who might be found fit might be passed on, so that in fact every encouragement would be given to all, however humble their birth, to place themselves in such a position as their talents and their industry would show them capable of supporting" (Williams, *History of the People of Trinidad and Tobago*, p. 202).

in the higher positions of life might have had to give way in point of intellectual culture to the pupils of popular education(18).

The "toe of the peasant," however, still remained far from the "heel of the courtier" in the school population. Ten years after the establishment of The Queen's Collegiate School, of the 206 pupils who had been admitted, "Less than a fifth . . . were coloured, none was black, none was Indian"(19). In addition to the restrictive entrance regulations concerning "legitimacy," a system of fees was established. The ordinance of 1870 provided for free government schools and government-assisted schools charging tuition, which created competition for the free places in the government schools. Establishment of "assisted schools" was slow since managers did not feel they could compete against the free schools, and in 1875 "the odd solution was adopted of imposing fees in Government schools. . . ."(20).

Education was still correlated with color and class, as it had been when the Keenan Report of 1869 pointed out:

> . . . the first thing likely to strike a person . . . is the strangness of the fact that whilst the white population, which is only between 5,000 and 6,000, furnishes 142 pupils to the collegiate establishments, the coloured population, which, exclusive of the Coolies, numbers from 60,000 to 70,000, furnishes only 37 pupils(21).

Although these figures in the report by Patrick Keenan(22) were used in support of more denominational control, they indicated the "pigmentocracy" in the schools. The conflicts of the society, competing national and group interests, were expressed in the philosophy of education and in the choice of who was to be educated:

> Emancipation laid the basis for a West Indian community and nation, but it did not go so far as to break the organic connection with England. For the rest of the nineteenth century the society was largely content with the provision of secondary education for the middle classes, with those who could afford it joining the upper classes in sending their children abroad(23).

18. Quoted in Gordon, p. 67.

19. Williams, *History of the People of Trinidad and Tobago*, p. 203.

20. Working Party on Education in Trinidad and Tobago, 1954, *Report* (Port of Spain: Government Printing Office, 1954), p. 4.

21. Williams, *History of the People of Trinidad and Tobago*, p. 203.

22. Keenan was appointed in 1869 to examine the state of public education (*Ibid.*, p. 200).

23. Braithwaite, "The Development of Higher Education in the West Indies," p. 15.

Education had thus far been exported to the colonies, and although the "organic connection" was not disputed, the suitability of the curriculum for territorial needs was beginning to be questioned. The Keenan Report had commented critically on shortcomings in the textbooks and recommended:

> ... a set of books whose lessons would be racy of the colony — descriptive of its history, of its resources, of its trade, of its natural phenomena, of its trees, plants, flowers, fruits, birds, fishes, etc. The pitch lake and the mud volcanoes, for instance, would supply materials for an attractive series of lessons. So would the growth, manufacture, value, and uses of sugar. And so, again, would the cacao, the bois immortelle, the cocoa-nut, the coffee plant, the cotton plant, the cannon-ball tree, the mora, the pine-apple, the mango, the star-apple, the sapodilla, the orange, the shaddock, the cashew, the guava, the plantain, the different varieties of palms, etc. — objects all familiar to the Creole. Interspersed amongst a number of such chapters there might be selections from the prose and poetical extracts in the Irish National school books — local matter forming, say, one-half, and general literature the other half, of each volume of the new series. The books would then possess the same general characteristics as the revised edition of the Irish series. As the Irish element preponderates in the Irish books, so the Trinidad element ought to preponderate in the Trinidad books, which would then be as popular with the Trinidadians as the Irish books are with the people of Ireland(24).

This was the forerunner of continuing criticism of the predominantly metropolitan orientation in primary and secondary curriculum. The metropolitan tie was firmly entrenched, however, when an external examination system was put into effect. In 1863, The Queen's Collegiate School established the Cambridge Certificate examinations, and they were adopted at St. Mary's by 1870. Even during its early period, the system of external examinations came under criticism. The French, still involved in securing their position, were concerned that education of their children had become "English." There was more severe criticism, however, in the light of growing concern about the metropolitan orientation of the curriculum: ". . . it raises the question whether, after all, the education given at our Collegiate Institutions is the one most suited to the wants of the great majority of those for whose benefits the Colleges were founded(25)." As the commercial and technical requirements of the country

24. The Report continues: "Lord Harris evidently contemplated such a series of books, for in his original instructions to the Board of Education he said — 'Still it is my opinion that, on some subjects, books might be written especially adapted to the children of this island.' No attempt, I regret to say, has hitherto been made to carry out Lord Harris' views. So far as I have been able to ascertain, the only publication of a local character that has emanated from the Board, or from any of its staff, is a little volume descriptive of the geography of the island, by Mr. Fortune, master of the Eastern Market Borough school" (Quoted in Williams, *History of the People of Trinidad and Tobago,* pp. 200–201).

25. Gordon, p. 253.

were increasing, it was questioned whether the subjects studied in preparation for the Cambridge examinations were "calculated to train the youth of this colony for those pursuits which by far the greater number of them will eventually follow." It was proposed that the curriculum be extended to include commercial education and agricultural chemistry(26). Popular demand for agricultural education continued, and by 1899 the Secretary of State for the Colonies, Joseph Chamberlain, put forward a comprehensive scheme of agricultural education, as part of a policy to make the British colonies more profitable(27). However, when courses in agricultural science were included in the curriculum of The Queen's Royal College, there was criticism to the effect that "the Agriculture the boys study is not tropical agriculture and their knowledge is theoretical. There is no opening here for a boy trained in that way"(28). The debate over curriculum continued as part of the larger debate over who should be educated and the place of the educational system in the development of the society.

By the end of the nineteenth century, primary education was still far from universal. Governor Robinson, in an address to the Legislative Council in 1889, stated, "There are still some 17,000 out of probably 36,000 in the island who are not receiving any education whatever"(29). In 1894, a report indicated that out of a total population of 200,028, the number of students with average attendance in the schools was 10,992. In actuality, "a very small and exclusive percentage of the population" was receiving secondary education(30). While more colored middle-class children were gradually being included, secondary education was still unattainable for the mass of Negro and East Indian children.

The "dual system" of secular and religious schools was further crosscut by ethnic and class factors. Keenan's report had been particularly critical of "the educational system, which fails to provide for their [East Indian] children acceptable schools."

> I cannot call to mind any other case of a people, who, having voluntarily come to a strange land which they enriched by their labor, were – morally and intellectually – so completely neglected as the Coolies have been during the past twenty-four years(31).

26. *Ibid.*, p. 254.

27. *Ibid.*, p. 140.

28. *Ibid.*, p. 145.

29. *Ibid.*, p. 119.

30. *Ibid.*, p. 242.

31. Williams, *History of the People of Trinidad and Tobago*, p. 211.

Continuing in a liberal vein, considering the social climate of the period, he noted: "No effort was made to induce him [the Coolie] through the awakening intelligence and dawning prospects of his children, to associate the fortune or the future of his family with the colony"(32).

Keenan had recommended that estate schools be established for "Coolie children" on the general principles proposed for the system of public education: "(1) They should be open to all comers and (2) all comers should be protected from even the suspicion of proselytism"(33). Recognition of the need for the expansion of education to East Indian children, however, was framed within the existing segmentation of the society — separate if not equal.

Individual colonial administrators and some members of the society recognized the need for developing a unitary school system in order to create a national culture and instill a sense of national identification in the heterogeneous society. But the dual educational system became even further partitioned with the "peculiar difficulties surrounding the education" of East Indian children.

A few plantations had provided some schooling for East Indian children, just as some schooling had been available to slaves. But since children were generally employed in the field, the establishment of an educational system might create an aversion to field work, and in turn a labor shortage on the plantations. Even in the post-Emancipation impetus to provide an educational system for the colony, the children of the East Indian indentured immigrants were effectively excluded through linguistic, religious, cultural, and social barriers. Although the Keenan Report had stressed the need for estate schools, there was little internal support for the recommendation. In 1856, however, following a cholera epidemic on the estates, an ordinance was passed "promoting the educational and industrial training" of the orphans of East Indian immigrants. The social and cultural as well as material benefits to the colony were spelled out by Governor Keate:

Independently of the motives of benevolence which have thus operated in providing a home and a Christian and English education for these poor children, I think this institution [the Tacarigua Orphanage] likely in the end to be productive of important results. The separation of even a small number of persons of Indian extraction at an age when lasting impressions are most easily formed, from the debasing influence of caste and heathenism, is in itself a gain; but when it is considered that this is to be done in a country so far removed as Trinidad from the land where those influences are rife, and that all other ties to that land are severed at the same time, it will not appear too much to predict that this asylum may prove to be the cradle, so to say, of a local Indian population, Indian that is in descent and natural characteristics, but English in education and

32. *Ibid.*

33. *Ibid.*

feeling, and having no home associations beyond the limits of the Colony(34).

Nevertheless rural education was available primarily through the ward system and assisted denominational schools attended by Negro children, and East Indians were reluctant to send their children to "Negro schools"(35). Attitudes of separatism engendered by the plantation society served to reinforce missionary efforts to educate the East Indians:

> An Indian will not send his child to a Creole school; he is afraid of injustice being done to his children by the Creole teachers, and of ill usage from Creole pupils. The Creole, as a rule looks down on the Indian, he is a semi-civilized being. He speaks a barbarous tongue and his manners are barbarous. He comes to Trinidad to make money, for there is no money in his own country. He takes work much cheaper than the Creole will do, hence he must be ill-treated when he can be ill-treated with impunity(36).

The conversion of non-Christian immigrants in the plantation colonies of the New World was effectively divided by historical circumstance between Protestant and Catholic missions, just as the Western Hemisphere had been divided between the Spanish and the Portuguese by the Line of Demarcation established by the pope in 1493. Spanish Catholic priests had worked among the Amerindians in the early period of colonization. Again, as the French settlers were Catholic, the Catholic Church had undertaken the conversion of the Negro ex-slaves on the estates and set up denominational schools; under the British plantation system Protestants undertook the proselytizing, and ultimately the education, of the East Indians. Canadian Presbyterian missionaries set up mission schools in the sugar areas, and the first "Canadian Mission" secondary school, for East Indians, was opened at Naparima in 1868. Education as well as salvation of the "heathens" came under denominational controls related to sectional interests. Once accepting the principle of conversion in a free society, conversion in the dominant denominational interest was preferred.

Although the system of separate denominational schools perpetuated ethnic cleavages in the society, Christianity became a channel to Westernization for the East Indians as it had for other converted groups. Evidence presented before the

---

34. Quoted in Gordon, p. 70. In 1876, the Tacarigua Orphanage became an industrial school, administered by the Church of England, open to homeless children of all races (Donald Wood, *Trinidad in Transition: The Years after Slavery* [London: Oxford University Press, 1968] p. 232).

35. Only three Hindu pupils were counted among the 1,221 pupils in 18 ward schools in 1868 (Wood, p. 230).

36. Robert Moor to the Governor of Trinidad, March 12, 1890, quoted in Gordon, p. 122.

Royal Commission on the Franchise in 1888 by the head of the Canadian Presbyterian mission stated:

> Their interest [in the franchise] has been awakened from education here, and I think the interest in those that recently arrived and perhaps those that speak the Hindustani language alone, has been created from contact with those who speak English here. I think I have ascribed it all to the influence of those who have been educated in the West Indies(37).

Despite the long-term realization that education was essential to a "free soul" and could provide an integrative mechanism for a multicultural population, there were still conflicting interests and attitudes with regard to the role of education in the colony, and the Commission appointed to study the schools in 1889 took the position "that it is the duty of the parent to educate his child, and not that of the state"(38). The Commission further declared "that it is not practicable to set up any idol of uniformity or national system of Education under the circumstances existing in the Colony"(39). The role of education in nation building, foreseen by Lord Harris, was not deemed "practicable . . . under the circumstances."

At the beginning of the twentieth century, attitudes toward universal education were still shaped by the requirements of the plantation society. A select committee inquiring into labor conditions in 1926 questioned witnesses about child labor on the sugar estates and whether children should start working before the age of ten or twelve years. Planters expressed the view that children "should go as soon as they are able to work, as long as this is an agricultural country"; that schooling "would be of no use to them"; and that "if children were not employed now, there would not be enough agricultural laborers in the years to come"(40).

Opportunities for higher education remained a distinctive social class prerogative. The 1870 ordinance had provided only four annual scholarships for study at universities in the United Kingdom. Eighty-four years later, in 1954, the Working Party appointed to study the development of educational policy reported the same number of coveted "Island Scholarships" in existence, with an additional one for girls as a concession to the times(41).

37. Quoted in Gordon, p. 123.

38. Williams, *History of the People of Trinidad and Tobago,* p. 207.

39. *Ibid.,* p. 208.

40. *Ibid.,* pp. 213–214. This attitude toward child labor recalls the position held by planters in 1860 (Wood, p. 227). See also Nath, pp. 166–167, for similar views expressed by planters in British Guiana.

41. Working Party on Education in Trinidad and Tobago, 1954, *Report* (hereafter cited as the Working Party Report), p. 12.

Lord Harris had proposed a liberal arts college as part of his broad scheme for secular education in Trinidad. The proposal was included in the Keenan Report, which went further and advocated the establishment of a University of the West Indies in one of the territories with a "large white population," which would, however, be open to students "irrespective of class, colour or race." At the time, "Anyone wishing for a higher education had to go to Europe and America. This placed a heavy burden on the wealthy proprietors, while it totally excluded from higher education 'the intermediate section of the community now rapidly increasing in number and respectability' "(42). That there was little support for the idea of a West Indian University at the time was partly a reflection of planter parochialism and, eventually, of the desire of the colored middle class to break away from provincialism and colonial status. Both the French and British upper classes wished to retain metropolitan cultural ties, and the colored middle class had also "inherited the tradition of education abroad." The model brought with it important extracurricular gains for the colored "intermediate section," as "they came to appreciate not only the virtues of a system taken over from the upper class, but positively to approve of the free atmosphere that the metropolitan country offered"(43).

For over a century, the educational system had been geared primarily to the needs of the planters and the middle classes. Adoption of the Cambridge Examination system ensured that secondary education was oriented toward Oxford and Cambridge and, in general, to the British academic tradition of liberal arts training for the upper classes. The curriculum as well as the selectivity of enrollment reinforced the social structure and its value system. Secondary school education was viewed as preparation primarily for the professions, or for civil service or teaching as somewhat less prestigious careers; essentially it was education for a "white-collar," gentlemanly style of life.

Higher education was interwoven with psychological as well as structural aspects of status:

> ... the conditions of West Indian life had produced among the colonial members of the society marked feelings of racial inferiority, which reinforced those arising from its status as a colonial society. Consequently, when there emerged a coloured middle class in the West Indies of some stature in the community, its members were quite happy and content to proceed to the United Kingdom for higher education. Completely Westernized themselves, their "nationalist" demands found expression in the desire to obtain identity and equality of treatment with the Europeans. Rather than develop any cultural life or tradition of their own they sought a passive absorption in the European cultural tradition. This was a factor immeasurably complicated by the absence of an indigenous

42. Braithwaite, "The Development of Higher Education in the West Indies," p. 13.

43. Lloyd Braithwaite, "The Role of the University in the Developing Society of the West Indies," *Social and Economic Studies, 14* (1965), 77.

tradition, and when West Indian nationalism did develop and began searching for distinctive symbols there were few to be found. These were largely to be discovered in the lower class or "folk" culture rather than in an intellectual tradition(44).

Since Emancipation, education had been seen by the colored population as a principle avenue of mobility; in the modern period the social compulsive for education was intensified with the pressure for broader social and political participation. Captain Arthur Cipriani(45) combined these popular themes in a speech before the West Indian Conference at Dominica in October, 1932:

Working men and women, I say tonight your greatest asset lies in education, and you must struggle and fight on and on, until you are the means of introducing compulsory education in every one of these colonies, and . . . you must never cease fighting until your children enjoy the same privileges of education in your schools as the children of the multi-millionaires. You will ask, how is that to be accomplished? It is to be accomplished by your standing together, and by your weight of numbers which is the greatest weapon that you can wield. Money you have none, influence none, but you have that one asset which is your weight of numbers, and mind you, if you do not make it felt, then the fault is at your own door(46).

It has been observed that "the plantocracy opposed compulsory general public education until they were literally coerced into accepting it by the British Government in 1935. The East Indians were the principal victims of their negligence"(47). East Indians, however, had also recognized that their "greatest asset" lay in education, and enrollment in the Canadian mission schools had steadily increased. Conversion to Christianity frequently resulted, especially when viewed as a prerequisite to professional advancement. Even if religious conversion did not take place, the mission schools "provided a way not only out of the cane fields, but also out of what remained of caste"(48).

Although the society at large tends to perceive the East Indians as a uniform group, they do not represent a homogeneous subculture. Rural, urban, social class, generational, and religious differences have been modifying elements in the

44. Braithwaite, "The Development of Higher Education in the West Indies," pp. 54–55.

45. Cipriani, a French Creole planter, had been captain of the West Indies Regiment, the champion of the "barefooted men," and was the "first genuinely national political leader to emerge in Trinidad" (Ryan, p. 32).

46. Quoted in Gordon, p. 165.

47. Ryan, pp. 30–31.

48. Clarke, p. 177.

process of acculturation. Conversion to Christianity, once seen as an essential prerequisite to social mobility, has slowed down in recent decades. Canadian mission schools are no longer the sole source of education.

With the upsurge of nationalist sentiment following the Independence Movement in India, East Indians of Trinidad started their own schools. In 1949, the government recognized Hindu and Islamic primary schools as part of the dual education system, and in 1950, for the first time assistance was provided to a non-Christian denomination, the Sanatan Dharma Maha Sabha. With the growth of this movement, the number of Hindu schools has recently increased and secondary schools are being established, further slowing the rate of conversion to Christianity.

By 1950 the social and political situation of the territory had changed dramatically, marked by a new constitution which signalized recognition of the movement for self-government. Awareness of the need for broadening nationalist sentiments beyond the middle-class elites was indicated in the minority report on constitutional reform: "Under such a Constitution the broad masses of the people can at last realize that this country is *their* country"(49). Efforts to deal with some of the basic problems of the multicultural society through the educational structure were initiated. Under the new ministerial system of the 1950 constitution, a Minister of Education was appointed for the first time and government support of secondary education was steadily increased during the 1950's. Constitutional change reflected basic social changes already in motion, including the idea that it was possible for the "broad masses of the people" to "enjoy the privilege of education."

There had been considerable expansion in secondary education. In 1959 there were two government secondary schools, sixteen government-assisted denominational schools, and about thirty private schools, recognized, but not aided, by the government. A parallel system of private education had developed to accommodate students who were unable to gain admission to government or government-assisted schools. These private schools mushroomed with the growing achievement orientation of the population. Most of the students came from the relatively deprived sectors of the population, both Negro and East Indian, that were unable to find places in or to meet requirements for admission to the government and government-assisted secondary schools.

Dr. Eric Williams, leader of the People's National Movement (PNM), which came to power in 1956, had written a decade earlier that "secondary education is so severely restricted to the few that the English education that it provides becomes a sign of class distinction"(50). The new government proceeded to broaden the base of education. In the first two years of its administration, the

49. Quoted in Williams, *History of the People of Trinidad and Tobago*, p. 241.

50. Eric Williams, *Education in the British West Indies* (Port of Spain: Guardian Commercial Printery, 1950), p. 31.

number of scholarships to secondary schools was increased from 250 to over 400. Since the advent of the new government, there has been "a dramatic increase in secondary education supported by a competitive free place system which enables a big cross-section of the public to aspire to a secondary education for the first time in the history of the West Indies"(51).

The new government also signalled the emergence of committees of inquiry composed entirely of nationals, as noted by the Maurice Committee appointed to study the schools in 1957: "It was the first time in the history of this country that an inquiry into its education system was put completely in the hands of a local committee"(52). National rather than metropolitan interests also finally emerged, and the report pointed out the need "to find some way to integrate the diverse elements which comprise our mixed population of many races and more creeds," given the "heritage of schools built for children of a particular religion or race"(53). Fifteen denominational School Boards were in existence when the Report was issued. Even in ethnically diverse areas, as many as 97 per cent of the students in some schools came from one ethnic group; the ethnic population however was multidenominational. The Maurice Committee Report documents the new values of nationalism as the committee expressed its concern "about the realization of our national aims and aspirations" and adopted the principle "that education is a national affair":

> Not only is education a national affair and everybody's business, but the fact is, that a people cannot develop its own national pride and consciousness and grow to nationhood except by using education to mobilise all its human resources which are found available in all sections and classes of its populations(54).

The instrumental role of education in nation building had finally been officially recognized and programmed. New secondary schools have been built since the Maurice Committee Report, and the expansion of the University of the West Indies to St. Augustine has also increased prospects for higher education. The "role" of the educational system, Dr. Williams wrote in 1945, "should be that of a midwife to the emerging social order"(55). The problem of bringing the

51. Gordon, pp. 298–299. For a digest of recent statistics on education, see Appendix A. Free Indian education was an important PNM campaign issue (Ryan, p. 347).

52. Committee on General Education, *Education Report 1959* (Port of Spain: Government Printing Office, 1960), p. 23. Hereafter to be referred to as the Maurice Committee Report.

53. *Ibid.,* p. 25.

54. Maurice Committee Report, pp. 23–25.

55. Williams, *Education in the British West Indies,* p. 10.

"malintegrated rural Indian population into the mainstream of the larger society"(56) was recognized; free education was to be universal. The "mood of the people" in 1957 reflected some ambivalence as well as buoyancy about the "emerging social order." It was in this atmosphere that this survey was undertaken.

56. Ryan, p. 500.

IV

Social Status and Perception of the World

Secondary school enrollment in Trinidad was traditionally largely a prerogative of the middle and upper classes, especially in the upper forms, consequently circumscribing social mobility. At the time of the first survey, enrollment in the upper forms of the secondary schools was still severely limited. In 1954 it was estimated that about 5 per cent of all government and assisted secondary school pupils enter the sixth form. Sixth-form enrollment at the time, however, represented less than 1 per cent of the age group in the total population(1). As there had been only a slight increase in secondary school enrollment by 1957(2), lower-class students in the sample constitute an upwardly mobile group whose world view reflects both their present status and their aspirations for achievement – and the tensions created by the disparity between them. The autobiographies graphically reflect structural variables of the society in the past and present as well as in the students' perception of the future. The findings fall into definite patterns or clusters of relationships.

The objective background factors of the students' social position are woven into their subjective perception of their environment and their perceived life chances. These factors also condition the different kinds of stress they expect to confront on the paths to fulfillment of their goals(3). Comparisons between the views of students at opposite ends of the social scale reflect structural

1. See the Working Party Report and Appendix B.

2. 17,050 students were enrolled in secondary schools in 1956. See Trinidad and Tobago, Ministry of Labour, *Report on the Manpower Situation in Trinidad and Tobago, No. 1* (Port of Spain: Government Printing Office, 1959).

3. The social class and ethnic composition of the students in the surveys provides the background for analysis of their attitudes. (See Tables 2 and 4.)

differences in such perceptions. These initial comparisons are mainly of a qualitative nature, based on the students' own descriptions of how they perceive their life problems and life chances. The discussion will be limited to three groups in the first survey – rural East Indians, Negro students from working-class backgrounds, and white middle-class and upper-class students(4).

While the essays of lower-class East Indian and Negro students provide a penetrating view of the psychology of social mobility, the essays of white students of higher-status groups illustrate expectations linked to status mainte-nance. Although their political power has waned since self-government was achieved, white members of Trinidad society retain relatively high economic positions and the prestige ascribed to European life-styles(5). Moreover, secondary education has been a normative expectation of white youth, and educational attainment has been associated with the maintenance of prestige positions.

The majority of the white students in the survey are the sons of professionals, senior civil servants, or businessmen, representing the upper and upper middle socioeconomic group(6). At the opposite end of the social continuum are the sons of rural East Indian and Negro workers who have attained the higher forms in secondary school, generally through considerable family sacrifice. As we turn to the subjective view of their life situation, we discern striking differences among Trinidadian youth, reflecting structural factors as well as individual reactions to the situation.

In general, the essays reveal that students on the threshold of assuming new roles express anxiety about either their own ability to meet successfully the challenge of the future or whether the opportunity for achievement will be available to them. However, anxieties stemming from perceived obstacles to social mobility differ from those related to status maintenance. To start with, anxiety about the financing of higher education is a dominant theme among lower-class East Indian and Negro students. White students, on the other hand, for whom college education is a normative expectation, do not express anxieties of this nature; their anxieties are of another kind. Lower-class students are also keenly aware that attending secondary school creates profound differences in their life chances. As one Negro student writes: "It is an opportunity that thousands of boys are craving for, and unfortunately may never get." These Negro and East Indian students are also more likely than either colored or white

4. The views of students of other social class groups – middle-class East Indian, Negro, and colored students – are not included in this section. References to the second survey will be indicated as such.

5. In the West Indies, "To be white was to be blessed, to have the gift of grace." See Ryan, p. 33.

6. About a fifth of the white students in the first survey fall into the middle category, including sons of junior executives and small businessmen, while only 8 per cent of this group falls into the working-class category (see Table 3).

students to mention schooling as one of the three most important experiences of their lives.

All the students recognize that the hopes and fortunes of the individual are closely linked to the changing social pattern. For lower-class students, primary emphasis is on the attainment of higher education to qualify them for participation in the changing society:

> What will become of the ordinary man who is uneducated and thereby will not have any qualifications? Evidently he will be the one who is going to suffer. The world will soon belong to the educated and not the uneducated. (Negro)(7)

Another student writes:

> In the world today, jobs are getting exhausted, so that every individual is learning something he prefers. Many students go away and study, qualify for degrees and still there are no jobs for them. Everywhere things are getting difficult, especially for the uneducated. (Negro)

Anxieties generated by aspirations for mobility are underscored by the hardships of the reality situation, which the student often perceives as intolerable and capable of being changed only through higher education, as in the following illustrations:

> When I think of my present situation, I become unhappy. My parents are poor and I have two brothers and four sisters. My father has no permanent job and he alone has to work to support our family. It is clear, therefore, very early I will have to support the home, but today jobs are already difficult to get and education plays a great part in this affair. (East Indian)

Another lower-class student writes:

> . . . living a life in the country and being influenced by its environment, a child sees almost nothing before him except the hardships his parents and forefathers have passed. How can a child raise his standard except through this ambition of receiving a University education? (East Indian)

Parallel themes of family sacrifice and personal striving to achieve higher "standards" occur frequently among students in this group:

> My parents have a large family and are very poor. My father and mother are around middle-age and still have to work very hard in our cane field. Sometimes I often cry to see them coming home after a day's work, wet down with perspiration. It hurts me so much, that sometimes I feel to leave school and help them in the fields; yet sometimes it encourages me to do my school work with great eagerness so in the future I will be in a better position to help. (East Indian)

7. Throughout the volume, all quotations from students are reproduced verbatim.

The essays vividly illustrate the disparity between the actual situation, characterized by frustration with the environment, and the hope for a better future.

Students' self-ratings, as well as social-class data, were used to determine to what extent perception of the social world was correlated with awareness of social stratification. Students were asked to rate their own social position in reply to the question, *To what socioeconomic class would you say that the family in which you were reared belonged?* The following answers were given as alternatives: upper class, middle class, working class, and lower class. The majority of Negro and East Indian students placed themselves in the working class, while the colored and white students tended to assign themselves to the middle class; 12 per cent of the white boys, 27 per cent of the white girls, and only a very small percentage of other ethnic groups assigned themselves to the upper class(8) (see Table 10). The same pattern is reproduced in the second survey; 14 per cent of the white students assigned themselves to the working class, as compared to 61 per cent of the East Indian and 49 per cent of the Negro students. Thirty-two per cent of the white students assigned themselves to the upper class, as compared to 10 per cent of the colored, 2 per cent of the Negro and 1 per cent of the East Indian students (see Table 11). These results

8. Among East Indian students, 60 per cent of the Hindus as against 49 per cent of the Christians ranked themselves members of the working or lower class.

Table 10. Social Class Self-Rating(a) of First Survey Sample, by Ethnicity
(in percentage)

Social Class	Colored	East Indian	Negro	White
Boys	(83)	(207)	(139)	(40)
Upper Class	4	4	1	12
Middle Class	55	41	39	60
Working Class	37	52	59	26
Lower Class	–	2	1	–
No Answer	4	–	–	–
Girls	(52)	(72)	(115)	(17)
Upper Class	7	7	2	27
Middle Class	56	44	47	53
Working Class	37	45	50	20
Lower Class	–	1	–	–
No Answer	–	–	–	–

a. Responses to the following question: *To what socioeconomic class would you say that the family in which you were reared belonged – upper class, middle class, working class, or lower class?*

Note: Because individual percentages were brought to the nearest one-half per cent, totals do not always equal 100 per cent.

Table 11. Social Class Self-Rating(a) of Second Survey Sample, by Ethnicity
(in percentage)

Social Class	Colored (21)	East Indian (104)	Negro (82)	White (28)
Upper Class	10	1	2	32
Middle Class	52	35	48	54
Working Class	38	61	49	14
Lower Class	–	2	–	–
No Answer	–	–	–	–

a. Responses to the following question, *To what socioeconomic class would you say that the family in which you were reared belonged – upper class, middle class, working class, or lower class?*

Note: Because individual percentages were brought to the nearest one-half per cent, totals do not always equal 100 per cent.

indicate that self-ratings on social class closely parallel objective ratings based on father's occupation(9) (see Table 3).

Perception of low status is linked with intense desire to overcome the position ascribed by social background and a high degree of hopefulness. Factor analysis of the data(10) from the boys' sample in the first survey reveals a cluster of variables indicating that feelings of deprivation are linked with striving orientation and with optimism regarding the future. Analysis of variance shows that this factor characterizes Negro and East Indian boys of the lower socioeconomic group, but is practically absent among colored and white youth(11). This cluster includes the following variables, based on responses to the questionnaire:

9. This does not lend support to the position of M. G. Smith, who maintains that in the West Indies family background, personal associations, education, and other social criteria are more significant in determining status than occupational criteria. See M. G. Smith, "Social and Cultural Pluralism in the Caribbean," *Annals of the New York Academy of Sciences, 83* (1960), 763–785. Cumper points out that there is no evidence of stratification based on occupational level in the West Indies comparable to that in an industrial society. See George E. Cumper, "The Differentiation of Economic Groups in the West Indies," *Social and Economic Studies, 11* (1962), 319–332. (Our data, however, suggest that this may not be the case.)

10. Factor analysis was carried out on all the variables derived from the coding of the essays, multiple-choice, and open-ended questions (see Appendix F for categories).

11. Analysis of variance shows mean score differences significant at .01 between ethnic groups; East Indians and Negroes rank first and whites rank last on that factor. Also significant at .01 were differences between socioeconomic groups, in decreasing order from Class III to Class I (see Appendix F).

Factor A: Deprivation and Striving	Factor Loading
Perceives family status as low	.39
Expects to achieve a higher living standard than that of his family	.33
Feels school failure one of the three most important events of the past	.30
Prefers discussing personal problems with people outside the family	.25
Perceives the distant future as more satisfactory than the near future	.21
Does not expect to enter father's occupation	.17
Believes taking part in community affairs one of the two things to be most proud of accomplishing	.17

Factor analysis of the girls' responses shows somewhat similar results. Among the girls, however, being underprivileged affects social perception less hopefully insofar as their situational anxieties do not seem to be balanced by optimistic expectations of a better future or of great accomplishments. Factor analysis of the data from the female sample reveals a "pessimism" cluster strongly linked to low socioeconomic status. The following variables comprise the cluster:

Factor B: Pessimistic Outlook Among Girls	Factor Loading
Feels present state of health to be poor	.37
Has fears about seduction and premarital pregnancy	.32
Does not mention successful family life among achievements to be proud of	.32
Does not mention children's achievements as an important life goal	.26
Does not expect to marry	.22
Feels pessimistic about personal future	.18

Comparison by socioeconomic status based on analysis of variance shows that the lowest group (Class III) ranks first on this factor, followed by Class II and Class I in decreasing order (significant at .01), demonstrating the close correlation between poverty and a pessimistic outlook, accompanied by general health complaints and dysphoria among the girls(12).

12. Analysis of variance shows differences between ethnic groups to be significant at .01, with East Indian and Negro girls ranking first, white last, and colored in between (see Appendix IV). Factor B is also significantly related to type of school attended. On this factor, girls from private schools rank higher than girls from government schools at a level of .01. As previously stated, private schools are attended primarily by pupils from the lower socioeconomic strata.

Lower-class boys who express optimism about their future on the questionnaire nevertheless recognize that they have to overcome hardships in order to achieve their goals. This awareness may even increase their goal striving, as may be seen in the essays: "Success only comes after much hardship," a Negro student writes, and continues:

> My parents are very poor but they are sacrificing to send me to a secondary school. . . . This year I am trying to get either a first or second grade because life is very hard in Trinidad at present. If I do not get a certificate I believe that my life outside will be very arduous. I have to work very hard to get to this goal of mine. I stay up late at night with my eyes glued to my books in order to learn my work for the next day. There are many educated people in Trinidad today, and if I do not get a good education I would obtain great privations in the outside world. Therefore, I am planning to get always a good job for which I can get money to further my studies. . . .

Lower-class students are also aware that achievement of their goals is problematical regardless of individual effort:

> If I got a good grade certificate I will leave and try to get some thing so that I can bear a shoulder to my father and brothers who all toil to support a large family of sixteen. Although I am from a poor and illiterate family, I do not have the intention of following this pattern. However, if misfortune overtakes me, I will be forced to follow the line of my father and my two older brothers. My future sometimes looks rosy as an apple and as a bed of roses to others; however, a slight slip and I can fall into the pool of misfortunes, hard work, misery. (East Indian)

One of the questions arising from the study is whether the means to mobility are viewed realistically by the students who represent the mobile group. Striving for mobility, which characterizes the lower-class students, frequently is seen in the framework of environmental stresses and strains. One out of three East Indian students and one out of four Negro students of lower socioeconomic background discuss external obstacles to achievement in their essays and emphasize their determination to overcome all difficulties in order to attain their goals. Similar determination is rarely mentioned by white or colored students, for whom, in reality, there are no comparable obstacles to achievement. Furthermore, the realization that social advancement is dependent on a university degree dominates the thoughts of most lower-class students:

> I am very ambitious as so many young people nowadays and would like to go far in this world and be somebody great. The restricted education would hinder me in achieving many things, even in writing in full sweetness this autobiography. It is with great strain that I stay on in school to try to obtain a grade. (Negro)

From this point of view, although distant goals may be viewed unrealistically (as will be seen in a later section), the near future is assessed with remarkable accuracy. Readiness to defer gratification and to make essential, immediate sacrifices in order to attain their goals is revealed with consistent regularity among both East Indian and Negro lower-class students.

Mobility represents a form of culture change, as well as of individual striving, and new values are brought to bear on behavior. Familiar stereotypes about the "national character" of East Indians and Negroes in Trinidad emphasize culture and personality differences, particularly in their work-and-leisure patterns and styles of life. Historically, East Indians have been characterized as hardworking and parsimonious to the point of extreme self-denial in food, dress, and recreation. Lower-class Negroes, on the other hand, have been reputed to be adverse to work and thrift but prone to pleasure and to living primarily for "fêting." This portrait of a "national character" dichotomy which appears in the historical records of the past century(13) has reappeared in some recent studies of lower-class behavior. One recent study reports that East Indian children are willing to defer gratification in anticipation of a greater reward but Negro children prefer immediate gratification(14).

A significant finding of the present study is that students in both groups recognize the necessity to defer gratifications in anticipation of later rewards, and there is a convergence of subcultural values in relation to striving for mobility. The theme of postponement of pleasures is a leitmotif in the essays of both East Indian and Negro lower-class students, as typified by the following excerpts, representative of many others:

> I would be exceedingly glad to leave at once to further my studies or rather to obtain knowledge about one of the above named professions but for the lack of financial backing I would be forced to spend some years working in order to get the money which I would need to see me through unless some strange incident occurs, such as getting a reasonable sum of money by luck. Before the amount of money which I would require can be saved, a lot of sacrifice would have to be made, and most of the things which I would like to have would have to remain where they are. Most of the parties and things which we, the people of Trinidad, have quite regularly would have to go by without me taking any active part in it. (Negro)

13. See Rubin, "Culture, Politics and Race Relations."

14. See Walter Mischel, "Delay of Gratification, Need for Achievement and Acquiescence in Another Culture," *Journal of Abnormal and Social Psychology, 62* (1961), 543–552. See also Helen Green, "Values of Negro and East Indian School Children in Trinidad," *Social and Economic Studies, 14* (1965), 204–224. Another recent publication shares the point of view that "East Indians . . . are more industrious and frugal . . . than the rest of the population." See David Lowenthal, *The West Indies Federation* (New York: Columbia University Press, 1961).

In the world today jobs are getting exhausted. All the universities are filling up. When a student plans to study abroad it is one of the hottest problems he is faced with. The conditions and hardships are discouraging, but if I want to further this I have to make a sacrifice. (East Indian)

A "kernel of truth hypothesis" has been postulated in assessing generalizations about "national character"(15). Contrasting patterns of frugality and "freeness" undoubtedly existed in the different social and cultural circumstances of each ethnic group, and acculturation to the dominant values of the society was conditioned by different historical imperatives. However, the structural requirements of mobility modify patterns of behavior that may have been functional in other contexts. It is evident that the students perceive the need for new patterns of behavior as prerequisites for social mobility, especially when the goals are high, even if they may clash with previous values:

My life would be empty without my being a doctor. Money is a grave drawback to me. The government never gives scholarships to study medicine so there is no hope to go free. I intend to work and get enough money for the first two years. Meanwhile I am trying to strengthen my character for the task ahead. I am trying to study very hard to pass the exams, then I avoid spending long hours going to dances, pictures, and chatting with friends. Lastly, I am trying to avoid women, or rather girls. Previous to this I was like the average teenager, chasing girls and going to dances and so. Suddenly I decided that all that is folly. (Negro)

Variations on this leitmotif appear with great frequency among the lower-class students who are thus set apart from the "average teenager" of their culture; they are part of a new subculture of mobility. White students, on the other hand, tend to express concerns about their personal shortcomings as drawbacks to achievement rather than anxiety about external obstacles. A recurrent theme in the essays of white students is that opportunities are within reach but that failure may result from "laziness" or "lack of ambition." Such concern, which is totally absent in the essays of Negro and East Indian boys, is revealed in the following excerpts:

I have lived in comfort and it is this comfort that breeds indifference to the future. I do not mean that I do not have plans for the future, but I am too lazy to try very hard to realize them. (White)

I take a quick look back into my life and see that I have all but failed myself. As I become older, I become lazier and slack off. I am almost on the brink of doing nothing. I came out with only a third grade on senior Cambridge. I . . . have just realized that . . . if I ever want to do something I must labor and sweat a little and never give up no matter what. My

15. Otto Klineberg, *Social Psychology*, rev. ed. (New York: Holt, Rinehart & Winston, 1954).

family is quite well off, so I know I will be sent away [to study] if I want and I sure do. (White)

Again, self-doubt is seen in the following excerpt from another essay:

> I need to gain experience of life itself and of people. I have got to grow up, to become mature in my approach and attitude to myself and my problems and other people, and life as a whole. At present I lack all this; of course I suppose that this is to be expected, as I am yet a young and immature adolescent. All this will gain through the rest of my life, by the time I start to study my career will be mature enough. Another thing I need is self-confidence. That can only be achieved through personal experience, by getting to know and understand myself, my limitations and capabilities; by getting self-knowledge to know how I will react under given circumstances. (White)

While the white student "knows" that, given the determination and ability to pass his examinations, he will be sent abroad to study, Negro and East Indian students, who have the determination and feel confident of their ability to succeed, have less assurance about the economic and social situation. Rural East Indian students, particularly, tend to emphasize external threats to achievement with very little indication of self-doubt (given freedom from "misfortune" or "unfortunate circumstances" and given the opportunity to move forward), as in the following:

> All my hopes, expectations, plans, aspirations depend on the successful outcome of this examination, but still if *by some misfortunate stroke of fate I happen to fail this examination,* then though the shock will be great I will not let it knock me over or conquer me, but I will be up and will get moving along other lines, which means that my hopes or ambitions will not be the same, but still that natural instinct or impulse will be there to promote and to lead me on like a bright heavenly star, never flinching from the duty I owe to myself, others, and most emphatically to my country.

Similar findings have been reported in studies in the United States indicating that lower-class individuals tend to perceive the external world as threatening while middle-class individuals are more prone to anxieties concerning personal inadequacy. Interpretations of such findings usually have been couched either in terms of social class differences in personality or in cultural differences in value orientation. Cultural formulations have been stressed, particularly in a number of recent studies of lower-class groups in the United States. An alternative interpretation, however, lies in differences in the structure of the situation, which engender different existential and experiential stresses(16). For example,

16. See Suzanne Keller and Marisa Zavalloni, "Ambition and Social Class: A Respecification" *Social Forces, 43* (1964), 58–70. See also Elliot Liebow, *Tally's Corner* (Boston: Little, Brown, 1967).

there are marked differences among Negro and East Indian students in the private and government schools in response to the statement, *The world is a hazardous place in which men are basically evil and dangerous.* While 61 per cent of the East Indian and 57 per cent of the Negro students in private schools agreed with this statement(17), the percentage agreeing dropped considerably among students in government schools — to 40 and 33 per cent, respectively.

The Trinidad data supports the premise of structurally patterned sources of psychological strain. The different types of vulnerability that characterize groups at opposite ends of the social scale may explain an intriguing pattern that emerges from the multivariate method of factor analysis. A "fear of failure" cluster is revealed by factor analysis of the data of the first survey, including the following variables (see Appendix IV):

Factor C: Fear of Failure	Factor Loading
Feels failure to achieve goals is one of the two worst things likely to happen	.47
Feels lack of ambition is one of the two worst things one could be accused of	.16

The analysis of variance shows that the lowest socioeconomic group ranks first on this factor, immediately followed by the highest group (significant at .05). Interestingly, then, both the most underprivileged and the most privileged students are likely to exhibit severe anxieties about failure. These results based on the questionnaire data match the findings derived from content analysis of the autobiographical essays; students from both the highest and lowest socioeconomic groups show marked anxieties about achievement. However, the essays reveal that the zones of strain differ substantially. Lower-class East Indian students, primarily, and Negro students, to a certain extent, tend to locate the threat of failure in the external world, while white students are more likely to reveal anxiety about failure due to their sense of personal inadequacy. Although rural East Indian students often perceive the environment as threatening and express feelings of being discriminated against, they have exceptional confidence in their own ability to realize their ambitions. The cumulative experience of over a century of social discrimination is particularly salient as the new opportunity structure reveals itself to the aspiring students, but it does not diminish their extreme self-confidence.

17. Private schools are generally attended by pupils who cannot gain admission to government and government-assisted schools, at the time of the survey usually lower-class students. (See Chapter III.)

THE FAMILY IN SOCIAL MOBILITY AND STATUS MAINTENANCE

How have lower-class students managed to reach the upper forms of secondary school in the face of many obstacles? We have no comparative data revealing outstanding mental ability relative to their siblings or to the majority of the age group who did not continue their schooling. Changing family circumstances are undoubtedly a factor in enrollment, but it must be assumed that, in the absence of compulsory secondary education, mobility values are differentially adopted by individuals as well as by subgroups of the society.

Among the forces that facilitate or circumscribe social mobility, family influence has been emphasized in various sociological studies(18). Even though in the present study no direct questions were introduced to determine the specific influences which oriented the lower-class youth toward higher education (and stimulated or reinforced accompanying patterns of delayed gratification), spontaneous references to supportive family attitudes appear with regularity in the essays:

> My father was not a rich man. He was a road overseer and used to receive a salary of $36 a fortnight. He had to support a family of five. The family consisted of my father, my mother, my grandmother, myself, and my sister. We grow rice which supports us throughout a year and other small garden crops. My parents usually reared at least a cow. I was encouraged by many people to go to the school. My mother also asked me many times to go, and then I made up my mind to go. I was kind of lonely that day in school, but from that day onwards I made friends and so got accustomed. The fee for attending the school was $16 dollars a term, and the uniform was blue shirt and khaki pants. My father bought a bicycle for me to come to school. Whatever my report was my parents always told me I should do better. Every year I had to pay $49 fees and approximately about $30 to $40 in books. At the end of this year I will have 17 years and I hope to write my school certificate examination. (East Indian)

Another student writes:

> My parents were not rich, in fact my father was barely able to keep the family going. It was a large family. As time went by, my parents thought it best that I should attend college, as I had made good progress at elementary school. I spent four years at Presentation College, but to the great disappointment of my family, I did not graduate. They insisted that I return to school the following year to repeat, but that time, I was fed up with school or at least I thought I was. Despite their protest, I started to work in the oil fields. For a time I enjoyed life in that atmosphere, but

18. See Joseph A. Kahl, "Educational and Occupational Aspirations of 'Common Man' Boys," *Harvard Educational Review, 23* (1953), 186–203; Hilde T. Himmelweit, "Social Background, Education and Work: A Conceptual Analysis Derived from a Follow-up Study of Adolescents" (Paper presented at the International Congress of Psychology, Moscow, 1966); David P. Ausubel, *Maori Youth* (Wellington, New Zealand: Price, Milburn, 1961).

soon, seeing how one can be pushed around without the proper qualifications, I quit the job with an intention to return to school. My parents received this news with joy. (Negro)

Although opportunities for mobility may be limited for the adult generation, parents look for fulfillment of their aspirations through their children:

My father, who was a small farmer, realized the use of a good education and he sent me here to do so. My father can read but to a very little extent. (East Indian)

In fact, the students sometimes spontaneously write like social scientists:

My parents, although poor, always wanted me to become a doctor, so my father has always inspired me on education and he said that I should fulfill his expectations by becoming a doctor. (East Indian)

The family may influence the rate and direction of social change by mediating ideal values to the new generation. Strong parental influence in the choice of education as a route upward is a frequent theme, especially in the autobiographical essays of lower-class students. The following is a typical excerpt:

Most of the inhabitants of this small, so-called town are unwealthy. In my case, it is very difficult to be educated. As a matter of fact, I am faced with many unfortunate circumstances, but as the world is getting each day more civilized, my parents are struggling to see that I am educated. (East Indian)

The instrumentality of parents in furthering the social mobility of their children is supported by significant findings about the family situation of the students in the sample. More than 90 per cent of the lower-class respondents in the study have legally married parents, with the father as chief breadwinner, which sets them apart from many lower-class youths in the society. This assumes special significance in the light of the Report of the Working Party in 1954, which listed 52.8 per cent of live births in 1952 as illegitimate[19]. High rates of illegitimacy have been concomitant with past and present conditions of West Indian society[20].

The so-called West Indian family, the matricentric or grandmother family, is characteristic of lower-class Negro groups in Trinidad. Visiting and consensual

19. Working Party Report, p. 23

20. R. T. Smith, *The Negro Family in British Guiana* (New York: Grove Press, 1956). See Lloyd Braithwaite and G. W. Roberts, "Mating Patterns and Prospects in Trinidad," in Trinidad and Tobago, Central Statistical Office, *Research Papers, No. 4* (1967), p. 121.

unions are patterns of domestic life in the lower class, and although legal marriage is part of the domestic cycle, it is frequently delayed until economic stability has been established. Thus high rates of illegitimacy and absence of the father in the household are to be expected(21). In the past, discrimination on the basis of illegitimacy could have excluded the bulk of the population from attending school, and bias against illegitimacy may still exist informally in some denominational schools. As previously indicated, the traditional East Indian family has persisted, and early marriage is characteristic of this group(22). White families also follow the traditional forms of "Western" or "Christian" marriage; although some of the white students in the sample have parents who are divorced or separated, most come from a two-parent family.

The fact that Negro students in the sample reveal the same degree of family stability as students in other groups strongly suggests that the relatively stable working-class family headed by the father as breadwinner is instrumental in establishing a basis for social mobility. Income, provided by the father as family head, is undoubtedly an important factor in releasing a young person from economic responsibility. Possibly a more significant cultural aspect is that, in the West Indies, both stable marriage and high value placed on education have been indicative of the internalization of middle-class norms, and are thus important aspects of anticipatory socialization for mobility. Psychologically, perhaps, the lower-class father provides a spur to achievement, if not an actual role model, and may thus be instrumental in transmitting achievement values to his children.

The other side of the coin of parental support is the sense of reciprocal obligation expressed by students in the underprivileged groups, though somewhat more frequently by East Indian students, possibly as part of a cultural pattern of obligation to parents:

> I would go about working for a few years to give my parents the best cooperation possible, for they themselves are very poor and all this toiling and sweating just to see to it that I am able to attend school regularly. My parents did this because they knew how hard the work in the fields are, and by obtaining a certificate it will be much easier to get a job. I would have to work and upkeep them now, saving some of my money so that I might be able to leave the island and go and further my studies. I would have to work very hard before attending such a University in Canada. I would like to become a barrister at law. I would try to secure a work not forgetting to send as much help to my parents. (East Indian)

> It would be my duty to see that my parents are provided with the necessary requirements since they have sacrificed their life in order to provide me with a proper education. (East Indian)

21. Discussed more fully in Chapter VIII.

22. See Braithwaite and Roberts, "Mating Patterns and Prospects in Trinidad," p. 122; and Chapter VIII of this book.

In the same vein, another student writes:

> I will do my best to help my parents because I see what pains they take in sending me to school. Ever since I realized the vast expense my parents have paid and their voluntary sacrifice to furnish me with books, pocket change, and with sufficient clothes, I resolved to help them as much as possible. (East Indian)

Desire to help parents is expressed by 22 per cent of Negro and of East Indian boys, 15 per cent of colored, and 13 per cent of white boys in the first survey. Among the girls, 27 per cent of the Negroes, 21 per cent of East Indians, and 25 per cent of colored students expressed this concern, while only one white student did so (see Table 12). In the second survey, 20 per cent of the Negro and 33 per cent of the East Indian students spontaneously expressed feelings of obligation towards their parents, as compared to only one of the white and none among the colored students (see Table 12). This is particularly striking in the rural schools where twice as many students as in the urban schools express a sense of obligation toward the family, either directly to their parents or to help other siblings attain an education:

> I am the oldest child that they really spend much money on to educate, so of course they will be expecting me to support them for a small period as a sort of repayment. (Negro)

The lower-class family expects to benefit from the achievements of their children through direct economic support as well as the enhancement of family status. Recognition of economic obligations and a sense of duty to parents, however, should be kept distinct from familial closeness or understanding. Education and the accompanying exposure to new values and new role models apparently create a psychological gap between lower-class secondary school students and their parents. Attitudes of students at polar social positions — lower-class East Indian and Negro students, and middle-class and upper-class

Table 12. Students Expressing the Desire to Help Parents, by Ethnicity

	Colored	East Indian	Negro	White
First Survey Essays:				
Boys	(83)	(207)	(139)	(40)
	15%	22%	22%	13%
Girls	(52)	(72)	(115)	(17)
	25%	21%	37%	(1)a.
Second Survey Essays:				
Boys	(21)	(104)	(82)	(28)
	–	33%	20%	(1)a.

a. One respondent.

white students – illustrate this point. To answer the question, *If you had a personal problem that worried you, whom would you prefer to talk it over with?* the majority of white respondents chose "my immediate family" among the various alternatives, while East Indian students preferred "specialists" or people unrelated to them as advisors. Social mobility tends to lead to psychological distance between the generations insofar as school and personal experiences produce a set of values quite distinct from the more traditional views of the students' families:

> My parents are not up to date people. I think it wise that I should let you know that I have never ever discussed my intentions with my parents or anyone else except now, and I don't have any intentions of doing so with them either. I intend doing some teaching in an elementary school for about three years, and with the money received I will support my parents. I will be about the age of 21 and will be entering the seminary at the age of 22 with a clear conscience and without anyone saying that I was ungrateful. (Negro)

These findings were confirmed in the second survey, in which lower-class East Indian respondents were twice as likely as those in other groups to select the category of a "trained person" as someone with whom to discuss personal problems. This may be an indication that anticipatory socialization in a situation of mobility engenders the need to establish new social networks, replacing the immediate family.

Social and psychological drift from the primary group is interrelated with the inevitable absence of appropriate role models within the lower-class family. White students, for example, while expressing no sense of economic obligation to their families, disclose more personal rapport with them and, in addition, often select their fathers or other close male relatives as role models:

> I believe that by becoming a doctor I can be of most use to humanity. My father is a doctor and he goes a long way toward fulfilling my idea of a good doctor. I must thank my father for having shown me how I can play the future.

> My father has a great love for politics and art. For me my father is a hero in both spheres. I should live following my father's footsteps, especially as far as art is concerned.

White students, whose secure position in the social structure has generational depth, may also select the grandfather as a role model:

> [I wish to] take up law in the pattern of my grandfather after whom I am named.

> I wish to accomplish the respect, honor and knowledge of my grandfather who had two doctor's degrees, one medicine and one law.

Colored students are also in a position to model their aspirations on their fathers', and sometimes even on their grandfathers', achievements:

> I have always wanted to become a doctor. This profession has always stood for what is good and helpful for our fellowman. My father was a doctor, and all through my early life I was surrounded by an atmosphere of medicine and the hospital. Those who have eyes only for the salary will never make good doctors.

While the working-class family can provide the incentive for mobility, by definition it cannot provide the ideal personal identity and new social roles to be emulated. Lower-class Negro and East Indian students, in contrast to colored and white students, need to turn to friends, teachers, or distant culture heroes as role models, as in the following examples:

> I am now treading in the footsteps of a very great friend who also recently won an island scholarship. He has been my closest companion for about ten years. I see that I am always in his trodden path and will with determination and his most valuable tutoring, ultimately win the island scholarship for the language group. (Negro)

> My family doctor has influenced me a great deal, and he is my ideal of a noble man to emulate him is my only wish. (East Indian)

For rural students, especially, the limitations of role models within the family are compounded by environmental factors. "The important people are a rarity in these parts," writes one Negro boy, wrestling with alternative role choices and not knowing whom to "contact." Life in small villages sharply limits contact with professional people who could serve as models for aspiring youth. Future careers and occupational norms can be envisaged only through reading or exposure to mass media, and grasped through imaginative empathy. Given the absence of local real-life models to emulate, and lack of contact with local reference groups against whom one may measure one's own aspiration and attainment, imagination, even fantasy, may play a large role in aspiration. The students are, themselves, aware of these limitations:

> I have always heard of great doctors and scientists and I said to myself that one day I might become one of these great men. My parents are very poor so if I am ever to become one of these men I have to work and save some money. (East Indian)

In situations of mobility, where a parent or other relative is unavailable as an appropriate role model, a substitute must be found. The more distant the role models are in time and space, the more shadowy they become, and the more unrealistic is the perceived pattern of greatness.

Inherent in the mobility situation of rural East Indian students is a disequilibrium between the experience of their immediate environment and the ideal identity inspired by reference groups not clearly accessible to them as models. As we have seen, the secondary school system of Trinidad has traditionally been oriented to provide education for the upper classes as a springboard to a university degree. While the base of attendance has been broadened, the secondary school is still a prestige-bestowing institution and implies the observance of middle-class standards as well as adherence to middle-class values. There is a very real discrepancy between the rural East Indian life-style and the school value system, and there may be conflict between the two major socializing agencies — the family and the school. The process of "anticipatory socialization," "the acquisition of values and orientations found in statuses and groups in which one is not yet engaged but which one is likely to enter"(23), differs structually among different groups.

White and colored students come from families and from a social milieu which provide middle-class role models and standards that are implicitly absorbed in the process of socialization. Lower-class students may need to draw their role models from distant sources — Schweitzer, Einstein, Churchill, and even more remote historical figures. Their long-range goals tend to assume heroic qualities in contrast to those of other students. Nevertheless, as has been indicated, all the students perceive realistically the immediate requirements for advancement in their pursuit of educational goals.

23. Robert K. Merton, *Social Theory and Social Structure*, rev. ed. (Glencoe, Ill.: The Free Press, 1957), p. 384.

V

Educational Goals

Not surprisingly, the autobiographies reveal that educational plans and choice of profession are universal student concerns; they constitute a major topic of the personal essays and underlie prevalent anxieties connected with passing examinations. The Working Party on Education pointed out in 1954 that "the examination system . . . is regarded as the 'main ladder of upward social mobility,' leading to enhanced status and a field of white collared, clean handed employment"(1). The importance of the examination "pass" to life chances is frequently spelled out in the essays. This concern is expressed by an East Indian student as "The passing or the failing would be the green light, or the red light for my future years." The fifth and sixth forms are especially geared to the examination system with its potential for status achievement and also for the validation of highly ascribed status, and the essays reflect these interlinked concerns:

> We wish to be looked upon. I hope the examination would be a further step in my achievement of being someone to be looked upon. (East Indian)

Successful completion of the upper forms opens the avenues to mobility, but it is not yet an "open sesame" available to all. In previous years, less than 3 per cent of the enrollment reached the top forms and qualified for taking the examination for a Higher School Certificate(2). Preoccupation with these decisive examinations is a strong leitmotif that runs through the essays; it is also

1. Working Party Report, p. 78.

2. Maurice Committee Report, p. 69.

both the "greatest hope" and the "greatest fear" that students reveal upon direct questioning. One boy writes:

> Can anyone realize how fervently I desire to succeed in this examination, which everyone realizes is to be the true test of one's ability. I imagine my whole future life depends upon it and how I pray for that intention. (Negro)

Even when financial and other obstacles to achieving higher education can be overcome, the magic door to the university can be opened only with the Higher School Certificate; its attainment is a primary goal. "Everyone of us in this island should know the importance of a Senior Cambridge," writes an East Indian student. Reaching the upper form is a major step toward "the green light," with the very important proviso of the level of passing grade attained on the Cambridge School Examination – first, second, or third grade pass(3). A first grade pass is the prelude to the Higher School Certificate Examination, which is a prelude to university admission. The second grade pass is considered a minimum qualification for certain jobs in government, commerce, and industry(4). A third grade pass may qualify the student for teaching jobs (a rather ironical situation, as the Maurice Committee noted in its report) but is not high enough to meet high aspirations, as the students note:

> These days when one has a grade three he is not thought of as a person who got through the examinations. Also I would like to please my parents by getting a good grade.

The major goal of students in the upper forms of secondary schools is to succeed in obtaining a first or second grade pass, and a good number may take the examinations two or three times until they obtain the coveted grades:

> Even though I fail at my first attempt, I will try again and again until I succeed. (East Indian)

The relevance of the students' preoccupation with qualifying examinations and the "fervency" of their desire to qualify may be seen in relation to the statistics on examination results. In 1956, of the 1,258 pupils who wrote the School Certificate Examination, 74 per cent passed, but, of these, 50 per cent received a third grade pass only, so that less than one-third could hope for

3. *Ibid.*, p. 68.

4. "Government and assisted secondary schools prepare pupils who will proceed to the Universities and other places of training after age 18, or who will enter professions, specialized industry, commerce and other occupations for which a *School Certificate* or *Higher School* Certificate is required as a condition of entry." Working Party Report, p. 81.

admission to a university(5). This is relevant in view of the fact that so many students in the present sample plan to enter universities.

The probabilities of obtaining "a good grade" are also conditioned by the type of school attended. Attendance at private schools, which have still been functioning even with the expansion of government secondary schools, considerably limits the students' chances. The striking difference in examination results obtained by students in the two types of schools (government and government-assisted, versus recognized private) was noted in the Working Party Report(6). In 1953, 82 per cent of the students at the government and government-assisted secondary schools passed the School Certificate Examination (832 out of 1,081), while only 47 per cent of students at the private schools (392 out of 883) passed(7). Moreover, 61 per cent of the private school students received only a grade three pass, which is unsatisfactory either for university entrance or to meet criteria for admission to desirable posts in the civil service. Examination results even at the recognized private schools have been consistently poor. Private schools do not have educational resources equivalent to those of the government schools and as a group reach lower achievement levels on the external examinations toward which all secondary education has been oriented. Since the examination system conditions career chances, the type of school attended becomes a significant factor in the opportunity for achievement. Aspirations of the students in the survey to attend a university must, therefore, be analyzed by type of school attended.

As may be seen in Table 13, more students at government and government-assisted than at private schools expect to attend a university; however, a very large proportion of students at both types of schools indicate that they are working toward this goal. Given their limited objective chances of attaining a high pass on the examinations, however, such aspirations seem more unrealistic for the private school students than for students in government schools. As may be seen, there is a considerable increase in the percentage of students who aspire to enter a university among those who have reached the sixth form of the government schools. Having attained this level through considerable effort, there is increased motivation to continue to university education.

Regardless of type of school attended, the percentage aspiring to attend a university is highest among East Indian students of both sexes. This is particularly striking among girls in the private schools, where 45 per cent of the East Indian and 25 per cent of the Negro girls express the hope to attend a university. Given the small percentage of private school students meeting requirements for university admission, there is great discrepancy between aspirations of the students and the realities of the educational situation.

5. Maurice Committee Report, pp. 69, 70.

6. Working Party Report, p. 87.

7. *Ibid.*, p. 86.

Table 13. Students Aspiring to Attend a University, by Form
and Type of School (First Survey Essays)

Schools	Colored N %	East Indian N %	Negro N %	White N %
Boys				
Private Form 5	(9) a.	(59) 71	(35) 64	(1) a.
Government and Government-Assisted Form 5	(56) 59	(121) 86	(71) 71	(32) 61
Government and Government-Assisted Form 6	(18) 87	(27) 100	(33) 88	(7) a.
Girls				
Private Form 5	(15) 20	(15) 45	(51) 25	(3) a.
Government and Government-Assisted Form 5	(27) 36	(37) 63	(42) 43	(12) 30
Government and Government-Assisted Form 6	(10) 42	(20) 70	(22) 67	(2) a.

a. The number is too small for percentaging.

In Form 6, as may be expected, the great majority of all students aspire to a university education. In Form 5 there are significant differences by ethnic group, with the East Indian and Negro students more likely to have university aspirations. Ethnic affiliation as a variable operates in the same way for both sexes, the rank-order of college aspirations by ethnic group being exactly the same for males and females in the fifth form. East Indian students rank first, followed by Negro, colored, and white students, in that order. Similar results have been obtained in studies comparing college aspirations of Negro and white high school youth in the United States(8). Apparently, in the United States as well as in Trinidad lower-class students perceive that their major channel of mobility lies in educational attainment.

Although the perception of educational attainment as a structural requirement for mobility is quite realistic, the probability of fulfilling this aspiration (in both the United States and Trinidad) may not be. For many of the Negro and East Indian students, study abroad is dependent either on securing a scholarship or on being able to support themselves in order to attend a university:

In the event of failure to obtain a scholarship, I intend to work at a local oil refinery or an industrial chemical factory for two or three years. During

---

8. Harvey C. Lehman and Paul A. Witty, "A Study of Vocational Attitudes in Relation to Pubescence," *American Journal of Psychology, 43* (1931), 93–101; S. Gray, "The Vocational Preferences of Negro School Children in Trinidad," *Journal of Genetic Psychology, 64* (1944), 239–247; A. Antonovsky and M. Lerner, "Occupational Aspirations of Lower Class Negro and White Youth," *Social Problems, 7* (1959), 132–138; N. P. Gist and W. S. Bennett, "Aspirations of Negro and White Students," *Social Forces, 42* (1963), 40–48.

this period I will live sparingly, saving as much money as I can, till I see it possible to support myself at a university for at least two years. Then I will have to work part time for the remaining four or five years. I have always been worried about being able to pay my way through. (Negro)

This may be contrasted with the assurance of a university education expressed by white students, as in the following excerpt:

I have a reasonably good chance of securing an island scholarship, failing this however, I shall in any case be given a university education by my parents.

The desire to attend a university with or without a scholarship is an essential element in the students' orientation to mobility. In fact, educational striving is so salient that it may be elicited by very broad and general questions. Factor analysis of the data (first survey among boys) reveals a cluster of variables indicating the linkage of high levels of educational aspiration, high levels of determination to reach goals, and a high sense of responsibility to the family(9).

Factor D: Striving Orientation	Factor Loading
Would spend a hypothetical large sum of money for his family	.60
Thinks education/profession one of the two most desirable things not yet acquired	.35
Would be willing to make the greatest sacrifice of personal time, comfort, and money to obtain higher education	.29
Desires to go to college	.27
Would be most proud to accomplish outstanding occupational and educational achievements	.24

Analysis of variance shows a significant difference between ethnic groups on this factor (.01). East Indian students rank first, Negro students second, followed by colored and white students. East Indian students in the study come from Hindu, Moslem, and Christian denominations; Hindu and Moslem students in the sample tend to fall into the lower socioeconomic groups. The percentage of both sexes aspiring to enter a university is higher among Hindu and Moslem students than among Christian East Indian students. Moreover, the Moslem-Hindu group ranked highest(10), well above the Christian group, on the factor of "striving

9. A similar cluster does not emerge in the factor analysis of data in the girls' sample; this is consistent with their generally lower striving orientation.

10. Significant at .01 in the analysis of variance.

orientation." Moslem and Hindu students also have higher aspirations and expectations concerning their distant future than the Christian East Indians in the sample, as will be seen in the following chapter.

The second survey reveals similar near-universal aspirations for higher studies among students in Form 6, regardless of ethnic background (see Table 14). The Form 5 sample reveals the same high aspirations among East Indian and Negro students as were found in the first survey. (Comparison of the two forms is limited to the East Indian and Negro groups due to the small number of colored and white students.)

Table 14. Aspirations to Attend University, by Form (Second Survey Essays)(a)

Colored		East Indian		Negro		White	
Form 5 (2)b.	Form 6 (19)	Form 5 (83)	Form 6 (21)	Form 5 (13)	Form 6 (69)	Form 5 (3)b.	Form 6 (25)
–	95%	92%	100%	85%	94%	–	100%

a. Both forms are in government-assisted schools.
b. Number too small for statistical analysis.

According to the 1960 population census, 4 per cent of the total adult population (fifteen years and over) had attained a secondary school level of education with a School Certificate. Seven-tenths of one per cent of the adult population had attained some university training. While the latter figure is somewhat higher than in the rest of the British Caribbean, there is still a "vast gulf separating the Caribbean islands from the industrialized societies" on this score(11). Both at the University of the West Indies and abroad opportunities for higher education have been increasing in the past few years, but they are still limited and were far more limited in 1957 and 1961 during the period of the surveys. In view of the objective situation, the majority of the students in this sample may be nurturing unrealistic aspirations. The probabilities are actually quite slim that the 100 per cent of the East Indian students or 88 per cent of the Negro students in Form 6 who desire to do so can go abroad to study (see Table 13). The results, therefore, reflect the value and prestige attached to higher education rather than the probability of actually attaining these goals. For the girls in the sample there seems less possibility of frustration on this score. Most of the careers they envisage do not require university training, and the percentage of girls planning to enter a university is considerably lower than that of boys in all ethnic groups. Many plan to seek training as teachers or nurses and to continue their careers after marriage, which is the ultimate goal of the majority.

11. See Appendix E and G. W. Roberts and N. Abdulah, "Some Observations on the Educational Position of the British Caribbean," *Social and Economic Studies, 14* (1965), 144–153.

Table 15. Countries Selected for Study Abroad(a), by Ethnicity
(First Survey)

Countries	Colored	East Indian	Negro	White
Boys	(58)	(190)	(116)	(25)
	%	%	%	%
England	36	27	25	35
Canada	29	42	42	35
USA	40	29	51	36
West Indies	7	3	5	–
Other	3	8	3	
Girls	(17)	(46)	(47)	(5)b.
	%	%	%	%
England	37	34	31	–
Canada	31	43	41	–
USA	28	20	60	–
West Indies	6	3	3	–
Other	6	11	–	–

a. More than one country may be selected.
b. Number too small for statistical analysis.

Probabilities of going abroad for a university education may be judged by available statistics for the period. The United Kingdom Central Office of Information estimated that there were 370 Trinidadian students in England, less than a third of whom were actually enrolled in a university, with the rest receiving non-university training(12). While the number of students going abroad has increased in the decade since the first survey, especially to the United States and Canada (see Appendix E), the total number studying at universities abroad nowhere matched the number of students in the sample who were imbued with this goal. Since the only university education available in Trinidad at the time of the surveys was in tropical agriculture at the Imperial College of Tropical Agriculture (ICTA), those aspiring to attend a university would naturally have to go abroad, either to the University College of the West Indies in Jamaica or to a metropolitan center.

Most of the students aspiring to go abroad for university study specify the country or countries they would select. Distribution of the countries selected may be seen in Table 15. The major countries selected for study abroad were Canada, the United States, and England, with the latter no longer the predominant choice for university training. It is interesting to note that the University College of the West Indies (UCWI) was seldom selected, and not at all by white students. UCWI, the first institution of higher learning in the area, was

12. U. K. Central Office of Information, *Education in the United Kingdom Dependencies* (London: H.M.S.O., 1955).

74

founded in 1945, but over a decade later it still seemed to have limited appeal to students in Trinidad. In discussing the development of the UCWI, Braithwaite noted that "the affiliation to London [University] guaranteed the middle classes that the 'standards' to which they were accustomed would not be violated"(13). Nevertheless, study in Europe or America was considered more desirable, as it provided opportunities for travel and new experience(14); undoubtedly it was also considered more prestigious. The importance of the scholarship system was noted by Braithwaite:

It should be observed that in all the islands the apex of the educational system came to be the scholarship and the scholarship examination for study at the university abroad. This system worked admirably as long as the chief candidates for these scholarships were of European origin or belonged to the upper classes, whose connection with Europe was intimate. However, with the rise of a coloured middle class this problem changed somewhat. The creation of some educational mobility in the school system led to the scholarship being popularly regarded as a most important means of social mobility. The winners of scholarships concentrated on the professions of law and medicine, because of their lucrative nature, their high status, and the independence of control which practice of these professions allowed. These positions became increasingly a source of inspiration to large sections of the population, in that although the actual number of scholarships were relatively few, they were sufficient in number to twist the whole educational system and the orientation of the educated away from the islands(15).

The period of dawning political emancipation saw the rise of aspirations in the emergent lower class of Negroes and East Indians, as well as in the rising colored middle class. Achievement might no longer be limited to the few fortunate Island Scholars, or to the white and colored segments of the population; color and class might no longer be a brake on ambition, but the path would still be arduous. Perhaps it is the distance which must be traversed between present reality and the actual attainment of aspirations which creates a greater sense of urgency among all lower-class students. Rather than discouraging the students, it appears that status distance strengthens their achievement motivation and enhances their dreams of accomplishment. The occupational and status aspirations of lower-class students, as we shall see, range from realistic goals of raising personal and family status and improving the community to grander ambitions of changing their entire society or even the whole world.

13. Braithwaite, "The Role of the University in the Developing Society of the West Indies," p. 79.

14. For a discussion of aspirations to travel, see Chapter IX.

15. Braithwaite, "The Development of Higher Education in the West Indies," pp. 54—55.

VI

Occupational Choice

Hopes and aspirations of youth are a product of their culture and society. In traditional societies, occupational choice may be as rigidly circumscribed as in caste societies, and the scope of youth's imaginings may be limited to fanciful deeds. In such societies, role identity is ascribed by the circumstances of birth, whether color, class status, or ethnicity, as determined by the particular stratification system, and there is little room for mobility between the strata. The peasant boy may dare to dream that he is a prince but probably not that he will become a school principal. Occupational choices broaden with greater social opportunity; however, the levels of aspiration may be lowered or heightened by the values and needs of the society, and personal goals may be bounded by social realities.

New nations bear the promise of new life chances and new potential identities, especially for the youth of formerly disprivileged classes. National development plans and the replacement of expatriates in former colonies provide new opportunities for a range of managerial and technical as well as professional skills. In the 1957 essays – even before Independence – some of the students explicitly state that they expect to inherit the positions vacated by the English:

> We Trinidadians are eager to take over all the places previously held by the Englishmen. Our nation will need more and more specialists. (Colored)

New horizons open up to a generation of youths eager to take their place in the changing society, and the students' essays reflect the promise of change in their country:

> Trinidad is experiencing a great change in political, social and economical life. The island will need men of integrity, knowledge and capability. Great

emphasis is being laid and will be laid in the industrial expansion of the colony. The men needed to direct, control, and supervise such, will be local men with knowledge and capability and I hope to fill a place in that field. By doing so, I hope to help in the uplifting of the social and economical standard of the community. I hope to fill a place especially in the oil industry for this is playing and will continue to play an important part in the island's economy. (Negro)

The lure of work abroad, which drew off many of the emergent elite of previous generations, is also affected by the changing social scene. As one Negro boy writes:

After my University studies I hope to return to my small country and set about by hard work and self-sacrifice to make a name for myself. The bigger countries offer more scope for success, but I have always had a burning love and loyalty for my small country, even to the house I am growing up in.

Love of country is enhanced by the new opportunity structure for East Indian as well as for Negro students:

When I am a specialist I will return to good old Trinidad, where as the legend says, I will end my days. Trinidad has great need for specialists and I sincerely hope to be one.

Perception of national needs and opportunities becomes a salient factor in the aspirations of students from ethnic groups who were formerly structurally disprivileged in their own country with regard to professional placement. Even for the traditionally more privileged colored group, the horizons widen:

At present, Trinidad is in great need of its own doctors, engineers, lawyers, priests, and other professional persons, and I think that I will be of some service to Trinidad as an engineer.

This is a pervasive theme in the essays of the students who see that their life chances are linked to a new social order. In the transitional period, however, there may be a problem of congruency between personal aspirations and national needs and opportunities. Emergent countries are faced with the tasks of expansion of educational facilities and broadening the opportunity structure to fulfill the rising aspirations of the population. The first opportunities for achievement in the old ascriptive social order usually came through openings in teaching, junior civil service, junior managerial posts, and, for some, particularly the colored middle class, in the professions. Such opportunities increase with political change, and the ethnic base of the traditional middle-class occupations broadens. A new nation must have at its command skilled manpower to meet new demands in technology, engineering, industry, and management; modern

Table 16. Occupational Choice among Boys, by Ethnicity (First Survey Essays) (in percentage)

Occupations	Colored (83)	East Indian (207)	Negro (139)	White (40)
Medicine and Dentistry	20	34	29	23
Law	4	9	9	3
Teaching	8	14	13	3
Pure Sciences (Biology, Chemistry, Physics)	4	8	8	10
Engineering and Architecture	30	13	13	18
Economics	1	(1)a.	4	–
Agriculture	–	3	–	3
Pharmacy	–	2	1	–
"Technician"	8	1	3	10
Civil Service	1	1	–	5
Pilot	5	4	6	3
Business	2	1	1	8
Art	3	2	1	5
Other(b)	14	17	12	9

a. Selected by only one student.
b. Miscellaneous category includes priesthood, unspecified, and undecided.

manpower skills are more essential to development programs than the traditional occupations of medicine and law. One of the objectives of this study was to examine whether the new national ethos of opportunity creates new projected identities concomitant with role integration in the society and to what extent occupational choice is guided by emergent technological and manpower requirements.

The 1957 essays indicate that medicine, the traditional and prestigious profession, is the career choice of 34 per cent of all East Indian students and of 29 per cent of all Negro students. One out of three East Indian students and approximately the same proportion of Negro students wish to become doctors (see Table 16). As one Negro student writes: "I want to study medicine so that I may be able to go through life without any serious obstacles." Parental pressure to achieve status mobility in this direction is sometimes mentioned by the students:

My parents want me to be a doctor; it is because they are poor people and medicine is one of the most dignified professions in Trinidad. (East Indian)

Sometimes, however, there are indications of a conflict between the generations in this respect, as in the case of the student who writes:

My parents, who are Indian, want me to study medicine. In my mind it is becoming too common. I want to study agriculture.

Another East Indian student writes:

> My mind is divided between becoming a doctor or an agriculturalist. My goal is not riches; all I crave is enough to be satisfied. I want to help the occupants of the district in which I was born.

Conflicts in choice between the traditional occupation of medicine and the modern occupation of engineering as a means to develop agricultural technology are delineated by another East Indian student:

> My mind is being destined in journeying to the U.S. to become an engineer. To become a doctor would not make my destination fulfill. Another reason is that in Trinidad there are too many doctors. ... In Trinidad now there are only a few engineers, so to become an engineer and working for the government of the country ... will help plenty in the development of the island. My intention also for being an engineer is to help in inventing machines for the cocoa, sugar, rice and many other plantations. I will return to Trinidad, while I will do my endeavor best to aid the people.

One of the few boys who indicated his intention to study at ICTA (Imperial College of Tropical Agriculture, now part of the University of the West Indies) also combined social and technical concerns in his choice of agriculture as a career:

> Would it not be important to know that by using scientific methods I can greatly increase the sugar content in cane, or the tomato can now grow to the size of a grapefruit. What has really instigated me to be an agronomist is the fact that I want my island to be self-supporting and mentioning again, it depends to a large extent on agriculture for its survival. (East Indian)

Agriculture is the rare choice, however, as Table 16 indicates, selected by only a very few East Indian and white students, and not at all by Negro and colored students. Informal interviews with the respondents after the survey was administered indicated that they still associate agriculture with the degrading status of manual labor and feel it ludicrous to even consider a career based on agriculture.

Judging by the students' choices, law is apparently declining as a prestigious profession. It is still selected somewhat more frequently by East Indian and Negro than by other students; however, it is generally thought of primarily as a springboard to a political career. Medicine, the first professional choice of East Indian and Negro students, is strongly linked with a sense of social commitment, and there is often an expression of passionate fervor in their aspirations. A Negro student, for example, writes:

My first love is medicine and only after this examination I can attain the Freedom to pursue my love. . . . I will remain a doctor as long as life blood flows.

The role of the doctor is seen as essentially humanitarian, and this aspect, rather than the status it confers, is generally stressed in the essays. In this vein, an East Indian student writes:

I like this medical profession not because of the benefits I can derive from it for myself or because of personal advancement, but because it is the way in which I can play my part in aiding humanity.

White students also frequently mention the humanitarian values associated with the medical profession:

I hope to become some day a fine surgeon who can help in some way to alleviate the sufferings of humanity.

Although all groups share the humanitarian view of medicine East Indian and Negro students are most likely to link medicine as a profession with a sense of missionary dedication and frequently with dreams of scientific discovery. A Negro student, for example, writes that he chooses medicine for various reasons:

. . . least of all my personal gain; I want to work as a missionary in Africa, or some similar place and be in charge of a small hospital.

His lengthy essay explains his view of medical needs in Africa and expectations of what he can contribute to the development of the African continent. East Indian students tend to combine the roles of physician and medical researchers, and envisage themselves as discovering "the cure for cancer, and other incurable diseases."

I see the need of myself as a doctor in my country. I will want to do some research work on some of the diseases. In so doing I will be doing a great service to my country and to humanity as a whole. I especially want to find an effective cure for cancer. I want all these cases to be quite cured when I will have made my research successful. I will have surely done something which would be beneficial to my country and to all other countries on the globe.

Medicine, then, more than other professions, fulfulls the mobility as well as humanitarian aspirations of East Indian and Negro students. This choice was consonant with the colonial social order, in which status could be achieved most readily through the medical and legal professions, and was the usual channel of mobility for the rising colored middle class. Among colored students in the survey, however, it may be seen that technological interests now take precedence over medicine as a career choice. Some of the other students may be concerned with "saturation" of the medical profession, as has been indicated, and with competing status-linked occupational choices. For the most part, however, they select the traditional occupations as mobility horizons are opened to them. The colored students are distinctive in the percentage selecting occupations in engineering and other technical fields, such as the oil industry, radio, television, and so on.

Although lagging behind medicine, engineering is one of the second most frequent career choices — teaching being the other — among East Indian and Negro students (see Table 16). Since an engineer is not an independent entrepreneur in the same sense as a physician, this choice is usually tied to available opportunities, particularly in the oil industry, as indicated by the son of a small farmer:

I will spend at least ten years in the States pursuing my Petroleum Engineering Studies. When I qualify as an Engineer, I will come to my native land where I hope to be employed by one of the Petroleum Companies. The West Indies has great oil possibilities and so work will be always there, for persons to explore the various oil resources. My plan is to be in the Marine Drilling Operations now progressing slowly. Then I hope to establish myself as a prominent figure in the Oil industry. (East Indian)

Contrasting "modern" trend choices of engineering and technology with "traditional" trend choices of medicine and law reveals significant differences in the occupational orientation of the ethnic subgroups, as indicated in Table 17. There are intragroup differences by social class, however. Twenty-six per cent of the upper strata of East Indian students choose "modern" occupations while only 11 per cent select "traditional" occupations (see Table 18), in contrast with over 40 per cent of students in the lower groups who select medicine and law as their preferred choice. A similar trend with regard to occupational preferences is found among the colored students. This pattern is reversed among Negro students, with the upper socioeconomic group selecting traditional occupations more frequently than the lower.

Table 17. "Traditional" versus "Modern" Occupational Choices
of Boys, by Ethnicity (First Survey Essays)(a)
(in percentage)

	Colored (83)	East Indian (207)	Negro (139)	White (40)
"Traditional" (Law and Medicine)	24	43	39	26
"Modern" (Engineering, Technology)	39	14	20	28

a. Categories derived from Table 16; other occupations are not classified in this table.

Table 18. "Traditional" versus "Modern" Occupational Choice, by Ethnicity and
Socioeconomic Status (First Survey Essays)(a)
(in percentage)

	Colored			East Indian			Negro		
	I	II	III	I	II	III	I	II	III
	(26)	(26)	(30)	(32)	(65)	(95)	(21)	(36)	(74)
"Traditional" (Law and Medicine)	15	19	32	11	49	41	35	36	24
"Modern" (Engineering, Technology)	30	32	26	26	9	12	13	34	20

a. Categories derived from Table 16; other occupations are not classified in this table.

There are also some rural-urban differences in the nature of occupational choice. Negro students at rural schools are relatively more traditional in their aspirations than those at urban schools. This may indicate differences in the modernizing influence of the urban schools, as well as in the general environment. In the 1957 study, colored students, as a group, outranked students in the other ethnic groups in their choice of "modern" occupations, while the East Indians, as a group, outranked the others in their choice of "traditional" occupations. Many of the colored students were responding to social change in terms of an orientation toward modern professions. "In Trinidad, a young and building nation, there will be needed more and more skilled men in these fields . . .," one colored student writes. Another says:

I consider that the present political situation in Trinidad has marked out a prospective course in which my further studies will lie . . . in economics.

The autobiographies of some of the colored students express their shift in orientation from "traditional" to "modern" occupations. As one explains:

When I was nine I wished to become a lawyer, I no longer wish to do so. At present I have a great respect for medicine, but I don't think I'll pursue my studies there. [Now] I would like to study economics, and in this field I believe I can be of service to our Federation, at the same time securing for myself and my family a stable position. In this field, Dr. Eric Williams is my model.

This shifting orientation may also be found among Negro students who have selected "modern" trend occupations:

When I was a little boy I always admired the medical profession, and then I wanted to become a surgeon. However, as I advanced in secondary school, the medical profession became a faded light in my mind. I was doing well in my mathematical subjects. Engineering took the place of medicine. I admired the huge steel framework of the modern buildings.

The fascination of a steel bridge stretching across a river, and the utility of cranes and moving huge planks. I look forward to getting a job in a firm where I can help to construct modern appliances which will be of use to man.

For most of the students who have to depend upon their own resources there is still a major step from secondary school to the university, and they expect to undertake intermediate occupations before completing their studies and attaining their final career goals. Whether or not they really believe they can achieve their ideal goals, most students in the non-privileged groups (Negro and East Indian) recognize that the path to achievement is an arduous one, and that necessary stepping-stones include a university education. Many indicate they will interrupt their plans for continued study to take an interim job. Undoubtedly this intermediate step will become the final destiny of the majority of the respondents; yet, as data from Trinidadian students abroad show, the few who succeed in going abroad to a university have usually undertaken such an intermediate occupation. The success of the few may thus give plausibility to the hopes of the many.

Table 19. Boys Who Specify Their Plan to Work
Before University, by Ethnicity (First Survey Essays)

Colored (55)	East Indian (180)	Negro (104)	White (25)
33%	47%	47%	20%

Table 19 gives the percentage of male students who specify their plans to work before attending university. As may be seen, approximately one-half of the East Indian and Negro boys who plan to enter a university expect to work beforehand. While lower-class East Indian and Negro students indicate that they expect to work for five years or longer before they can attend a university, white students indicate that they expect to work for six months or one year before continuing with their education. Thus, working may represent an interim experience for boys whose university education is assured.

Lower-class students frequently specify the intermediate occupations they hope to undertake — teaching, clerical work, civil service, or work in the oil fields — in order to earn enough money to attend a university abroad. Teaching, especially, is seen as a stepping-stone to a university degree and achievement of higher status.

I will work for a few years after college [secondary school] to help my family because we are poor, and save money to further my studies. I would borrow books from the library, which I would study, and teach for a few years. I would teach them well and try to make Trinidad a better place for everyone to live in. I would like to see the young boys and girls of Trinidad prosper, just as much as if I were in their position. When I have about 18 to 19 years, I would like to further my studies. Trinidad might have its own University, if not, go to U.S. to study medicine or mathematics. I know that it is not easy to study these professions, but I would have to sacrifice my time and put my mind to it. If, due to financial difficulties, I am unable to further my studies, I would find a better profession than teaching – join a large firm and after a few years service I would run for elections. If nominated I would do my best to see that a university is set up in Trinidad and that many more schools be built in rural areas; also try for more hospitals. In general, I would try to make Trinidad a better place. If, however, I am successful in medicine, I would like to work in a hospital in Trinidad, to help in the prevention and cure of diseases first in Trinidad and then in other parts of the world. But suppose I study mathematics – I would automatically become a teacher and strive to have a large percentage of passes in my subject. (East Indian)

Negro and East Indian students tend to select teaching, a traditional occupation which has served as a channel of mobility, as their final occupational choice more frequently than other students. Although it is seldom an ideal choice for these students, it is the most common choice for one's first job, particularly among East Indian students; they tend to idealize the teaching role, as can be seen in the following excerpt from the essay of an East Indian student who aspires to be a doctor, but says this is unlikely for financial reasons:

Teaching may not be financially attractive but it is the best medium through which I can hope to share my knowledge with others. It would give me a sense of helping humanity.

When teaching is selected as the final occupation, it is usually presented in a humanitarian, sometimes in a messianic, framework:

Every man, woman and child should try in his own way to make his world, his continent, and his island a better place in which to live. Suppose one day I may have under my tuition chaps who would be the men of tomorrow, whose hands would sway the rods of government and fellows who will achieve fame in the wide field of science, arts and literature. This would be a chance to implant into the youthful minds of the growing generation their duty as men to make this world a place of peace, permanence among races, and bonds among countries all working for one aim, that nothing can break. I in my own way would like to solve the problems of all these injustices, through the hands of my pupils in my career as a teacher. My first intention is to try to raise from the pit the low standard of morality which is corrupting our youth. (East Indian)

In the same vein, another East Indian student expresses his concept of the teaching role:

Should I be a teacher, I would impart to those entrusted to my care all I have learned by trial or error in nineteen or twenty years so that they would not stumble over the same blocks which hindered my way. I would instill in them the need for unity among the many classes, colors, creeds which abide in our island, so that it would be ever shining in its example of unity among black, white, yellow and brown.

Although it is questionable whether the anticipated messianic role of the teacher will be realized, teaching may nevertheless satisfy a significant mobility requirement of lower-class students "to be looked upon." As one student explains: "A teacher is the person looked upon by his pupils and the people." A student who expects to become "a master of a secondary school" invests his future role with anticipated status rewards:

No more will I be considered the son of a poor peasant, for apart from working in a government department for a good salary, the honors I will receive, the respect I will demand, and the position I will hold in my rustic community would be of an elevated standard. (East Indian)

East Indian students, then, who list teaching both as an intermediate occupation and as their probable final occupation foresee an "elevated standard" measured by the "honor and respect" they will secure from pupils and community. Frequently they frame this choice in terms of the vicarious prestige they will derive through the achievements of their pupils.

In the United States, as in Trinidad, teaching has been a channel of social mobility(1). For many of the students in Trinidad it may also be the link to generational mobility, providing status as well as psychological satisfaction through the careers of one's students, and may become in due course a stepping-stone to mobility for one's own children. Imbuing the "probable" role of teaching with idealized values would also diminish frustration in not achieving higher goals. An East Indian student indicates that if "fate" interferes with his major goal, he will become a teacher:

In my opinion there is no other field of endeavor which can contribute so much to one's country as the field of education. The school stands as a center of civilization and around it all modern cultures cohere. Without it all civilization would probably crumble and fall. My duty, therefore, will be to perform my part unselfishly and my future as far as money is concerned is dimly prospected. I will be the helmsman of the ship of the class and steer it amidst the rough waters till I reach safely to the shore. I will try to be a guiding light to shine on the children I teach and not only show them the way to pass their examinations, but also to be better men and women of tomorrow who will undoubtedly follow in my footsteps walking in the grace of God and man. All my plans are based on my idea of contributing my share to my country, myself, and others, unselfishly so

1. Anne Roe, *The Psychology of Occupations* (New York: John Wiley, 1956).

that when I die I will be satisfied that I have done my duty and I have left this place a better world.

The results of the first study had revealed high levels of educational and occupational aspirations, which, given the reality situation, did not seem capable of realization. In the second survey two additional questions were introduced to determine whether the students saw any discrepancy between their occupational aspirations and expectations. These questions were: *State the occupation which you are most likely to enter,* and *If you had your choice of any occupation in the world, the necessary ability, and the full opportunity to enter it, what occupation would you choose?*

Table 20 shows the results obtained on these two questions side by side with the results of the essays, indicating the students' perception of the relationship between opportunity and aspiration. It is only among white students that ideal and probable occupations almost completely coincide, while the reverse is true for all other students. A considerable proportion of the latter consider teaching as their probable future occupation, even though most of them would prefer other occupations were optimal opportunities available. In contrast, white students tend to shun teaching as a career.

Political and social change has undoubtedly been a salient factor in determining career choices, especially of the Negro students; however, comparison of the 1957 data with that of the second survey requires a cautious interpretation due to the differences in the sample. In 1961, the emphasis on engineering remains almost the same for the white and colored students, but there is a notable increase in the selection of engineering as an occupational

Table 20. Occupational Choice, by Ethnicity (Second Survey) (in percentage)

Occupations	Colored (21)			East Indian (104)			Negro (82)			White (28)		
	Probable	Ideal	Essay	Probable	Ideal	Essay	Probable	Ideal	Essay	Probable	Ideal	Essay
Medicine and Dentistry	5	25	30	7	26	26	18	28	18	25	33	29
Law	5	7	–	–	4	4	1	2	9	14	10	18
Teaching	33	4	5	53	18	25	28	2	15	11	–	5
Pure Sciences (Biology, Chemistry, Physics)	10	14	15	1	7	8	9	13	12	7	14	19
Engineering and Architecture	24	21	30	8	17	13	16	22	27	18	19	25
Agriculture	–	4	4	1	3	2	5	1	6	4	–	–
Business (Pharmacy)	–	–	10	–	–	–	–	–	–	–	–	–
Civil Service	14	–	–	11	–	–	5	–	1	–	–	–
Pilot	–	7	–	1	10	1	2	9	4	–	12	–
Other	10	18	5	19	21	20	16	22	15	21	12	4

choice among Negro youth(2). Fewer Negro students in the second survey indicate medicine as their ideal choice in their essays — 18 per cent, as compared to 29 per cent in the 1957 survey. The number of colored students who select medicine as the ideal choice in their essays, however, increased from 20 to 29 per cent. A high proportion of East Indian students in both the urban and rural areas still maintain their orientation toward medicine and law as preferred choices. Colored students, as in the first survey, tend to select engineering as their probable occupation both in the questionnaire and in the essays. One out of four indicate in replies on the questionnaire that medicine would be their ideal choice, but only 5 per cent consider that it will be their probable occupation. East Indian and Negro boys frequently list as their probable occupation on the questionnaire the one described in their essays as only an intermediate occupation to accumulate savings for higher studies. As noted previously, this intermediate step may well become the final destiny of the majority of the respondents, and they are realistic about the gap between aspirations and expectations. The least degree of discrepancy in terms of occupational choice exists for the white students. White students are the only group for whom any chosen occupation seems both ideal and possible. This congruency between desire and reality may well define the concept of opportunity.

Few of the boys in either sample are undecided about career choices. Indecision may hinge partly on the uncertainty of examination results:

> This exam is very important to me because it is going to have a great effect on my future life. I am 17, and would be leaving school this year. If I am a failure I would not brood over it but would try to further myself by taking lessons in bookkeeping or typing, as good jobs are being offered in those lines. But if I am successful I will go abroad and study engineering, for this is my line. I intend to sacrifice five more years of my youthful years to become a master of my art, whatever that may be. (Negro)

Career indecision may reflect personal dilemmas about temperament or skills, as expressed by the boy who writes, "I never liked the sight of blood, so unlike many of my school chums, medicine is far from my thoughts. I am tongue-tied and stutter a great deal so there goes my hopes of being a barrister." He also considered the ministry, but rejected that, and "comes to engineering, as I am good at mathematics" (Negro). Indecision about career choice may also stem from a general attitude of resignation about one's life chances:

> You have noticed that I have not mentioned my desire for an upper education, or to become a man with a great profession. The truth is that I, unlike so many of my friends, have no big ambition or ideals. I have

2. See also the similar findings of A. C. Sieuchand, "A Study of the Aspirations of Three Racial Groups in the Grammar Schools of Trinidad, West Indies" (Thesis, Diploma in Social Psychology of Education, University of Leicester, 1961).

learned by bitter experience that it is best to take things as they come, not to hope for much out of life. (East Indian)

This sense of resignation, however, is not always imbued with bitterness:

I should like very much to go abroad to study aviation for my life's ambition is to become a pilot and see the world. However, should not my wildest dreams come true, I would not be greatly disturbed by now I have grown accustomed to disappointment and have learned to accept it. (Negro)

Optimism or pessimism may stem from a variety of personal, cultural, or social factors which condition individual orientation to the environment. The study did not include psychological questions per se to determine individual personality traits that may be quantified. The essays are personal documents, however, and reveal idiosyncratic as well as subcultural factors in attitude formation. Cultural factors seem to influence the orientation of Hindu and Moslem students to regard the external environment as a prime determinant of personal destiny(3). As one student writes:

We may get our joys and happiness from riches, power or from influence, while sorrows may be derived from some misfortune. (East Indian)

One concern of the study was to examine the students' perception of their life chances in their social environment. To investigate this more precisely, specific indicators were introduced into the second survey to throw light on whether high individual aspirations are set within the framework of optimism or pessimism concerning the economic future of the country(4). As may be seen in Tables 21 and 22, the preponderance of students expected that the standard of living in Trinidad would be higher in the future. While white and colored students were most optimistic about a higher national standard of living in the future, Negro students tended to be most optimistic about the availability of good jobs within the coming ten years for persons with their qualifications and were less likely to anticipate severe competition for a limited number of

3. In a discussion of religious and social change in India, Milton Singer speculates about whether belief in Karma "may be used more often to explain failure than to explain success" ("Religion and Social Change in India: The Max Weber Thesis, Phase Three," *Economic Development and Cultural Change, 14* [1966], 500). "In the first place, I do not believe we can deduce realistic consequences from basic beliefs, values, or motives postulated in isolation from concrete social and cultural contexts. The influence of such beliefs, values, and motives on behavior depends on what they mean in a particular context, and this in turn depends on how particular actors in that context define the situation" (p. 501). As Singer points out, it is necessary to ask how such beliefs function in specific situations.

4. See Appendix D, questions 7 and 8, p. 221.

Table 21. Expected Standard of Living as Compared to Present,
by Ethnicity (Second Survey)
(in percentage)

	Colored (21)	East Indian (104)	Negro (82)	White (28)
Higher	95	78	89	96
Lower	–	5	4	–
About the same	5	14	8	4

positions. East Indian students were most likely to anticipate severe competition and limited employment opportunities.

GIRLS' CAREER CHOICES

The girls in the sample represent an even more special group of students than the boys in relation to their age grade in the population as a whole. In 1957 it was still somewhat unusual for girls, particularly East Indian and lower-class Negro girls, to continue to the fifth and sixth forms and to prepare for examinations for higher studies(5).

The general fields, aside from medicine, in which the girls indicate career interest are similar for all the groups – teaching, nursing, and secretarial work are the leading choices, with a variety of other sex-linked occupations randomly selected. These choices fall into the occupational categories which have been considered as "characteristic" occupational choices for females(6). The matter of male-female occupational preferences is largely conditioned by social requirements and perception of appropriate roles, including the role of housewife. Whether or not women are more suited than men to "expressive roles," this image tends to be reinforced by the value system and by the "cultural messageways"(7).

Although the cultural messageways loom large in the girls' choice of occupations, there are subcultural differences in occupational preferences and in

5. "The average male child can expect to spend about 9.3 years in primary school and 1.8 in secondary school, and 11.2 years in school in general. . . . Female . . . 9.1 years in primary and 1.7 in secondary school or 10.8 years in schools of both types. It is also clear that females tend to leave school at a somewhat younger age than males" (G. W. Roberts, "A Note on School Enrolment in Trinidad and Tobago," *Social and Economic Studies, 16* [1967], p. 116).

6. See Roe.

7. See Ellen McDonald, "Educated Women: The Last Minority?" *Columbia University Forum, 10,* 2 (1967), 30–34.

Table 22. Expectations of Future Occupational Opportunities,
by Ethnicity (Second Survey)
(in percentage)

	Colored (21)	East Indian (104)	Negro (82)	White (28)
There will be many well-paying, secure positions available ten years from now for a person with my future qualifications.	29	22	48	37
There will be competition for good jobs for a person of my qualifications since there will be more people seeking work than positions available.	48	38	38	41
There will be severe competition for good jobs for a person of my qualifications since there will only be a few openings available and many people seeking employment.	24	36	14	22
No answer	–	4	–	–

levels of professional training requirements. Sixty per cent of the East Indian girls select occupations requiring a university degree, in contrast to 30 per cent of the white girls, 33 per cent of the colored girls, and 39 per cent of the Negro girls (see Table 23). Approximately 23 per cent of the white girls specifically eliminate career considerations from their plans for the future and envisage careers only as wives and mothers, while only 4 per cent of the girls in the other groups specify marriage alone in their essays.

Although the girls are less likely on the whole than the boys to select occupations requiring higher education, the rank order of university-linked career choices among the ethnic subgroups is the same as for the boys, with East Indian girls by far the most likely to aspire to become doctors, lawyers, or secondary school teachers, despite economic obstacles. The relatively high level of aspirations of East Indian girls is especially noteworthy in that a few of them also aspire to political careers, an unusual goal in 1957(8):

I will go up for the Legislative Council Elections. If I am successful I can then help the people of my country most of all whether I am the Minister of Health or not, though I would be extremely happy if I am the Minister of Health or Education. (East Indian)

Like any other young person of my age, my hopes and expectations for the future are very high. I am studying very hard in order to make a good

8. Recently, a woman has, in fact, been appointed as Minister of Health (although subsequently replaced by a male physician in this post, she remained in the Cabinet as Minister of Housing) and several women have been appointed to seats in the Upper House of the Legislature by the Government, which is interested in advancing the position of women.

Table 23. Girls' Choice of Occupations Requiring and Not
Requiring a University Degree, by Ethnicity(a)
(in percentage)

	Colored (52)	East Indian (72)	Negro (115)	White (17)
Occupations Requiring				
a University Degree				
Medicine and Dentistry	15	26	15	6
Law	–	5	2	–
Teaching (MA, BA)	15	26	16	12
Pure Sciences (Biology,				
Chemistry, Physics)	–	3	5	6
Architecture	–	–	1	6
Unspecified	3	–	–	–
Subtotals	33	60	39	30
Occupations Not Requiring a				
University Degree				
Teaching (Elementary School)	15	4	10	–
Nurse	10	13	19(b)	12
Secretarial Work	12	8	14	–
Other (Home Economics,				
Dietician, Beautician,				
Decorator, Fashion, Librarian,				
Interpreter, etc.)	14	6	5	12
Unspecified	2	3	7	–
Art	6	2	3	12
Air Hostess	4	–	–	11
Marriage only	4	4	3	23
Subtotals	67	40	61	70
Totals	100	100	100	100

a. Girls in both private and government schools included.
b. In the private schools this percentage was 35 per cent.

grade. If I do well in this examination, my parents have promised to send me abroad to study and as any one can imagine, I do not intend to let such an opportunity slip. In fact I even have hopes of attempting to win a scholarship, so that I may not expense my parents, who are not very wealthy. [She plans to study law at Manitoba University in Canada.] After my university career which I intend to be a success, I shall take up a post as a barrister-at-law in my native country, which is Trinidad. [She also plans to take an active part in politics.] ... and then would have the respect and admiration of the people of my country. (East Indian)

Some of the girls with high ambitions found it difficult to transcend economic difficulties, family obligations, and the expected priority of education for brothers. They may also have been concerned about prevailing attitudes toward women's occupational roles.

I want to be a doctor, yet everything is against me there. . . . I want that in spite of everything but of course I get no real encouragement. Those who encourage, think it a grand idea, but they think nothing of the difficulties; they don't even know they exist. The others who know of them try to discourage me. They think it foolish that a girl should sacrifice so many years to study and then at the end of it, or somewhere along the way, she'll get married. And even if I do decide to go ahead in this idea there is the very real difficulty of being accepted at a university, being maintained abroad, finding fees. My father has four children to provide for, who are younger than I am; two of them are boys who really need a good start in life. (Colored)

The percentage who plan to work before entering a university is given in Table 24. As is the case with the boys, more East Indian and Negro girls envisage the need of working before entering a university. Perhaps the most crucial problem confronting the girls is the perceived conflict between marriage and career aspirations; and they weigh alternative accommodations as they write about their future.

MARRIAGE-CAREER CONFLICTS

Many of the girls who are faced with a genuine dilemma about their future roles discuss this problem, indicating various modes of adaptation, from ambivalence to conflict to compromise, as in the following excerpts from the essays of East Indian girls:

The result of this examination would have a great part to play in my life. My secret ambition is to become a doctor or rather a surgeon and should the result of my examination be favorable, I intend to take a job, and from my wages, and with my mother's help (my father is dead) to save a great deal in view of reaching my goal. In Trinidad the wages are quite reasonable for one who has the Higher School Certificate, therefore it might not be very difficult to save. However there is still another point to consider. The fact that during my working period, I might fall in love and marry. Well that indeed would be fatal to my intended medical career. My plans would shoot up in space. . . . The fact is however that whether I become a doctor or whether I fall in love before, my greatest hope for the future would be to get married.

Table 24. Girls Who Specify Their Plan to Work before University, by Ethnicity (First Survey Essays)

Colored (17)	East Indian (43)	Negro (34)	White (5)a.
15%	38%	27%	—

a. Sample is too small for statistical analysis.

I live in hopes for that day when married women could become head mistresses — right now in our country no married woman can hold such positions. I think that married women can do just as well in any such field. Marriage here, I feel, is regarded as a handicap, but I think it is an asset.

However, as the essays show, a career is often seen as a stage before marriage or an interlude from full-time family responsibilities. Having a career is perceived as a "modern" role for women, but one which should antecede marriage.

As every modern girl, my plans and hopes for the future take the form of a career, and, perhaps later, marriage, home and children. (Negro)

A third of the sample follow this pattern of aspirations to achieve professional status, with recognition of their competence, and then to marry and become full-time housewives. "My ambition is first career, and later, home life." More than half of the girls in all the groups, however, mention the problem of conflict between marriage and career, as shown in Table 25. Fewer of the Negro girls may have anxiety on this score, as it is customary for the women they know to work for wages and be economically independent. East Indian girls may choose one of two alternative solutions — avoid marriage entirely or become full-time housewives. The white girls apparently have the greatest frequency of conflict over traditional versus modern roles.

Five per cent of the Negro and colored girls discuss at some length the dilemma of career versus marriage for girls, and the cost of education as a consideration in life choices:

A large sum of money must be spent to gain a profession. All that money will be wasted if I marry and become a housewife. (Negro)

They are perplexed by the perceived conflict and find no solution to the dilemma. Retreat into either-or solutions, however, is atypical. One out of four girls (one out of three for the East Indians) feels she can make the adaptation of a double-track career of "working and homemaking" (see Table 26). More of the East Indian girls plan to work after marriage, and, as has been indicated, East Indian girls also rank highest in university aspiration. The results of cross-tabulating aspirations for higher education with expectations of being exclusively a homemaker, as the final life goal, are shown in Table 27. High educational goals apparently reduce the expectation of giving up a career to

Table 25. Girls Mentioning Marriage-Career Conflict, by Ethnicity
(First Survey Essays)

Colored (52)	East Indian (72)	Negro (115)	White (17)
65%	63%	57%	69%

Table 26. Girls Planning to Work after Marriage, by Ethnicity
(First Survey Essays)

Colored (52)	East Indian (72)	Negro (115)	White (17)
20%	34%	27%	25%

become a full-time homemaker. The higher percentage of East Indian girls who plan to work after marriage is correlated with their high educational aspirations.

There are apparently multiple factors involved in the decisions the girls must make about their future. For middle-class girls, the role of full-time homemaker, with some voluntary community activities, is still the accepted one.

> Like most young girls I should like to get married and I should like to do so before my 28th birthday. I want to have children, boys preferably, I want to mind them myself so I shall give up my career until my children are of school age, when it will once more be welcome to me. During these years of wifehood and motherhood I shall, no doubt, need outside interests to prevent me from being a boring companion so I think I shall join a club, maybe a drama club. (Colored)

For some of the mobile girls, such a role may contribute to the elite status of the husband and also fulfill the middle-class concept of the husband as provider and the wife as "mistress" of the home.

> I do not wish to be a married woman with a career. I will spend most of my time caring for my children and husband. (Negro)

Table 27. Girls Who Expect Their Final Goal to Be Homemaker and Girls Who Expect to Work, by Occupational Aspirations and Ethnicity (First Survey) (in percentage)

	Colored	East Indian	Negro	White
Girls aspiring to an occupation				
requiring a university degree	(17)	(43)	(39)	(5)a.
Who expect to be				
full-time homemakers	17	17	23	–
Who expect to work	83	83	77	–
Girls aspiring to an occupation				
not requiring a university degree	(33)	(26)	(73)	(12)
Who expect to be				
full-time homemakers	36	42	40	72
Who expect to work	64	58	60	28

a. Number is too small for percentaging.

Most of the girls who plan to work, however, recognize that there may be economic pressures until elite status is established, and they are prepared to work in order to help support the family rather than to fulfill career aspirations:

When I am married, I think the woman's place is in the home. So, unlike many women I would be at home instead of going to work. I would like my husband to feel that *he* is the bread winner and consequently the head of the family because I thoroughly disagree with this idea of women wanting to wear the pants; or henpecked men. The marriage vow is — to love, honour and obey and I think that is really as it should be. Yet, I would not be a drain on my husbands neck, and if at all it becomes necessary for me to work, I will have had my qualifications and will be perfectly capable of doing so. (East Indian)

Whether education for a girl is for achievement of elite status through marriage or for personal fulfillment and advancement is a question which needs long-term study in a society where the public status of women has advanced only comparatively recently. In the past, social advancement has been possible for attractive girls, particularly light-skinned girls, as a result of the "high market value of a white skin"(9) in the "marriage market," where "marrying a light-skinned woman came to be almost a sign and symbol of occupational and professional success"(10). In this context, a secondary school degree, let alone a university degree, did not particularly enhance a girl's chances for marriage. Being attractive, despite the calypso song(11), is seldom a deterrent to marriage, though this may not be so rigorously tied to color as in the past. In the present situation, it is possible that professional men are expecting more intellectual companionship in their marriages(12), or that girls are actually planning to pursue careers.

In fact, these may not be incompatible goals. It has been suggested in studies in the United States that the contemporary role of housewife provides "a kind of secondary professionalization," since life-style has become an important aspect of middle-class society. By maintaining appropriate life-styles, the wife

9. Eric Williams, *The Negro in the Caribbean,* Bronze Booklet No. 8 (Washington, D.C.: Associates in Negro Folk Education, 1942).

10. See Braithwaite, "Social Stratification in Trinidad."

11. "If you want to be happy the rest of your life,
Never make a pretty woman your wife,
From a personal point of view,
Get an ugly girl to marry you."

12. Sieuchand reports that 17 per cent of the Negro, 17.6 per cent of the East Indian, and 11 per cent of the white students in his sample preferred wives with a university education. For 28 per cent of the white students, university education as a requirement "doesn't matter," as compared to 37 per cent of the Negro and 9.4 per cent of the East Indian students (p. 43).

Table 28. Index of Achievement Orientation, by Ethnicity (First Survey)
(in percentage)

	Colored	East Indian	Negro	White
Boys	(83)	(207)	(139)	(40)
At least two mentions of concern and striving for occupational or educational goals	69	85	85	53
Three or more mentions of concern and striving for occupational or educational goals	12	19	21	9
Girls	(52)	(72)	(115)	(17)
At least two mentions of concern and striving for occupational or educational goals	21	78	64	–
Three or more mentions of concern and striving for occupational or educational goals	6	11	7	–

and children support the status position of the husband-father and are linked to the new elite class(13).

This point is further illustrated by correlating university orientation with expectations of becoming full-time housewives. Only 17 per cent of the East Indian girls as compared to 50 per cent of the white girls intend to make the home a post-career focal point. Higher education has apparently become a normative expectation for middle-class and upper-class white girls as preparation for marriage. For the East Indian girls securing an education entails greater sacrifice and more of a break with their culture; it is consequently seen as a channel to a career and personal independence, rather than as preparation for the housewife's role.

ACHIEVEMENT ORIENTATION OF BOYS AND GIRLS

High levels of educational and occupational aspirations are logically distinct from actual commitment to their achievement; it is necessary to examine the saliency of commitment (or achievement drive) in order to distinguish between desire and intention. A variety of measures have been used to determine the degree of commitment to educational and occupational goals. An Index of Achievement Orientation was developed to measure the saliency of the students' concern with educational and career success as spontaneously elicited (Table 28). The Index includes all students who, in the first survey, mentioned

13. McDonald, p. 32.

achievement themes more than twice in response to five broad open-ended questions(14).

There is a greater concern with educational and occupational achievement in the groups which were highest in levels of aspiration, that is, East Indian and Negro. Even though boys are more achievement-oriented than girls, the rank order on the Index of Achievement Orientation is the same by sex and ethnicity; East Indian students are first, closely followed by Negro, then by colored students, with the white students last. For the former, then, the desire to achieve is supported by a strong sense of commitment.

The strong achievement orientation of Negro and East Indian students is further confirmed by the results obtained on a Profile of Achievement Orientation (see Appendix G). On each of the indications used for the Profile (derived from both the essays and the questionnaires in the first survey), Negro and East Indian students (boys and girls) are consistently higher than white or colored students. It is difficult to determine cause and effect relationships in this achievement pattern. Whether it is because East Indian and Negro students have had to overcome serious obstacles, as described in their essays, that they have higher motivational investment in their goals than other students or that their high motivation has enabled them to reach a high educational level is a moot question. Whatever the reason may be, it is relevant for the understanding of social change to recognize that, when opportunity is available, a reservoir of striving can be uncovered, regardless of previous "cultural" differences in orientation.

In the second survey, additional data were obtained on the importance attached to various kinds of occupational gratification. The students were asked to rank a series of ten possible sources of gratification as "very important," "somewhat important," or "of little importance." As may be seen in Table 29, stability and security (category 2) are considered very important career elements by all groups, ranging between 81 per cent of the colored students and 65 per cent of the East Indian students. The category of "being helpful" (4) also ranks high among all groups. For the category of "status and prestige" (9) however, the East Indian and Negro students score highest, each group totaling 34 per cent on this dimension, in contrast to 10 per cent of the colored and 18 per cent of the white students. Colored students are most likely to select the category of opportunity to be "creative and original" (3).

In Table 30 the nature of career requirements which the students consider *most* important are examined. There are two categories which are selected as the

14. *What two things would you most like to have that you don't now have? What two things would you most like to know about the future? As a parent, what two specific lessons will you try hardest to teach your children? If you should get a large sum of money five years from now, what would you do with it? What two things could you conceivably accomplish during your lifetime that you could be most proud of?*

Table 29. Importance of Various Career Requirements, by Ethnicity (Second Survey)
(in percentage)

Consider to what extent a job or career would have to satisfy *each* of these requirements. For each of the following ten statements indicate with a check whether it is very important, somewhat important or of little importance to you.(a)	Colored (21)				East Indian (104)				Negro (82)				White (28)			
	1(b)	2	3	NA	1	2	3	NA	1	2	3	NA	1	2	3	NA
1. Provide an opportunity to use my special abilities	57	43(c)	–	–	53	25	11	11	71	21	4	4	77	23	–	–
2. Enable me to look forward to a stable, secure future	81	14	5	–	65	19	9	7	77	16	4	3	71	18	7	4
3. Permit me to be creative and original	43	19	38	–	18	36	36	10	23	43	29	5	21	43	29	7
4. Give me an opportunity to be helpful to others	66	24	10	–	72	18	5	5	65	28	5	2	57	36	4	3
5. Provide me with a chance to earn a good deal of money	38	33	29	–	33	40	20	7	31	45	22	2	18	61	18	3
6. Give me an opportunity to work with people rather than things	62	28	10	–	37	42	13	8	49	24	24	3	58	21	21	–
7. Give me a chance to exercise leadership	14	48	38	–	23	32	35	10	16	37	45	2	25	43	29	3
8. Leave me relatively free of supervision	19	19	62	–	18	26	47	9	23	32	41	4	32	29	36	3
9. Give me social status and prestige	10	57	33	–	34	39	15	12	34	39	24	3	18	43	32	7
10. Provide me with adventure	33	19	48	–	33	27	31	9	22	33	43	2	18	39	39	4

a. The question was adopted from the Cornell University Study. See Goldstein et al.
b. 1 = very important; 2 = somewhat important; 3 = of little importance; NA = no answer.
c. Percentages all to be added horizontally within ethnic categories.

Table 30. Most Important of Ten Career Requirements, by Ethnicity
(Second Survey)
(in percentage)

Career Requirements(a)	Colored (21)	East Indian (104)	Negro (82)	White (28)
1. Provide an opportunity to use my special abilities	–	11	15	11
2. Enable me to look forward to a stable, secure future	27	29	35	56
3. Permit me to be creative and original	5	3	2	3
4. Give me an opportunity to be helpful to others	43	41	34	27
5. Provide me with a chance to earn a good deal of money	5	7	2	–
6. Give me an opportunity to work with people rather than things	10	1	5	3
7. Give me a chance to exercise leadership	5	1	2	–
8. Leave me relatively free of supervision	–	3	–	–
9. Give me social status and prestige	5	4	2	–
10. Provide me with adventure	–	–	3	–

a. See Table 29.

most important by all ethnic groups: (1) "A stable and secure future," and (2) "being helpful to others." The majority of white students (56 per cent) select "a stable and secure future" as the most important career requirement, while 27 per cent select the category of "being helpful to others." East Indian and colored students most frequently select the category of "being helpful to others" (41 per cent and 43 per cent respectively), with stability and security as the second most frequent category (29 per cent and 27 per cent respectively). Negro students select with equal frequency the categories of security and helpfulness. Although the category of "a stable and secure future" is a frequent choice among all the students, there are marked differences among ethnic subgroups. The groups which are more optimistic and have high expectations appear to express less concern about a stable future.

It is interesting to compare these findings with the study originally conducted among Cornell University students in the United States (by Goldsen, *et al.*). Only 10 per cent of the students in the Cornell study selected the category of "being helpful to others" as the primary career consideration. As may be seen in Table 30, students in the Trinidad survey select the altruistic category with considerably more frequency than the students in the United States sample. Gillespie and Allport also found altruistic orientation more frequently among the youth of the modernizing nations than among Western youth (1955). They observed that social and personal goals were frequently closely interrelated among the youth of new nations. This pattern of the close intertwining of personal and social aspirations also emerges strongly in the Trinidad data (see Chapter X) and is one of the striking findings of the study.

VII

Long-Range Goals

The students' essays are personal documents, earnestly and often vividly written, and they make engrossing reading. The opportunity to talk about themselves and their future plans seems to have let loose a flood of thoughts and feelings, and the autobiographies cover a broad spectrum of life interests. The students write of relations with parents and friends, of their hobbies and current interests; they discuss political problems and social change; they give their ideas about love, marriage, and children; they describe with great intensity their present preoccupations, and most ardently, they write of their future hopes and aspirations, particularly of the desire to elevate their standards: "Every man wants to be something." Both reality and fantasy are involved in the evocative thoughts they express about the future and in their hopes and dreams of achievement.

Autobiographies of the future are particularly effective in capturing dimensions of fantasy, for desires and expectations are projected into the distant years ahead and thus freed from the contingencies of present reality. Fantasies about future roles and statuses are undoubtedly typical of adolescence and may be considered an aspect of anticipatory socialization(1). Intuitively, one student asks, "How can a child raise his standard except through ambition?" Even when the free latitude of fantasy is tapped, however, subcultural influences in levels of fantasy emerge.

The importance of fantasy or fictional goals in mediating between individual needs and reality and in facilitating or hindering certain behavior has long been recognized. Sometimes the function of fantasy goals is characterized as a compensation for the inevitable disappointments and frustrations inherent in

1. The related concepts of ego-ideal, idealized self-image, and level of reality have been used to describe these mechanisms.

human life(2), and sometimes as preparation for and incentive to action(3). Adolescent fantasy, in particular, has been subjected to a great deal of theoretical speculation. Fantasy goals represent a typical stage of adolescent development according to Inhelder and Piaget, who believe that adolescent cognitive patterns are characterized by a temporary return to "autistic" thinking which produces an inflated self-image and extravagant illusions of future achievements(4). It is implicit in the work of Inhelder and Piaget that such dreams of grandeur represent a universal pattern of cognitive development in adolescence. There are some indications in recent studies, however, that the use of fantasy as a mode of adaptation to reality may be affected by sociocultural factors as well as by general psychological mechanisms. The overt expression of fantasy is also modified by cultural factors.

In their comparative study of the aspirations of youth, Gillespie and Allport found that the expressed desire to become a great person was much more usual among students from emergent nations than among youth from industrially developed countries. Similar results have been reported on intranational differences by Danziger, who compared autobiographies of the future of African and European high school students in South Africa(5). Jahoda(6), comparing occupational choices of high school students from Ghana with those of British secondary school graduates studied by Veness(7), found the former much more ambitious and fantasy-oriented in the choice of professions. In another study, comparing Maori youth with Pakeha (white) youth in New Zealand, Ausubel found that the Maori youth had more unrealistic aspirations, especially in relation to remote goals, than the Pakeha(8). Given these findings, the assumption of "autistic" thinking as a universal phenomenon of adolescent development needs to be further explored. In this context, the data from

2. See J. Lampl-de Groot, "Ego-Ideal and Super-Ego," in Ruth S. Eissler et al., (eds.), *The Psychoanalytic Study of the Child, 17* (New York: International Universities Press, 1962), 198.

3. Henry Murray et al., *Explorations in Personality* (New York: Oxford University Press, 1938).

4. Bärhel Inhelder and Jean Piaget, *The Growth of Logical Thinking* (New York: Basic Books, 1958).

5. Danziger, "Psychological Future of an Oppressed Group."

6. Gustav Jahoda, "Social Aspirations, Magic and Witchcraft in Ghana: A Social Psychological Interpretation," in P. C. Lloyd (ed.), *New Elites of Tropical Africa* (London: Oxford University Press, 1967), pp. 199–212.

7. Veness, *School Leavers: Their Aspirations and Expectations.*

8. Ausubel, *Maori Youth.*

Trinidad may contribute to a comparative perspective of the relation between these psychological mechanisms and sociocultural backgrounds of youth.

The Trinidad students' spontaneous descriptions of their final goals cover a broad range, from comparatively modest levels of self-fulfillment to expressions of grandiose achievement. For some students, dreams of the future are reality-oriented, as reflected in their stated goal to achieve professional skills and appropriate styles of life. Others, however, express ardent expectations of achieving "immortal recognition" as the result of "great deeds," or the amassing of "great wealth," or both. In fantasy they sometimes see themselves in multiple roles of global scope — as world-renowned scientists, discoverers, sports heroes, statesmen, philanthropists, and national models for future generations. The expression of very high fictional goals is not simply the expression of universal "school boy" dreams of grandeur, however; the study indicates that such visions of grandeur do not occur idiosyncratically, but follow consistent subcultural patterns. The following excerpts indicate some of the range of daydreams and aspirations expressed by the boys in the sample:

> I have always wanted to become a doctor. This profession has always stood for what is good and healthful for our fellowman. . . . What I want out of life is not only security and position but a way of relaxation and pleasure as often as the occasion permits. (White)

Another student writes:

> I am among those young men who prefer to go ahead if not to achieve great things to live a worthy life to myself and to my fellowman. . . . After that [a university education] I want whatever the ordinary man would want, a good home and family. To play music to be able to enjoy myself. I want to live a good and hardworking life, but all I can say is I desire a peaceful and fairly comfortable existence. (White)

Such relatively modest expectations may be contrasted with the following:

> I will certainly try to make this world a better place in which to live, so that in the year 2000 AD when some film producer in Hollywood is filming a review of the advances of the last 1000 years, my name will appear along with other great men for a brief period of time on the screen, along with other names belonging to men who tried to improve our world. (Negro)

> I will be the greatest footballer and athlete in England. After this I would like to settle down to be a lawyer or engineer and also a scientist. In the field of my chief profession, medicine, I would like to do something spectacular, so that the eyes of everyone would be upon me. I would like to discover a paramount cure for cancer. In science also I would like to do something spectacular. (East Indian)

The first striking difference in this dimension which emerges from the data is that between the sexes. Fantasies of heroic deeds and great accomplishments occur almost exclusively among the boys. One of the most ambitious girls in the sample is a fifteen-year-old East Indian girl of the Arya Samaj denomination who plans to be a barrister-at-law:

> If I do well in the examination, my parents have promised to send me abroad to study, and as anyone can imagine, I do not intend to let such an opportunity slip.

She is nevertheless attempting to win a scholarship, "so that I may not expense my parents, who are not very wealthy." She is one of the few girls who plans to take up a political career:

> I shall be met with much opposition, but if a person's mind is made up to accomplish something, nothing but death or serious illness will be able to stop him. I therefore am determined to clear any obstacles which may stand in my way, and to proceed with my work to the very best of my ability.

The very high final goals of this student may best be expressed in her own words:

> Again, I may meet with great success, and then would have the respect and admiration of the people of my country. They would be everlastingly grateful that I had proved that I could be of such a great ability and would try to assist me in my work of making the world a better place to live in. . . . In later Life . . . I will take to writing books. In this way I hope to present to the world my view of life and the standard to which the world has progressed. This may help unprogressive states and communities to reach the higher standard of the more civilized parts of the world. . . . Having accomplished all these things, and attained the standard I hope to reach, I would then be able to rest peacefully, assured by the fact that I had done all that was necessary of me and that after my decease, I would always be remembered as one who had spent her life trying to make the world a better place to live in.

A few of the girls express such comparatively modest sentiments as:

> When I die I will like the people to say, "This was a good woman who gave her life to the welfare of her people." (Negro)

Aspirations even of this nature are rarely expressed by the girls and, moreover, do not match the intensity of the desires for recognition expressed by boys. Social and cultural, as well as educational factors, tend to limit women's roles to the traditional, and there are few other feminine role models in their society for girls to emulate, even in fantasy. The Hollywood star image is apparently too

Table 31. Boys Expressing Very High Final Goals, by Ethnicity
(First Survey Essays)(a)
(in percentage)

Goals	Colored (83)	East Indian (207)	Negro (139)	White (40)
Great Wealth	11	13	19	16
Scientific or Literary Accomplishment	5	17	9	10
Political Power	2	13	11	—
Heroic Achievement(b)	—	3	—	—
Total Expressing Very High Final Goals	18	46	39	26
Total Not Expressing Very High Final Goals	82	54	61	74

a. Aspirations to become famous sports figures are not included, but would have increased the proportion of East Indian and Negro students expressing high aspirations.

b. These students imagine themselves becoming "great noble heroes" or "the most praised man in the world because of my bravery."

race-bound to provide even a fictional role, and, in 1957, very few women had emerged on the national scene to capture the imagination of young girls. It is also interesting that, aside from Florence Nightingale, no female figures of historic or international fame were selected as role models by the girls. Whether or not women are constitutionally "more realistic" or less achievement-oriented than men, early socialization based on sex role differentiation may function to make them so.

The following analysis of the 1957 data on the incidence and content of "very high final goals" is, therefore, based only on the autobiographies of the boys in the sample. The total frequency of fancies of great achievement varies significantly by ethnic group, regardless of social class(9). As Table 31 indicates, East Indian and Negro students are more likely to spontaneously express fantasy goals of great achievement than either the white or colored respondents. As may be seen, East Indian students rank highest in expectations of great achievement, closely followed by the Negro students. This would indicate an inverse relationship between ethnic status and the predominance of a highly idealized self-image. Moreover, social and cultural factors interact not only to condition goal-striving but also to provide the expressive style for the fantasy material. These differences can best be illustrated in the respondents' own words, starting with excerpts from the essays of East Indian students(10).

9. No significant statistical difference was found by social class. Among East Indian boys in the sample, however, Christians tend to be less fantasy-oriented than Moslems and Hindus.

10. All quotations are reproduced verbatim. Each excerpt is from a different respondent.

I would like to be that man well respected and talked of by all such as Abraham Lincoln, Pandit Nehru, and Sir Winston Churchill. My death should be a shock to all and the decease of a great human being.

I will write a book called the "Romance of Music and Literature." I will make this book as great as any Shakespeare play; then I will return to India to endeavor to become a genius in the film industry.

If my life could be like the negative [film] of the great Einstein, that is all I could ask. I would be satisfied I will have contributed my share to the world.

I hope in the future to be an international cricketer, and an international footballer. To let my parents and friends hear over the radio that I am a great cricketer. Let the people of my island listen to how I am batting or bowling. When I was about 12 years I was thinking how I can make myself very famous, and that my parents will think highly of me.

I am always thinking that one day I will be one great man in the world; that thought is constantly reverberating in my mind. When I have lived the life all the world would stand up and say he was a man.

Craving for recognition is a pervasive theme in these essays, and the desire for posthumous fame may also be a salient note in the fantasies:

I am sure that when I am buried and gone away my name will still be ringing in the hearts of men and my name will go down in the history of the world. (East Indian)

Writing about the distant future particularly lends itself to the projection of heroic self-images:

By the year 2000 the world will be in disorder, turmoil, ruin. I will rise at the top first, try to alert the coming destruction, to manoeuver to bring our Federation through trials and tribulations; to promote freedom and liberty. (East Indian)

I want to develop an adventurous spirit. I will tour the earth by air, by sea, and by land, I shall become a peacemaker among hostile people. (East Indian)

Multiple role achievement is another characteristic of the fantasy goals of some East Indian students. This multiple heroic role projection is shared by some of the Negro students, but is not found in the essays of any of the white or colored students in the sample. The range of fictional roles fantasied may encompass all possible fields of human endeavor:

I wish that I may do very well at that coming exam. My abilities and aspirations should be planted in a respectable ground that people may have good thoughts and look at me as a decent and brilliant man of generosity. If not successful, I would repeat it until my result would be successful; then obtain an HSC [Higher School Certificate] , and get a good job with a reasonable salary. When I have planted a strong foothold of myself in my country, about financial and educational responsibilities, I would then look to the economical development of my country. I would try to raise the standard of the present to a more serious and capable dignity. I would exterminate all those troublesome politicians who argue foolish subjects day after day. When my work is accomplished in the political field, I would then turn my thought to the agricultural conditions which are being prevailed in my country. I would deliver my utmost best and try to help the poor generation who suffer from many disastrous floods which sweep through the crops. Sluices, dikes and bridges would I center my concentration on. About the year 1966, when my country would be undergoing experience of jobs and luxury, I would turn my attentions on foreign affairs. Be friendly with all countries, so in case of help those countries would willingly submit to my helpful petitions. I would like to be a member of parliament where my authority would be even greater, not only to my country but also on worldly things. When I should reach the age of 33 my position would be so great that men would look at me with a clean heart and would be pleased at my generosity. I would like to become a noble scientific scientist and try and complete many wonderful experiments than my industrious studying of night and day. With my devoted studying on experimental subjects, one day I might be successful at discovering a plan for some outer space land. I would like to be seated myself in my fast travelling rocket and conquer and be the first human being to reach the moon. Then I would try to colonize lands for human existence, and I hope and pray that I might be successful on that subject. (East Indian)

This theme of world fame through multiple roles may also be seen in the following excerpt from the essay of a Negro student:

I would like to be a great man not only in music but also in sociology and economics. In the U.S.A. I would like to marry a beautiful actress with plenty of money. I would also like to be famed abroad as one of the world's foremost millionaires.

Far-reaching visions of glory involving leadership and political roles appear in the essays of 11 per cent of the Negro and 13 per cent of the East Indian students; the following are excerpts from the autobiographies of East Indian boys:

I have made all plans when I receive my grade (Senior Cambridge) I want to become a politician. I want to become a historian so that I can be a very good politician. I will like to be the premier of Trinidad and Tobago to become as the Hon. Dr. Eric Williams. Also to be one of the leading statesmen of tomorrow I will become one of the leading historians of the world if possible. I have great confidence that I will be one. My intention is to be one of the leading statesmen of the world, as Mr. Nehru.

After securing a good position in the minds of men I would then fight elections. If I am not successful I would try again but should I be successful Woe be to the corrupters! I would do everything to help the poor, yet not displeasing the rich. I would sincerely devote my life to them as I have been doing in the past. I would try my best to be the leader of Trinidad, I would lead it as Alexander led his people and should it be necessary I would prefer to die as Caesar for I am ready to face anything for the good of my people. After leading Trinidad I would like to try my luck to lead the West Indies. Of course, such day dreams may seem impossible for any one without the ambition but take heed, it is not from a "say and cannot do person."

High-achievement goals of Negro students also fall into the realm of lofty roles of political leadership, as in the following excerpts:

In politics I hope to come up against men like Krushev and other enemies of freedom. I hope I will be able to overcome them with my words, and put them to shame. It may seem that I am speaking of impossible things, but I hope to be renown, as a man like Sir Winston Churchill and to do as many great things as he did. I would like my entire family to be world-famous.

I expect to be a man of international fame, a man who by virtue of his political genius has acquired so much respect from his people that he will be fully capable of living in peace with his people.

I want to be a West Indian diplomat, I would like to have a magnetic power over men and a stronger magnetic power over women. I must be very intelligent and quick-witted; I must be fluent in at least seven languages. I must be very resourceful and I must say the correct thing at the correct moment. With these qualities and a wonderful foresight and with other necessary abilities which I can't forsee, I would be able to do wonders for the world by doing wonders for my nation.

The high aspirations of these Negro students may be fantasy(11) in terms of individual ability or the probabilities of individual opportunity for fulfillment; nevertheless in 1957 they were a sociopsychological reflection of the new channels of mobility in the emergent nation and although fictional roles, they may be closer to reality than they were in the past. Reality and fantasy assume different dimensions where there is a complementarity of personal identity and social ideology; the life history of the students coincides with the history of the new nation.

However, as previously noted, the element of self-doubt may sometimes enter into even the fantasy goals of Negro students, disturbing their dreams:

11. Sieuchand classified aspirations to become Premier, Governor-General, Governor, or Chief Justice as "phantasy choices."

Frankly, I would like to be a great person who would be remembered always; a person whose name would be used very much as Dr. Salk's, Galton, Einstein, etc . . . but there is always a barrier. If it is not my social standing, maybe I have not enough brains. I am thinking of inventing a flying submarine, but I am not very good at physics and maths.

Naturally, I expect to obtain a great accumulation of wealth after leaving school but so far it seems impossible. The only person I can rely on is my father, who is working strenuously to keep me on my legs.

Again, as previously noted, the element of self-doubt is entirely absent from the essays of East Indian students; none of their essays express uncertainty about personal capacity to achieve very high goals. Cultural differences in this regard are striking. The following lengthy excerpt from the autobiography of an East Indian student is literally a "high flown" daydream:

My great aspirations plans and expectations for the future rely upon the results of the Cambridge Examination. What I want to be is some great person, that people may look on me with pride, admire me, and after my death I want to be remembered by all as a great personage of my time. My desirous longing to be this person has always remained within me, and it will always remain, until I fulfill my want to be this great personage. I want to be a great scientific engineer, and I hope in the near future to fulfill this great desire. I spend many a day dreaming of my future in solitary places. Sometimes I am lost away in my dream, and I see myself pictured as the great scientific engineer that I wanted to be. I also see myself at the head of all scientific engineers and my name constantly repeating itself at the top of world news in a daily newspaper. What I like best in my dream is when I see myself pictured as a great explorer, exploring the other planets above us. In my dream I am filled with emotional feelings. I am stunned at the sight of how the people get along in space. They behave better than the people on earth, and their thinking and way of living are superior to ours. When I usually awake from my day dream, I think myself to be another person, the great scientific engineer, but soon I recollect my senses, and then I am myself again. I plan to go through all the hard ways of becoming a great scientific engineer, my great hope will not be stopped by any obstacles. The only obstacle will be nature itself, and death.

Wealth, prestige, and power represent three of the ideal values associated with Western society. Little is known, however, about subcultural differences in the importance given to each of these values and the motivations for achievement in these spheres which are transmitted to new generations. For some groups, prestige derived from scientific or literary achievement may take precedence over wealth derived from enterprise or over renown attained through political power. Young people will be motivated in the direction of the social and cultural values they experience. There are group differences among the students, as Table 31 shows, not only in the total incidence of fantasy goals, but also in the sphere of preeminence selected. The themes that predominate in the essays of those students who aspire to great accomplishments fall into three major categories: (1) scientific or literary achievement, (2) political power, and (3) great wealth.

We find that, in fantasy, the East Indian students are more likely to emphasize fame based on scientific or political achievements than on wealth, although wealth may be an inherent corollary of these achievements. Negro students choose evenly between the attainment of scientific or political fame and the attainment of wealth. White and colored students, on the other hand, tend to give priority to the attainment of wealth per se whenever high final goals are depicted. When socioeconomic differences are examined, intragroup variations may be seen in the content of these goals only among the East Indian students. Wealth as a primary goal is more likely to be emphasized by East Indians in the upper socioeconomic group than by either the middle or lower socioeconomic group of students (45 per cent of the upper group emphasize wealth as opposed to 10 per cent of the lower). Correspondingly, only 14 per cent of those in the high socioeconomic groups express the wish to "become a great person," as opposed to 45 per cent in the lowest socioeconomic group. The ethnic variable as a determinant of fantasy goals is evidently crosscut by socioeconomic status among East Indian students. This finding is especially interesting in the light of variations in the mobility and "creolization" of East Indians.

The expressed desire to achieve fame through political power and outstanding leadership also reveals interesting ethnic differences. Political office, particularly the mantle of leadership, is selected by only 2 per cent of the white and colored students as a life goal, as compared to 11 per cent of the Negro and 16 per cent of the East Indian students. Political power, the traditional monopoly of the white minority in the colonial society, has only recently shifted to new elites. White students openly discuss the racial shift in power and their feelings of exclusion from the political power structure. It is curious, however, that colored students in the sample also seem to ignore the path of personal achievement through political power. In contrast, Negro students, who still have to make their mark upon the society, are highly motivated toward political careers, while the East Indians, who feel excluded from top-ranking political positions, indicate the highest motivation in this direction(12).

Although colored students seldom express interest in politics as a primary career, they frequently indicate that they may consider a political role after they have attained success in their primary profession:

> Toward the latter part of my life I would like to enter myself in politics, and to do some little bit for the improvement and uplift of this young Federation of ours.

12. Political attitudes of students in the survey are discussed by Vera Rubin in "Culture, Politics and Race Relations."

The few colored students who selected a political career as their primary choice typically opt for the more sedate British model as seen from a distance, rather than the demagogic style they perceive as characteristic of some local politicians:

> I am obsessed with the idea of becoming a statesman, a classical statesman, and not a mere rabble-rouser who acts impulsively and makes much ado about nothing.

Not only the levels of fantasy and the sphere in which fantasy life is enacted but also the style in which the students express themselves reflects cultural and social class variables. The intensity and emphasis with which these aspirations are described and elaborated constitute different expressive styles. Expressive or personal style is not an easily quantifiable variable; nevertheless, there are a number of distinctive dimensions which can be selected analytically, as follows:

Intensity — The primacy of the fantasy level in the essay as a whole; extravagant imagery of anticipated achievements.

Emphasis — Regardless of the goal selected, emphasis is placed on the high honors, praise, and universal admiration received for accomplishments rather than on the accomplishments per se. Correspondingly, if extreme wealth is the final goal, value may be attached primarily to its intrinsic enjoyment or to the status symbol aspects, e.g., the East Indian boy who writes, "I will be one of the world's biggest businessmen. A big name, being recognized everywhere and honored wherever recognized"; or the one who flatly states, "I love to live in luxury."

Reality Orientation — Distinction between fantasy and reality and the recognition of possible and probable levels of achievement are also an aspect of expressive style.

These dimensions can best be captured through the students' own words. Intensity of feeling, desire for high recognition, and blurring of boundaries between dreams and reality characterize many of the essays of East Indian students with very high goals. These dimensions are found to a lesser extent in the essays of Negro students, who, as noted, sometimes express self-doubts about the possibility of attaining the lofty goals they have set for themselves. White and colored students, who are less likely to evince fantasy in writing about the future, also manifest considerably less intensity in their expressive style.

The white students who come from a privileged social background very seldom express grandiose expectations; when wishful thinking is expressed, it is characterized by relative restraint, as in the following excerpt:

> Like countless other young boys and girls, I hope some day to bring fame to my country with an achievement in some professional field. However, I do not picture myself as a dashing noisy politician, a khaki-clothed engineer opening the scenic Trinidad countryside with new roads and

bridges or some intelligent young lawyer fighting feverishly for justice in a world which may at times be unjust. I hope to be a medical doctor with the gift of skilled hands and a clear, quick thinking brain. This is the profession in which I hope to achieve something while in the service of my people and my country. . . . These are not high-handed dreams but fervent wishes that I cherish very deeply and feel confident of achieving somehow, someway in the future.

Where status maintenance is the imperative for occupational choice, the fervency of anticipation is apparently diminished, even when broader roles of community service are envisaged, as in the following excerpt:

I think that being a good husband and father, methodical and efficient in my profession as an engineer, fighting for the erection of more institutions for those who cannot help themselves, and lastly trying to make people happy and bringing the world to a state of peace is quite sufficient for any man to hope to achieve in the future.

Morever, awareness of reality as a highly contingent factor in the realization of aspirations is pervasive among white youth, the means to their goals are clearly perceived, and their "definition of the situation" is relatively "moderate":

I want to live a moderate life, earning a moderate pay, slowly but surely working my way in the law firm, but I don't want to be chief justice of the Federation or anything like that. In the rat race to get to the top, famous men have forgotten what happiness is like. Why do I take this attitude? Look around. All the other boys must be writing about their ambitions to be famous. They all cannot be, for hope is an elusive thing. To many it brings fame, but to many others it is a mockery of their folly-born desires. The middle way is always the best.

Since many of these students are relatively wealthy and are concerned with status maintenance rather than with social mobility, obviously the psychological meaning of their aspirations is very different from those of lower-class East Indian and Negro youth. The poor boy's fantasy is the rich boy's reality, as seen in the following excerpt from the essay of a white student:

By this time my father may be a share-holder in the company, I will take over the business. I will expand it and try to live up to the traditions that my father has built up.

Since this student expects to achieve high status, he has been included in the category of "very high final goal"; given his life situation, however, this goal can scarcely be defined as fantasy-oriented, and comparatively little intensity is manifest in expressing his intention to maintain his high family status.

Among the very few white students who express the desire for fame, there are accompanying expressions of self-doubt and feelings of insecurity:

I find myself despairing of ever achieving the plan which I have for the future. What, if any real worth have I achieved for the eighteen years of my existence as one of God's creatures on this earth? I desire a brilliant future. What hopes have I of seeing this desire fulfilled?

Another white student who feels he is "too lazy to try very hard" to realize his goals nevertheless charts the successful course he expects to follow:

With the seriousness and gravity of a few more years I am going to apprentice myself to a Chartered Accountant's firm and then to learn the trade. When I want to, leave the Firm and go to any other big business concern and work my way up to the top.

However, despite self-doubts, working one's way "up to the top" is a normative expectation for many white youth.

Feelings of uncertainty and conscious distinctions between reality and fantasy are also likely to be expressed in the essays of the colored students:

There are few people whose lives seem to matter and not be a mere passing away of years. Among these I rank the serious composer of music or the poet who are absorbed in their art. I have always longed for a life, painful and vain though it may seem, of a Beethoven or a Shelly. But seeing that I most probably will never approach anything like either, what am I going to do with the few years of life alloted to me? . . . it is time to leave off dreaming and turn to reality. Most probably I shall turn to one of the professions. My aim is to have an occupation which will procure for me a comfortable living but which will leave me plenty of time to pursue my other interests.

Among students in the more privileged milieux, imagination is given a free rein, but illusion is curbed by close proximity to role models and first-hand knowledge of means of attainment.

Factor analysis of the data in the first survey reveals a cluster of variables reflecting "great expectations." It includes the following variables:

Factor E: "Great Expectations"	Factor Loading
Does not see leisure time as an important source of satisfaction in life	.43
Expects to be more successful in his field than the average person with the same amount of education	.40
Feels optimistic concerning his personal future	.34
Expects to achieve a higher living standard than his family's	.26
Hopes to achieve fame, wealth, or power	.22
Would be most proud to achieve an important role in national affairs	.22

114

This cluster demonstrates that variables indicating high self-esteem, the expectation of being more successful than the average person, optimism concerning the future, and very high final goals are interrelated. The association between variables reflecting manifest high self-esteem and manifest optimism concerning the future, and those variables reflecting very high final goals, is of particular interest and reinforces the data previously presented.

Analysis of variance by ethnic groups shows that East Indian boys rank first on the factor of "great expectations," closely followed by the Negro students. Colored students rank third on this dimension, and the white students are lowest (differences were significant at .05). When religion was used as an independent variable, the Moslem-Hindu group ranked well above Catholics and Protestants (.01). No significant differences were found in terms of socioeconomic status, type of school attended, or age(13). Moreover, this cluster did not emerge at all in factor analysis of the girl's sample, regardless of ethnic affiliation.

The assumption has frequently been made that very high goals are associated with low self-esteem and feelings of insecurity. The well-known view(14) that the self-image of members of minority groups is characterized by feelings of worthlessness and inferiority is not supported by the present data. East Indian students in this survey rank highest on Factor E, which combines great expectations and optimism, confirming their expressed self-assurance as seen in Chapter IV. Low self-esteem is apparently not a necessary concomitant of membership in a minority status group. This finding fits into a pattern that extends well beyond the West Indian scene. Rosenberg, in a study of the self-image of adolescents in the United States, reports that Negroes are not characterized by low self-esteem(15). Bloom, comparing self-attributes of white, African, and Indian college students in South Africa, found that unfavorable self-attributes were common among whites but were seldom expressed by African and East Indian students(16). As the present analysis has indicated, there is a functional interrelationship between high self-esteem, optimism about the future, and very high final goals. Apparently, high expectations must have a complement of high ego-involvement to support even the fantasy of achievement.

The world today is not at peace. There are many hostile factions who are endeavoring to provoke others. One has to follow the code and help

13. See Appendix G.

14. See Erik H. Erikson, *Childhood and Society* (New York: Norton, 1950).

15. Morris Rosenberg, *Society and the Adolescent Self-Image* (Princeton: Princeton University Press, 1965).

16. L. Bloom, "Self-Concepts and Social Status in South Africa: A Preliminary Crosscultural Analysis," *The Journal of Social Psychology, 51* (1960), 103–112.

others. This is what I propose to do. People may be in distress, there may be disputes and severe combats among my people which I will endeavor to bring to a solution and discover some means by which to terminate them. I would like to be an architect and an artist to imitate Leonardo Da Vinci. I would like to paint the famous Last Supper. I am sure that it will be a great success. I would aspire to attain or even to exceed that point, thus I will be quite confident that I have endeavored to assist mankind and elevate the needy and incompetent. (East Indian)

HIGH FINAL GOALS IN THE SECOND SURVEY

One of the questions left unanswered by the results of the first survey was whether the difference in incidence of expressed desire to become a great person was due to difference in cognitive representations of the self or to cultural and social class differences in style of expression and freedom to express fantasy. Consequently, the problem arises as to whether a more sensitive instrument could elicit the pattern of "autistic" thinking that Piaget postulated as a universal pattern of adolescence.

To further examine these aspects of fantasy and to control for possible group differences in style of expression, a series of open-ended and multiple-choice questions was included in the second survey as an additional means of inducing expressions of the desire for greatness. An Index of Expectation of Greatness was developed on the basis of these additional data. The Index was designed to measure the occurrence rather than the intensity of the individual's expressed desire for great achievements; every student who expressed the desire for greatness one or more times was, consequently, included in the scoring. The results obtained from the essays in both surveys will first be compared to establish a base line for the results of the Index.

The results of the two surveys based on the essays (Table 32) are strikingly similar and validate the findings of the first survey on subcultural differentials in

Table 32. Expectations of Fame Through Scientific, Literary, or Political
Achievements, by Ethnicity (Based on Essays)(a)
(in percentage)

	Colored	East Indian	Negro	White
First Survey	(83)	(207)	(139)	(40)
	7	33	27	10
Second Survey	(21)	(104)	(82)	(28)
	5	33	20	11

a. These figures are partially reproduced from Table 31. The category of wealth was not included in the analysis of expectations of becoming a "great person," and, therefore, has been omitted in Table 32.

Table 33. Index of Expectation of Greatness(a), by Ethnicity
(Second Survey Questionnaires)

Colored (21)	East Indian (104)	Negro (82)	White (28)
32%	50%	47%	15%

a. The Index is based on the following variables: expectations of becoming a "great person" expressed in the essays and/or in reply to the following questions: (1) *What do you most hope to accomplish in the course of your life?* (2) *What two things could you conceivably accomplish during your lifetime of which you would be most proud?* and selection of *To achieve fame by doing something outstanding* as the primary goal among the seven alternatives given on the questionnaire. (See Appendix G.)

expressed high levels of aspiration. Comparison of Table 32 with the Index (Table 33), based on the questionnaire, shows a considerable increase in manifest expectations to become a "great person" among colored and Negro as well as East Indian students. Thirty-two per cent of the colored students express very high goals in a structured situation, as compared to 5 per cent based on spontaneous mention in the essays. Even though they are less likely than Negro and East Indian students to spontaneously express very high expectations, they disclose a considerable increase in very high aspirations in response to structured stimuli; apparently the middle-class imperative to follow British role-models of restraint may be modified when such measures are introduced. However, no significant increase is found among white students when Tables 32 and 33 are compared, confirming the previous finding of a relative lack of expressed very high aspirations among the white students. This parallels a number of findings, the most recent of which is a similar study by Thelma Veness (1962) of several thousand white students in the final form of secondary schools in England. Veness found the students to be strikingly lacking in ambition and with only modest aspirations for the future. The relative absence of expectations of greatness among white students in the Trinidad sample is further confirmed in factor analysis of the data from the second survey. A factor emerged that indicates non-achievement orientation(17). This factor comprises the following variables:

Factor F: "Non-Achievement Orientation" (Second Survey)	Factor Loading
Occupational achievement is not an important source of satisfaction in life	.44
Wealth is not the main goal in life	.27
In the choice of one's career, social status and prestige of an occupation are considered of little importance	.24

17. See Appendix G.

Analysis of variance of this factor of "non-achievement orientation" shows significant differences (.01) between ethnic groups. White students rank highest and East Indian students lowest, followed by Negro students, who are slightly higher than the East Indians, thus reproducing exactly in reverse the pattern of achievement orientation that emerged from the first survey. However, "non-achievement" is a relative matter when it involves maintenance of a comfortable status, as may be seen from the following excerpt written by the son of a customs broker:

> I have no wish to amass a fortune but I suppose, in common with the rest of men, it would be pleasant not to have financial worries once one has reached middle-age. (White)

Achievement is necessarily measured from the point of departure; the son of the cane farmer has a longer way to travel than the son of a customs broker in order to achieve status, and more fanciful goals may be necessary to motivate him:

> I would like. . . to be a man such as Lincoln or even one of the greater sportsmen in the world. I expect to be a great scholar as well as a great sportsman. (East Indian)

FUNCTION OF FANTASY

As has been amply illustrated, there is a striking incidence of lofty, essentially unobtainable or unrealizable goals among lower-class students, which sometimes seem to flow in a daydream-like sequence. Are they consequently to be dismissed as socially inconsequential? The function of extremely high goals for the adaptation of the individual to social reality has been a matter of considerable speculation. Fantasy in the regulation of personal behavior has been alternately viewed as compensatory, dysfunctional, energizing, or paralyzing. Freud observed that unsatisfied wishes are the driving power behind every fantasy and that fantasies contain the fulfillment of wishes and improve an unsatisfactory reality. Socially as well as personally induced frustrations can thus be remedied in fantasies of becoming a great, powerful, or illustrious person.

Other writers, like Schachtel, however, consider fantasy a dysfunctional adaptation to reality(18). Still others believe that lofty goals are a reaction to feelings of inferiority and "diminished" ego(19). We must keep in mind that these are speculations and there is little empirical data to provide corroborating evidence to validate any of the theories. Validation would call for longitudinal studies in an effort to determine to what extent the fantasy goals of youth

18. See Ernest G. Schachtel, *Metamorphosis* (New York: Basic Books, 1959).

19. See Rosenberg.

hindered or favored later achievement. For the present analysis, the data sheds light on possible theoretical constructs, and the insights of the students on this score are quite interesting. The students themselves, in psychosociological fashion, sometimes analyze their flights of imagination:

> Several have been the times that thoughts of greatness enticed me and lifted me above the sphere of solid work. For this laxity I have suffered, a fact that has led me to put less trust into elusive dreams, and that has inspired me to more endeavor. (Negro)

The positive function of fantasy is quite clear for some of the students in the sample:

> As young people delve into the future they find their hearts leaping with secret ambitions, plans and expectations which may never be realized, but the fact of their presence encourages and urges one onward to the road of success in life. My chief ambition is to amass enough money so that I can go away to study to be a doctor. (Negro)

An East Indian student whose essay encompasses a series of free-flowing fantasies writes:

> I am very ambitious. I want to be a recognized person in my future life.

The content of fantasy is necessarily conditioned by culture; the traditional visions of Plains Indian youth, for example, are materially different from those of youth in Western society. While subcultural correlates of the incidence and intensity of fantasy in the student sample are essentially "Western," we find a dimension which is specific to East Indian students. They frequently discuss the cultural concept of self-perfection as an essential path to achievement, as in the following excerpt:

> My principal aim and object in receiving education is to be able to give assistance to mankind, and this can only be accomplished by perfecting myself. There is no limit to perfection; there will always be an opportunity for assisting mankind as one travels on the road to perfection. My ambition is to become perfected and to specialize in surgery, not in order to be able to acquire a lot of money or fame as some low thinking people might believe, but to assist mankind.

Another writes:

> My aim in life, therefore, will be self-perfection, which is the only means which can be used to accomplish the great and noble deed of assisting mankind which I believe is the sole duty of each of us on earth.

Whether or not the accomplishment of "great and noble deeds" is a realistic or realizable goal, the concept of self-perfection may buttress the drive to achievement:

> We can't exist without a purpose in life. I have come to the ultimate conclusion that my prime purpose in life will be to help humanity, not physically but mentally, and if possible, morally. This I am sure I can do through the medium of self-perfection and a good profession.

This concept appears only in the essays of East Indian students and provides an interesting example of cultural conditioning for achievement. We have no data on child training differences in the different subcultures[20] and their effect on achievement orientation; we do not know whether East Indian mothers, directly or indirectly, inculcate their sons with values of self-perfection, duty to humanity, and striving toward high goals. These values, however, are part of the fabric of the Hindu world view which stresses salvation through individual effort and self-improvement. This view is expressed in the writings of an Indian psychologist, who states:

> If we make proper use of our power of discriminative control, and shape ourselves into the ideal picture which the great seers and leaders of humanity have placed before us, we can become divine and our society heavenly[21].

Internalization of this "divine" ideal is evident in many of the essays of East Indian students: "I want to educate the entire world which is corrupted today". Some students indicate they would like to go to India to study yoga in order to attain self-perfection. This value system apparently provides psychological supports for many of the boys of low social status by emphasizing the potential power of the individual to change the environment and overcome his ascriptive position of status inferiority. Nevertheless, they perceive that low status, in actuality, can only be overcome through social recognition; consequently the preoccupation with self-perfection is inevitably linked to the expressed desire to "assist mankind" and thereby obtain recognition and even fortune:

> I am born of poor parentage, but of Hindu ancestors who had given up their lives as martyrs of Trinidad for their love for their religion. My motive is to attain self-perfect first, and then I shall see about others doing the same. Thus, in this way I shall be able to live happily in luxury and free from lust, pride and jealousy, and resultingly I will try to make others happy. I should free disseminate to others the little I possess so as to make this world pure and noble and one fit to be dwelt in, rather than the

20. See Green, "Values of Negro and East Indian School Children in Trinidad."

21. B. L. Atreya, "Indian Culture: Its Spiritual, Moral and Social Aspects," in United Nations Educational, Scientific and Cultural Organization, *Interrelations of Cultures* (Paris: UNESCO, 1953), p. 130.

human dregs of society. I'll try until one day fortune may perhaps smile on me who is so meek, eager and interested.

While in the traditional society of India individuals could not overcome low caste status, in the modern achievement situation in Trinidad it appears that the "divine ideal" can be realized in professional statuses as new opportunities are opened; perhaps reincarnation can be realized within one's lifetime.

I might as well study for some high position that only a few men have been able to achieve. I expect to pass through this world only once and I would like to do some great deed that will long be remembered. (East Indian)

The problem of unfulfilled achievement drives is a sociological as well as a psychological question. Looking at the matter from an essentially psychological point of view, Schachtel is severely critical of the dysfunctional aspect of fantasy:

The persons who resort to the magic feeling of omnipotence, in an attempt to deny the difficulties of reality will be particularly vulnerable to the encounter of obstacles and frustrations, because they are in such a glaring contrast to the narcissistic fantasy of omnipotence. Often these people react with despair or hopelessness to realistic difficulties(22).

The Trinidad data show that fantasy thinking, even though predominant among adolescents belonging to groups who historically enjoyed little prestige in the society at large, is correlated with a very favorable "self-image." This is contrary to Erikson's view that underprivilege and discrimination undermine one's sense of self-identity(23). "Great expectations" are characteristic of the Negro and East Indian youth in the study who have had to face objective conditions of stress. "Great expectations" and "wishful thinking" do not coexist psychologically with pessimism and dysphoria. Pessimism and dysphoria would be too undermining to a youth striving for achievement. Given the reported worldwide orientation of non-Western youth toward "ego-inflation," it may be surmised that undetected cultural elements rather than environmental pressures influence this pattern. One possibility to consider is that an insecure ego is a deviation or a peculiarity of Western industrial man. It is necessary, however, to examine each situation in its social context.

A final consideration should be introduced here. Within the framework of the total social structure, in which only 6 per cent of the youth of the same age group reached secondary school, the East Indian and Negro students in the

22. Schachtel, p. 37.

23. See Erikson, *Childhood and Society.*

sample represent an exceptional minority. Attainment of the upper forms of the secondary school against heavy odds is an exceptional achievement in itself; this may foster or reinforce the perception of being different and exceptional. Both social and motivational forces may reinforce each other to produce the kind of idealized self-image seen in the following examples:

> I am the sort of person who thinks he is above the average man, perhaps because I am generally superior in the line of sports and education. (Negro)

> The HSC [Higher School Certificate] exam requires an intelligent and industrious good student which fits into my position very perfectly. (East Indian)

It is extremely significant for both personal and social development that the idealized self-image of the students is essentially related to people and to society. The students may have great fantasies, but they are not alienated from their society as are some of the youth in other countries. They are not "deviants with deviant commitments"; they have a deep involvement in their era and in the future of their country.

> If I could be the leader of the island in my future days, I would be happy to lead and to make a better and more prosperous community. Let us hope that one day I may achieve what would be an achievement for the betterment of the island as a whole. (Negro)

VIII

Marriage and Family Life

Marriage and family life are a major concern of the future projections of almost all the students in the survey. Marriage expectations and plans, regarded universally as the "normal" aspirations of youth, assume a special sociopsychological saliency for youth in the survey. Social class and subcultural differences in social organization in the West Indies are especially marked in family life and the different patterns of mating and marriage which have emerged historically. Due to their difference from conventional European models, Negro lower-class patterns of mating have been a particular focus of attention and have been demarcated under the rubric of the "West Indian Family."

Also called the matricentric or matrifocal or grandmother family, the West Indian Family is characterized by the presence of a female head, with children and grandchildren or other female relatives comprising the functional household unit. A major characteristic of the matricentric family is the absence of the adult male in the regular role of household head and chief provider and the sporadic presence of visiting males in the roles of father and lover. Unlike these "visiting" or "living with" unions, common-law unions are characterized by the regular presence of the male as mate-father in the household, forming more traditional "nuclear" family unions which are of longer duration.

The various types of union lead to different sets of reciprocal duties and obligations; in common-law unions, deeper relationships between mates and parents and children may be formed, and may lead to legal marriage, according to the social norms of the greater society. Consensual unions, although stable, do not carry the binding obligations of legal unions. Legal marriage (in the juridical and ritual sense) is sometimes referred to as "Western" or "Christian" marriage to differentiate it from "folk" forms which are considered to be "deviant."

There has been a good deal of scholarly interest in seeking the sources of these variant forms of mating. A number of students have traced their origins to the imperatives of cultural continuity; Herskovits found antecedents in polygamous forms of family organization in Africa(1); a study of lower-class family organization in Barbados concludes that the patterns are old English in origin(2). Whether family type "origins" are presumed to be African or English, causality is found in cultural continuity. Others have traced the antecedents of contemporary West Indian family forms to slavery, pointing out that the intensive process of acculturation, the massive uprooting and purposeful derangement of family and tribal groups, effectively destroyed the possibility of retaining traditional African forms of family organization. In the New World, patterns of casual alliances were conditioned and necessitated by the structure of the slave society. With the abolition of the slave trade, the planters' requirements for increase of the slave population led to slave "breeding" practices, in which production of progeny was the major interest, without regard for interpersonal relations of the parents. Furthermore, short-term or long-term concubinage alliances initiated by masters with female slaves not only removed such women from the pool of permanent partners, but established concubinage as a normative model. The institution of slavery is thus seen as the antecedent of contemporary family forms in the West Indies(3). Other students have pointed to the post-slavery plantation system as the chief determinant, asserting that it created structural regularities which mitigated against "Western" types of marriage among the plantation workers(4).

Whatever the explanation has been, whether historical or functional, the designation of such types of union under the general rubric of the West Indian Family stemmed from their alleged predominance in the Caribbean, as opposed to other world areas. In fact, the peculiarity of the West Indian Family as a Caribbean social institution or a particular attribute of Negroes in the New World can no longer be maintained. A number of studies have reported the existence of matricentric family forms among lower-class, semiskilled, irregularly employed sections in other countries among diverse ethnic groups(5). The matricentric family is considered a characteristic of the "culture of poverty"(6):

> matrifocality, a high incidence of consensual unions, and a large percentage of households headed by women, which have been thought to

1. Herskovits, pp. 295–296.

2. Sidney Greenfield, *English Rustics in Black Skin* (New Haven, Conn.: College & University Press, 1966), p. 172.

3. See E. Franklin Frazier, *The Negro Family in the United States,* rev. and abridged ed. (New York: Dryden Press, 1951).

4. See Rubin, *Plantation Systems of the New World.*

5. R. T. Smith, *The Negro Family in British Guiana.*

6. Elliot Liebow, however, challenges the idea of attributing matricentric family forms to "culture," arguing that they are "predictable responses to conditions in [our] society

be distinctive characteristics of Caribbean family organization, or of Negro family life in the United States turn out to be traits of the culture of poverty and are found among diverse peoples in many parts of the world and among peoples who have had no history of slavery(7).

Despite the disapproving views of "promiscuity" taken by the "establishment," lower-class family forms in the West Indies tend toward a continuum – from casual unions, to common-law unions, to formal marriage; each individual, however, does not necessarily pass through such a cycle of family forms(8).

The "Western" ideal of marriage is pervasive throughout the society(9), but "marriage got teeth;" it is serious and is not lightly entered into(10). Among lower-class Negroes, formal marriage is primarily dependent on the position of the male as a stable wage earner as prerequisite to being the household head. It has also become functionally tied to a specific set of social and economic attributes, such as ability to provide the costly validating feast, independent ownership of a house and furnishings, and, ideally, the ability of the husband to maintain the social role of his wife as a non-wage-earning mistress of the household. All of these conditions are seldom fulfilled among the under-

---

rather than persisting patterns." As Liebow notes (p. 208), "There is, fortunately a growing suspicion that 'culture' and 'historical continuity' may not be the most useful constructs for dealing with lower-class behavior. Hylan Lewis, for example, suggests that 'It is probably more fruitful to think of lower class families reacting in various ways to the facts of their position and to relative isolation rather than to the imperatives of a lower class culture' ('Culture, Class, and the Behavior of Lower Income Families,' p. 43)."

7. Oscar Lewis, *A Study of Slum Culture: Backgrounds for La Vida* (New York: Random House, 1968), p. 19.

8. G. W. Roberts, "Some Aspects of Mating and Fertility in the West Indies," *Population Studies, 8* (1955), p. 211.

9. The prevalent attitude to formal marriage as an ideal goal does not necessarily bear out the Goode-Blake hypothesis that lower-class individuals regard the non-legal union as deviant. It underscores the fact that legal marriage and middle-class status are correlated; consequently, marriage as a goal is a corollary of mobility. See William J. Goode, "Illegitimacy in the Caribbean Social Structure," *American Sociological Review, 25* (1960), 21–30; and Judith Blake, *Family Structure in Jamaica* (New York: The Free Press, 1961).

10. There is an Anansi story about Compére Tiger being judged for cursing his mother by Compéres Lapin, Chien, Cheval, etc. When the judges sentence Compére Tiger to get married, he says that his punishment is harder than he can bear. Anansi (the spider who lives by his wits) is the chief character in the folk tales of the Ashanti. See Philip M. Sherlock, *West Indian Folk-Tales* (London: Oxford University Press, 1966). Folk values can be found to sanction every type of union; non-marriage is an acceptable alternative under certain circumstances. For those who wish "to be looked upon" by the greater society, however, there is no alternative to formal marriage. See Hyman Rodman, "The Lower Class Value Stretch." Revision of a paper read at the annual meeting of the Eastern Sociological Society, April, 1961.

employed. Marriage is consequently delayed, but ultimately the majority of the population, whether under the pressure of children or grandchildren, of church or community, attains the status of formal marriage(11).

Legal marriage is the normative pattern among the middle class as well as the upper class(12). Outside unions traditionally have been maintained by men in the upper ranks as elsewhere in plantation societies, but middle-class women are expected to retain premarital chastity and their fidelity to marriage vows. Male extramarital relations were formerly with lighter-colored lower-class women, although now, with changing sex norms, such liaisons are increasingly intra-class. Nevertheless, middle-class girls are not expected to enter premarital unions, and illegitimacy is strongly tabooed, though not nonexistent. Consequently, for mobility-oriented youth, and particularly for lower-class Negro girls, marriage and legitimacy of offspring are particularly salient concerns.

East Indian family organization has followed another course of development in the West Indies. In the early period of indenture, rural isolation, social exclusion, and the expectation of returning to India fostered cultural retentions. Arranged marriages, marriage at an early age, and the joint family system were maintained according to traditional Hindu and Moslem practices, and ethnic endogamy was rigorously observed. There have been, consequently, significant sociocultural contrasts in East Indian and Negro marriage patterns and family life. A study of mating patterns in Trinidad points out that "in spite of the shortage of women among these immigrants, the decay of the caste system and the pressure of Western influence, the Indian family structure has persisted." As the authors note, however, "there has been some change in family organisation, noticeably improvement in the status of women, the decay of arranged marriages and a decline in the joint family system"(13).

Caste endogamy, the structural prerequisite of the traditional Hindu marriage system, began to be modified in the early period of indenture. Due to imbalance in the sex ratio of the immigrants, it was not possible to maintain the rigorous

11. See Vera Rubin, "The West Indian Family," in *Family Relationships: 4th Caribbean Conference for Mental Health, Curacao, Netherlands Antilles, 1963* (Caribbean Federation for Mental Health, 1965), pp. 53–65.

12. An early observer noted that "rank and privilege which are strongly marked in every thing seem to turn marriage into a distinction somewhat of the nature of nobility and to reserve it in general for the proprietors and leading men of the country" (J. Walker, *Letters on the West Indies*, quoted in Orlando Patterson, *The Sociology of Slavery* [London: MacGibbon & Kee, 1967], p. 165).

13. Braithwaite and Roberts, "Mating Patterns and Prospects in Trinidad," p. 121. These authors point out another interesting change that has taken place under contact, though in reverse of the rural lower-class Negro family pattern which starts with casual unions and is characterized by later marriage: "Due to the existence of early marriages and arranged marriages in a new culture which permitted of greater personal freedom, marriages broke down and new 'common-law' relations possessing neither legal nor religious sanction were entered into. In consequence of the disorganization of family life, visiting unions similar to those among Negro populations also developed" (p. 122).

Table 34. Mention of Marriage Plans, by Sex and Ethnicity
(First Survey Essays)

Colored		East Indian		Negro		White	
Boys (83)	Girls (52)	Boys (207)	Girls (72)	Boys (139)	Girls (115)	Boys (40)	Girls (17)
75%	88%	74%	83%	76%	88%	81%	100%

patterns of endogamy characteristic of the system in India(14). Ethnic group and religious endogamy became more significant than caste endogamy(15), although caste endogamy is still considered the ideal pattern for the older generation. The increase in caste and varna exogamy "probably indicates the extent to which class has successfully competed with caste as a determinant of social status among Hindus"(16). The breakdown of caste endogamy may also become a salient factor in status mobility for lower-class East Indian girls. It has been reported that "the higher castes are much less likely to object to unions with lower caste girls, especially if they are light-skinned, beautiful, wealthy, or have a secondary school education"(17). Levels of acculturation have varied, largely with individual mobility; in general, cultural traits have persisted more among Hindu groups, and Christian East Indians have been the most acculturated. However, there has necessarily been some modification of traditional marriage patterns among all the denominations.

The attitudes of the youth in the survey toward marriage and marriage partners can be examined against the background of traditional and changing cultural patterns and modification in the social structure and in light of the impact of mobility strivings on their aspirations for the family of procreation. In the essays, as might be expected, there is more frequent mention of marriage by girls than by boys — a constant which overrides ethnicity, confirming general findings from other countries that girls' aspirations are primarily centered on marriage and the family. Trinidad girls not only spontaneously mention marriage more often than the boys, but focus their autobiographies on marriage and family life as may be seen in Table 34. On direct questioning, however, responses concerning marriage plans are almost universal in every group (see Appendix J).

14. Schwartz, "The Failure of Caste in Trinidad," p. 119. A recent study of marriage among East Indians in a rural community concludes that "endogamous marriage is not of sufficient frequency to allow the existence of caste, much less its perpetuation." See Schwartz, p. 142.

15. Schwartz, p. 125.

16. Clarke, p. 190.

17. Ibid., p. 187.

Among the girls, as has been seen, preoccupation with family life is greater than among the boys; however, there are striking qualitative differences in the discussion of marriage in their essays which reflect subcultural differences. This is especially salient in the autobiographies of lower-class Negro girls, who are often preoccupied with ideals of romantic love and idealization of marriage and the wedding ceremony itself. A Negro girl writes, "My wedding will have all the grandeur and respect of a real noble wedding." "Respect," that is, respectability, is as important an ingredient, structurally, as the romanticizing aspects of "grandeur" and "nobility." While the ideal of romantic love and achievement of status through marriage may be a compensatory "fantasy" for many of the girls, there is also some indication of an avoidance reaction among lower-class Negro girls who "fear" and "dread" marriage. "I do not like marriage; I am somehow afraid of it." "I had always dreaded the marriage tie — Now I start to accept the fact that it is something necessary." In contrast, none of the respondents in other ethnic groups express overt fears of marriage in terms of interpersonal relations.

Table 35. Expressed Fear of Seduction, Abandonment, and Illegitimacy(a) among Girls, by Ethnicity (First Survey)

Colored (52)	East Indian (72)	Negro (115)	White (17)
21%	11%	30%	—

a. In reply to the open-ended question, *What are the two worst things that could conceivably happen to you during your lifetime?*

Lower-class Negro girls also tend to be more concerned with avoiding premarital pregnancies and with the possibility of abandonment. From the psychiatric point of view, it may be considered desirable that "there is a place in the society for the unmarried mother"(18), but for "upward looking girls," this is clearly not a desirable prospect (see Table 35). The unusually high concern of Negro girls with the possibility of traumatic interpersonal experiences may be seen as a counterpart of their fantasies about romantic love and marriage. The

18. Commenting on a study of slum families in Puerto Rico, the psychiatrist Edwin A. Weinstein observes: "It is of interest to contrast these attitudes to those in other economically deprived societies in the Caribbean. In the English-speaking West Indies there is much more sexual equality and less need for women to achieve identity in the role of the virtuous wife resisting the lustful advances of men. Sexual intercourse and pregnancy are not necessarily aimed at marriage and there is a place in the society for the unmarried mother. In situations where marriage is not economically feasible, the pattern of the unmarried mother may be a good deal more functional not only in providing premarital sexual experience but in serving as a means of population control" (Review of Lloyd H. Rogler and August B. Hollingshead, *Trapped: Families and Schizophrenia, Caribbean Studies*, 6, 3 [1966], 59).

strain may be heightened by the conflict between lower-class non-legal mating forms (and consequent *de jure* illegitimacy) and the model of "correct" behavior emphasized in the school and perceived as a middle-class norm. A Negro girl, who is herself "illegitimate"(19), projects:

> On hearing of my pregnancy my husband must be overjoyed and call me all the wonderful names in the world.

A Negro boy also raises the issue:

> I would like to have six children, four boys and two girls, all legitimate of course. I do not want the misfortune of having any illegitimate children. I want to be a devoted husband. Normal middle class is what I want.

Legitimacy as well as formal marriage are thus middle-class imperatives.

It is sometimes overlooked that marriage also validates the role of the male(20), but lower-class students establish the correlation:

> After I have myself to be a man and can support a family, I will search for a peaceful home and get married. I will carry on my home the best I can and will give my children the best education as possible and place them in a better position than I was in. (Negro)

Changing attitudes toward early marriage, parental choice of partners, and traditional women's roles are evident among East Indian girls. In their autobiographies, they spontaneously indicate plans to delay marriage, and eventually to combine it with a career. There are two alternative orientations to female roles. The first is the traditional pattern:

> . . . work should be left entirely upon the husband who is there to provide for his wife and she in return should always be home doing his homework; . . .

The second is an avoidance pattern — to dedicate oneself entirely to a profession and avoid marriage altogether:

> Marriage was the great and sole ambition in the seventeenth century, but I don't think that it is considered such a great achievement today. I think that people can devote their lives otherwise.

19. As previously pointed out, most of the students in the survey come from two-parent, married families. No questions were asked concerning *de jure* "legitimacy" of the students; nonetheless the faculty would mention the few children who were illegitimate. In one case "illegitimate" was written by a faculty member on the cover page of a student's paper. This boy wrote: "I was intended for the priesthood, but I am an illegitimate child. Everytime I think of that I wish I was dead. Not for being illegitimate, but for not getting into the priesthood." (Negro)

20. See Rubin, "The West Indian Family."

East Indian girls are the only ones who express the view that marriage is anachronistic; avoidance however is expressed in terms of perceived career conflicts. Emphasis on the traditional role of the housewife also is less frequent among East Indian than among white, colored, or Negro girls. Most often, East Indian girls state they would like to combine the role requirements of marriage with a profession, straddling their ambivalence.

> My duty will be divided between the home and the school [teacher]. I shall try to do the best I could in these two places. I hope I shall not neglect the one for the other.

Apart from anticipated delay in the age of marriage, there are other indications of both traditional patterns and breaks in cultural continuity. A minority of East Indian students specify that they will seek parental consent for their marriage, as tradition requires: "I will ask for my parents' approval, because even though I have reached such a height, I don't want to disrespect them." Twenty-five per cent of East Indian students who mention desired attributes of a spouse, in contrast to 11 per cent of Negro students and no mention by colored and white students, stress endogamy as a cultural requisite of marriage: "I will marry someone of my own nationality(21), a promise which I owe to my mother and father." Combining religious, ethnic, and social-class imperatives, another student writes: "Religion forbids marriage to any other person but a cultured Indian." On the other hand, completely breaking away from endogamous patterns, more East Indian boys than those in any other group (35 per cent) who discuss their future spouse in their autobiographies spontaneously express the desire to marry a white girl.

Sociological studies in the West Indies and the United States have indicated widespread preference among Negro and colored males for a lighter spouse, and the phenomenon of "lightening the race" is well known. However, only 13 per cent of the Negro students who discuss attributes of a wife specify preference for a white wife, while 11 per cent specify that they will marry a "brown" girl, or a girl of the same race. One boy writes of his potential spouse, "she must be dark." This trend seems to fall within the nationalistic orientation of this group as a whole. Ten per cent of the colored students mention preference for a white wife, and there is no specific statement about endogamous marriage either among colored or white students (see Table 36).

Desirable attributes of the ideal spouse fall into several categories. Traits of kindness, manners, charm, wittiness, and the like have been classified as the "expressive dimension." Factors of profession, education, ability to provide (or care) for the family, and so on are classified as the "performance dimension."

21. "Nationality" here more likely refers to ethnic group than to "nation," the term used by rural East Indians for caste.

Table 36. Principal Attributes Desirable in a Wife (First Survey Essays)
(in percentage)

Attributes	Colored (50)a.	East Indian (52)a.	Negro (51)a.	White (9)b.
Expressive Dimension	40	35	30	–
Performance Dimension	25	40	22	–
Physical Attractiveness	45	35	30	–
White Partner	10	35	13	–
Same Race Partner	–	25	11	–

a. Number who mentioned attributes of spouse in essay.
b. Number is too small for statistical analysis.
Note: Total percentage may exceed 100 per cent as multiple attributes were mentioned.

Beauty and physical attractiveness as desired traits in the partner have been set into a separate category. Finally, in this historically race-conscious society, mention of the preferred race of the spouse has also been separately categorized.

In terms of specific attributes, most of the boys stress the expressive dimension of the desirable marriage partner – charm, good manners, and good character – as well as physical attractiveness(22). It should be pointed out that even such personality traits are frequently class-conditioned. "Charm" and "good manners" are seen as middle-class attributes; such values, which form part of an idealized image, are reinforced by the women's pages of local newspapers and by radio programs as part of socialization to middle-class styles of life. These media of communication provide a technical literature which prescribes and standardizes behavior appropriate to elite status(23). In the social-class context, expressive as well as performance traits may thus be considered as part of a generalized image of status. East Indian boys, however, more than others, specifically stress the performance dimension as well as the expressive(24).

East Indian and Negro girls, who showed the greatest degree of personal ambition in the female sample, also accentuate the performance dimension as an

22. See Sieuchand for comparative data.

23. See McDonald.

24. In answer to a sentence completion question, *A wife* . . . , 14 per cent of the Negro and colored boys write, "should be faithful," a concern that is not expressed by students in any other group. On the same sentence completion, 14 per cent of East Indian students gave responses concerning "obedience" as expectations of the role of wife, an attitude expressed uniquely by this group. Again, while 17 per cent of the Negro and colored students associated the concept of companionship with the word "wife," only 1 per cent of East Indian students gave such a response. On the other hand, 14 per cent of the East Indian students, but none of the other students, conceive of a wife as a "source of inspiration." Data from the sentence-completion questionnaire are not included in this text.

Table 37. Principal Attributes Desirable in a Husband (First Survey Essays)
(in percentage)

Attributes	Colored (19)a.	East Indian (27)a.	Negro (57)a.	White (8)b.
Expressive Dimension	48	26	41	–
Performance Dimension	35	70	62	–
Physical Attractiveness	17	30	14	–
White Partner	13	–	–	–
Same Race Partner	–	–	5	–

a. Number who mentioned attributes of spouse in essay.
b. Number is too small for statistical analysis.
Note: Total percentages may exceed 100 per cent as multiple attributes were mentioned.

attribute of the ideal husband, as may be seen in Table 37. East Indian girls score highest (70 per cent) on this dimension, followed by Negro girls (62 per cent)(25).

Mention of desirability of a white spouse among girls is limited to 13 per cent of the students in the colored group, while 5 per cent of the Negro girls mention preference for a partner of the same race. Perhaps girls in other groups do not mention ethnic affiliation of the spouse because either intragroup or intergroup marriage is taken for granted, but other significant status attributes can be singled out.

While East Indian girls stress the performance dimension and physical attractiveness of the desired spouse, Negro and colored girls also stress the expressive dimension. Expressive attributes such as kindness and courtesy, even the image of a "loving and pleasant companion" may be idealized concepts of middle-class male behavior patterns; Trinidadian girls, however, also appreciate a "witty" and "chatty fellow" as a life companion(26). Idealized middle-class performance attributes are linked to the girls' cherished hope for lower-class Negro male dependability and trustworthiness, as may be seen in the following excerpt:

He should not be perfect, as no one is perfect, but he will have the marks of a true gentleman, honesty, kindliness, a cheerful disposition, religious minded and of the same religion, industrious, intelligent, neat, dependable, loving, and above all trustworthy to his country and to me. (Negro)

Normative mating patterns by social class and ethnic group, the sequence of types of marital union, and preferred age of legal marriage provide a frame of

25. Significant at the .001 level.

26. See Sieuchand for similar findings.

Table 38. Expected Age at Marriage, by Sex and Ethnicity (First Survey)
(in percentage)

Age	Colored	East Indian	Negro	White
Boys	(83)	(207)	(139)	(40)
24 or under	22	14	12	13
25–29	59	60	57	70
30 and over	19	26	31	17
Girls	(52)	(72)	(115)	(17)
24 or under	42	52	41	93
25–29	48	41	48	7
30 and over	10	7	11	–

reference for analysis of the students' attitudes with regard to age of marriage. In the essays, the students usually indicate the stage of life at which they expect to marry rather than a specific age: after completing secondary school, on returning from studies abroad, or after entering a profession. Most students state their preference to marry after they have returned from their studies abroad and have spent some years in professional activity(27). Delay of marriage until professional goals are achieved is a common expectation, especially among Negro and East Indian boys:

I do not intend to get married while at University. It would hinder my chances of getting through and would decrease my chances of reaching my goal. It does not mean that I will shun women, but I will not endanger myself by exposure to circumstances that would most certainly end in my getting married. (Negro)

If a man is married he can no longer study as when he was a bachelor, because he would have to look after his wife and children. If a man is poor he can never be married with a good woman. (East Indian)

Another, who plans to study law at Oxford, explains:

In the meantime I would possibly have several girlfriends and having an enjoyable time, but I would not marry until after I qualify as a lawyer. (East Indian)

To examine the links between educational and occupational aspirations and perception of the need to postpone marriage until professional goals are achieved, the students were asked: *"At what age do you expect to marry?"* Replies on expected age at marriage by ethnic group are given in Table 38. As may be seen, 31 per cent of the Negro and 26 per cent of the East Indian boys

27. See Sieuchand.

expect to marry after they are thirty, as compared to 17 per cent of the white and 19 per cent of the colored boys. As one boy writes:

> Many times as a youth I have thought about the happiness to be derived from a happy marriage and good living with a fine family. This would also wait on its turn which might come in my late 30's. (Negro)

Delayed marriage is a variable which has often been linked to upward mobility(28), and results from the present studies (both 1957 and 1961) confirm this relationship. Variation of mating patterns, and consequent postponement of legal marriage, complicate comparisons between age of marriage in Western industrial societies and the West Indies. The national average age of marriage for Trinidadian men in 1959 was 29.1. In terms of the requisites for marriage, this may be seen as confirming the pattern. Moreover, the data reveals that postponement of marriage is clearly perceived by the most ambitious boys as a necessary strategy to a high career goal, and they spontaneously discuss this problem.

Recent demographic studies have indicated that "early mating is much more prevalent among East Indian than among the other racial groups"(29). It is, consequently, especially interesting to find that East Indian students, more often than others in the sample, spell out the link between career achievement and postponement of marriage as a prerequisite to goal attainment.

> I have promised my dear old mother that I will not marry until I have obtained my doctorate.

> After having settled down as a dentist and having made a sufficient amount of money I would then have my own private office. Then and only then I would think of having a family.

This is a frequent theme in the essays and is linked with the perceived effect on achievement plans of falling in love. Avoiding any possibility of involvement, one boy writes: "Since marriage is closely connected with love, I would do my best to avoid all attack of it, and wait until I am about 30."

There is a good deal of discussion of relations with the opposite sex, in terms both of future plans and of the present — sometimes poignant, as with shy boys:

> I am very shy and everytime I am around girls I get flustered and cannot speak. Right now I am thinking of one special girl. She knows that I like her but it seems that she too is very shy. I hardly ever speak to her and

28. See Seymour Lipset and Reinhard Bendix, *Social Mobility in Industrial Society* (Berkeley: University of California Press, 1959).

29. Braithwaite and Roberts, "Mating Patterns and Prospects in Trinidad," p. 122.

whenever I get a chance no words ever seem to come out. I would like to marry her. (East Indian)

sometimes lyrical:

We are here on earth to love and enjoy life. If it were not so we would not have been given an ear for music, an eye for beauty and an appreciation for nice smooth things like the touch of a girl's arm. (Negro)

The students, however, clearly distinguish between their dreams of the future and the need for postponement of immediate gratifications. This may necessitate the postponement of marriage, as well as reinforce the ethos of mobility, in order to provide the appropriate style of life, in due course.

... marriage will have to wait until I can provide for a wife and children every luxury that is known within my sphere. I will get married about my thirtieth year. (Negro)

Before going on further I would like to state that I have already planned out that I would not marry any person unless I am working an easy job and obtaining an "Okay" salary to support my household. (East Indian)

Marriage is perceived as a normative pattern of the society, particularly as a symbol of middle-class life-style, and students in all the groups mention expectations of marriage with the same frequency. Postponement of marriage plans until professional goals have been attained reflects a strong achievement orientation among students from groups which traditionally marry late as well as groups which traditionally marry early: "At the age of 36 I would get married, as this is the only way you are looked upon."

In both surveys the students were asked to rank three out of six possible sources of life satisfaction including family, career, political activities, religion, leisure pursuits, and community activities. The results indicate certain regularities in career aspirations versus family aspirations as expected sources of satisfaction. All the students, as has been noted, include family relationships as an important factor of present and future orientation. However, the primacy of these goals varies: Negro and East Indian boys and girls emphasize career achievement and success rather than the family per se as a source of primary satisfaction; for white students (boys as well as girls) establishing the family of procreation is stated as a major life goal. White boys were more likely than the other students to rank "family life" as the source of greatest satisfaction in life (30) (see Table 39).

30. The Cornell study carried out among university students in the United States revealed an even greater emphasis on family life as a source of satisfaction; 55 per cent of the respondents selected family life as first choice on the same question. See Goldsen et al., *What College Students Think*, p. 60.

Table 39. Career versus Family Life as the Most Important Source
of Life Satisfaction, by Sex and Ethnicity
(in percentage)

	Colored	East Indian	Negro	White
First Survey				
Boys	(83)	(207)	(139)	(40)
Career	35	57	51	36
Family	20	17	40	40
Girls	(52)	(72)	(115)	(17)
Career	41	57	47	47
Family	37	23	20	27
Second Survey				
Boys	(21)	(104)	(82)	(28)
Career	20	50	46	36
Family	20	17	21	36

Actually, even though the essays of the girls are more universally oriented to family life than those of the boys, the girls select a career more frequently than family life as the greatest source of satisfaction. As may be seen in Table 39, the girls in every group, except for the colored, overwhelmingly select a career as the highest source of satisfaction. Apparently the idea of having a career is a powerful attraction to most of the girls, which indicates a widening chasm between traditional expectations concerning the role of women and their own feelings about personal fulfillment and possibly reflects changing norms.

Although white girls, more than any other group, unhesitatingly stress marriage as a life goal in their essays, they are somewhat ambivalent about the burdens of assuming family roles. The girls may be aware of latent problems arising from changing attitudes to careers for women and the cultural norms which pressure them to seek marriage as a means of achieving or maintaining elite status. They tend to accept the cultural norm of marriage without career, however, and given the strong position of white boys in this regard, they apparently feel they have little choice.

A multiple-choice question was added to the second survey specifically to examine the attitudes of boys toward careers for women(31). Responses to the question are given in Table 40. Various dimensions of traditional-modern attitudes emerge: White boys disapprove more frequently than any other group of women having careers at all (21 per cent)(32); colored students are by far the most emphatic in approving a career for a woman, provided that she is not

31. Goldsen et al. p. 48.

32. This is practically identical with findings in the United States, where 22 per cent of boys give this response *(ibid.)*.

Table 40. Boys' Attitudes to Women Working, by Ethnicity (Second Survey)

	Colored (21)	East Indian (104)	Negro (82)	White (28)
Which of the following statements concerning women working do you come closest to agreeing with?				
In general, I don't approve of women having careers.	5	12	9	21
I approve of a woman having a career if she wants one, providing she is not married.	62	36	34	39
I approve of a married woman having a career if she wants one, providing she has no children.	10	10	13	7
I approve of a married woman having a career is she wants one, providing her children are older than:				
Infancy to preschool (up to 5 years)	–	–	–	–
Grade School (6–10 years)	–	1	1	4
Junior High (11–14 years)	5	1	5	1
High School (15–17 years)	10	1	10	–
18 or older	–	5	10	7
I approve of a married woman having a career if she wants one, regardless of the age of her children.	10	31	17	10

Note: Total percentages do not always equal 100 per cent because figures were brought to nearest 1 per cent in computing tables.

married (62 per cent); while East Indian students are least traditionally oriented in this regard, 31 per cent – three times as frequently as colored or white students – approve of women having a career if they want one, regardless of the age of children(33).

It is also interesting to note differences in response to the question, *Who will have more influence in family affairs, wife or husband?*, by sex and ethnicity. As may be seen in Table 41, the majority of boys select the alternative of equality of marriage partners, however a higher percentage of the girls expect equality in marriage. The least discrepancy by sex is found among the Negro students. East Indian girls appear most eager to achieve a position of equality with their husbands. Given their high level of aspirations, it is interesting that they also

33. In breakdown by religious affiliation, Hindu students are highest on this score: Hindu, 35 per cent; Moslem, 28 per cent; Christian, 30 per cent.

Table 41. Attitudes toward Husband-Wife Influence in Family Affairs,
by Sex and Ethnicity (First Survey Questionnaires)
(in percentage)

	Colored		East Indian		Negro		White	
	Boys (83)	Girls (52)	Boys (207)	Girls (72)	Boys (139)	Girls (115)	Boys (40)	Girls (17)
Husband	22	13	22	6	19	13	29	20
Wife	6	7	8	9	6	4	7	–
Equal	69	80	70	83	74	81	64	80

Note: Because individual percentages were brought to nearest ½ per cent, total percentages of boys and girls do not always equal 100 per cent.

aspire to break with the traditional pattern of male dominance in the East Indian nuclear family. The authority of the female is eventually recognized in the joint family, but is generally ascribed to the traditionally potent mother-in-law and denied to the daughter-in-law(34). In contrast to the 20 per cent of white girls who feel the spouse should be more influential in family affairs, only 6 per cent of the East Indian girls gave this response. On the other hand, 9 per cent of the East Indian girls, as opposed to 4 per cent of the Negro and none of the white girls, indicated that they would be the more influential. East Indian girls are apparently more anxious and willing than the others to break with traditional sex roles.

Individually expressed concepts of sex roles, occupational roles, and family roles are socially conditioned psychological factors. Whether girls are more "affectively" oriented than boys is undoubtedly as much an aspect of sociocultural value systems as of psychobiological factors. Gillespie and Allport reported much greater discrepancy in Egypt, Japan, and Mexico in anticipation of equality of husband-wife roles(35). Among these groups many more girls than boys express a desire for equality in marriage, while the boys expect to take the dominant role. By comparison, the Trinidadian students are considerably more egalitarian.

In addition to the opportunity for spontaneous discussion of family life (past and present) afforded by the autobiographies, there were a number of areas in the questionnaire which could elicit responses concerning the salience of family life as a major preoccupation. On the basis of these responses an Index of Orientation to Family Life was constructed.

The greater orientation toward family life of girls as compared to boys may be seen in this Index (see Table 42). One striking ethnic difference is the lower

34. See V. S. Naipaul, *A House for Mr. Biswas* (London: Deutsch, 1961).

35. Gillespie and Allport, *Youth's Outlook on the Future* (1955).

Table 42. Index of Orientation to Family Life, by Sex and Ethnicity
(First Survey Questionnaires)(a)

Colored		East Indian		Negro		White	
Boys (83)	Girls (52)	Boys (207)	Girls (72)	Boys (139)	Girls (115)	Boys (40)	Girls (17)
48%	75%	41%	56%	40%	70%	51%	79%

a. The percentages in the Index include all the students who mention their future family at least once in response to the following questions: *If you should get a large sum of money five years from now, what would you do with it? What two things could you conceivably accomplish during your lifetime that you would be most proud of? For what end would you make the greatest sacrifice of personal comfort, time and money?*

percentage of East Indian girls who express the need for family orientation. Family life is more likely to be salient among white and colored students of both sexes, but much more so among the girls.

Confirming this pattern, 83 per cent of the white students in the second survey, as compared to 43 per cent of the Negro students, stated "a successful family life" or its equivalent in response to the question: *What do you most hope to accomplish during your life?* Responses to this question by white students are strikingly similar, as may be seen in the following examples:

A successful marriage, a successful career.

A harmonious marriage. With this accomplished most other things will follow.

I hope to work so that I may secure the welfare and happiness of my family.

To be a good husband and father and to attain such a position in my career as to be a credit to my family and benefit to my community.

To be a good family man, live a good life, die a happy death and go to heaven.

As noted above, approximately half as many Negro as white students included family life among their most hoped for accomplishments. Even among this group, however, priority was generally given to professional achievements, as may be seen in the following responses of Negro students:

Respect, prestige, a good stable home.

To become a doctor and have a high standard of morals and to have a happy marriage if I marry.

To be a respected man who can leave his children with something to hold on to.

To be a doctor of medicine who is accomplished loved and respected in the community and be a very good father and husband.

To have a good job and raise a good family.

In response to this question, colored and East Indian students also tend to cite career accomplishments primarily:

I hope in my lifetime to become recognized and accepted as one who has done much for the general uplift of mankind. (East Indian)

To be a prominent famous Economist to be a humanitarian in principles and possibly to lead my country onward with the world progressive ideas. (Colored)

I would like to do some great deed so that I could be knighted by some Queen or King. (East Indian)

I would like to do something that would be of benefit to my country and to all mankind. (Colored)

Another striking confirmation of the strong family orientation of the white boys comes from the factor analysis of all the data in the boys' sample for the first survey, which revealed a privatism cluster that closely resembles the description of privatism by Gillespie and Allport — orientation toward family life, lack of involvement in political and national affairs, and religious leaning(36).

Factor G: Privatism	Factor Loading
Expects to have many children	.70
Would like to have many children	.67
Does not believe participation in national and international affairs to be an important source of satisfaction	.27
Would be most proud to achieve a successful family life	.26
Expects to marry	.25
Would most like to have, among two things now lacking, a family of procreation	.20
Feels need for a religious orientation or belief	.18

36. See Appendix G.

Analysis of variance shows significant differences between ethnic groups (.05) on this factor. The means obtained by the various groups show that the white students rank first on the privatism factor, followed by the colored students. East Indian students rank lowest. (See Appendix F.) Factor analysis of the girls' data did not reveal any clear-cut cluster of privatism in any group.

The family of procreation assumes a prominent place in the autobiographies, and children are mentioned almost as frequently as marriage. The girls are slightly but consistently higher than boys in their mention both of marriage and of themes centered on children, with the exception of the East Indian girls, which is consistent with their greater emphasis on careers than on family life. Girls are also more specific about the number of children they plan to have, again with the striking exception of the East Indian girls, who are in the lowest percentile of any group in the size of family anticipated.

It is striking that both the East Indian boys and girls express the least interest in having large families (five or over), in contrast with the high East Indian birthrate on the island(37). However, decreases in fertility in urban areas have been generally reported with a rise in the levels of education(38). Demographic studies indicate that among East Indian women who have had six or seven years of schooling the fertility rate is lower than among those with no schooling(39). It is, therefore, not surprising to find the same trend among East Indian upper form students. Some express fears of the dangers of over-population, which may take a lurid turn: "People will die of hunger, and there will be a form of cannibalism again."

Essentially, East Indian students are concerned with the domestic problems of large family size. As one vehemently states:

My purpose for not having more [children] is because when I realize the

37. The Caribbean is one of the high-fertility regions of the world, with a crude birthrate of 30 per 1000 and over, and with a level of 2.0 in terms of gross reproduction rates. G. W. Roberts reports in "Reproductive Performance and Reproductive Capacity in Less Industrialized Societies," *Annals of the American Academy of Political and Social Science, 369* (1967): "East Indians who have migrated to Africa and to the Caribbean continue to show very high fertility rates, rates, in fact, higher than those of the other elements of the populations in their country of settlement" (p. 44). In Trinidad itself, "the figure for the East Indians (5.36) is 55% higher than that for other races (3.45)," in terms of total fertility (G. W. Roberts and Lloyd Braithwaite, "Fertility Differentials in Trinidad," in International Population Conference, Vienna, 1959, *Report* [Vienna: The Working Committee of the Conference, 1959]). Island-wide demographic studies have indicated that as a result of differentials in fertility rates, East Indians may in due course "constitute in fact a majority of the population" (Braithwaite, "Social Stratification in Trinidad," p. 15). Cultural rather than biological factors underlie these differentials in fertility.

38. Roberts, "Reproductive Performance and Reproductive Capacity in Less Industrialized Societies."

39. Roberts and Braithwaite, "Fertility Differentials in Trinidad."

Table 43. Number of Children Expected and Desired, by Sex and Ethnicity
(First Survey Questionnaires)
(in percentage)

Number of Children	Colored		East Indian		Negro		White	
	Expected	Desired	Expected	Desired	Expected	Desired	Expected	Desired
By Boys	(83)		(207)		(139)		(40)	
0–2	11	12	16	18	16	7	7	7
3–5	70	70	63	68	64	60	61	60
5+	20	18	21	14	20	33	32	33
By Girls	(52)		(72)		(115)		(17)	
0–2	17	19	16	17	17	17	–	–
3–5	69	59	70	76	63	66	53	53
5+	14	22	14	7	20	18	47	47

Note: Total percentages do not always equal 100 per cent because figures were brought to nearest 1 per cent in computing tables.

"trials and tribulations" my mother underwent with her large family, it just breathes hate in me to have more than three.

Among mobile families generally reductions in family size have been reported in the literature(40), and the East Indian students seem conscious of the relation of social mobility to family size.

Negro students also express concern regarding problems of family size:

I would like to have not more than four children so that I can take better care of them.

I have always wanted to have a large family and provided I can afford to take care of them (clothe, feed and educate them) properly, I should like to have as many as five or six children.

Responses to two questions about the number of children desired and the number of children expected reveal only slight differences within each group between the two dimensions, as reported in Table 43. Both desire for and expectation of large families (five or more children) are much higher among white boys and girls than among students in other groups.

Results of the second survey are presented in Table 44. There are no striking differences with respect to the number of children expected; about one-third of each ethnic group in the sample expects to have more than five children. There are differences, however, in the number of children desired; the number of East Indian students desiring a large family (more than five) drops to 18 per cent; colored students in the sample express the desire for more children than they

40. Lipset and Bendix.

Table 44. Number of Children Expected and Desired, by Ethnicity
(Second Survey Questionnaires)(a)
(in percentage)

Number of Children	Colored (20)(b)		East Indian (97)		Negro (80)		White (27)	
	Expected	Desired	Expected	Desired	Expected	Desired	Expected	Desired
0–2	10	10	6	12	8	9	11	11
3–5	58	35	63	70	64	61	57	52
5+	32	55	31	18	28	30	32	37

a. Boys only in the second survey sample
b. Differences in number are due to fluctuations in number of responses.

expect; the number of children expected is approximately the same for Negro and white students.

Family planning programs are being instituted on a national scale in response to the high rate of population growth and projected population increase. Previously, this had been in the realm of tabooed topics, and little public information or education about family planning was available. It is evident, however, that although the majority of students plan to have as many as three to five children, they are still concerned about providing for them "properly."

Where the possibility of attainment of their own goals is uncertain, the students tend to project their aspirations onto their children, as a form of generational mobility. This is especially true of the lower-class Negro girls. As one writes in her essay:

With the money I have saved I will pay for the education of my offspring, so they will not suffer the same fate as I.

Other Negro girls write in a similar vein:

I would not like my children to have just a secondary education as father and mother have, but some higher profession as a doctor, druggist or engineer.

I would really like to make some worthy contribution to the world and the only way I think it could be done is by making out of someone a great and dynamic personality, which the world could admire.

In fact, whether through career accomplishment or family role, the desire for status achievement is paramount among lower-class girls as well as boys: "There is nothing so rewarding as looking upwards" (Negro girl). One way out of the personal dilemma of career versus family life is through vicarious aspirations for children. As one girl who would give up her medical career for marriage writes:

> I do not think I would regret it either, because I might even be the proud mother of a family of doctors. (East Indian)

The theme of high aspirations for children is pervasive.

> I would like my child to have a higher education than I have. I would like my child to have a happier upcoming. (Negro)

The percentage of spontaneous mention of high educational aspirations for children is presented in Table 45. Boys and girls mention the desire to have their children attain a university education with the same frequency. East Indian students, followed by the Negro students, are outstandingly higher in this dimension, as in the previous variables related to personal achievement (desire to attend a university; expectation of very great achievement; emphasis on performance dimension of spouse; low family size). The striking similarity of boys' and girls' scores on this variable should facilitate the fulfillment of this aspiration. The second study confirms the pattern of greater frequency of expressed high educational aspirations for children among Negro and East Indian students than among colored and white students.

Table 45. Aspirations for University Education for Children, by Sex and Ethnicity
(First Survey Essays)

Colored		East Indian		Negro		White	
Boys (55)(a)	Girls (42)	Boys (149)	Girls (48)	Boys (100)	Girls (92)	Boys (24)	Girls (13)
27%	22%	45%	45%	37%	37%	25%	25%

a. Number who spontaneously discuss children in essays.

Table 45a. Aspirations for University Education for Children, by Ethnicity
(Second Survey Essays)

Colored (21)	East Indian (104)	Negro (82)	White (28)
14%(a)	22%	23%	11%

a. Percentages are based on total samples, not restricted to those who mention children as in Table 45.

The moral and religious values associated with middle-class life-style are emphasized by Negro and colored students, especially, in their discussion of the training of children. Respectability, moral worthiness, charity, church-going, and obedience to authority are frequently stressed as essential attributes for status achievement, with its social group participation components, as in the auto-biography of a lower-class Negro girl attending a private school:

> My children must enjoy life more than I did. They should partake in all social activities as possible. Attend parties, go to selected dances, take part in football, cricket, basketball, netball, and be acquainted with many decent crowd. They should help the poor, sick, and simple, and be "lawful" to superiors. They should also try to be nice to one another. They must go to church every Sunday and pray sincerely to God.

The frequency of those who mention the need for moral and religious training for children is presented in Table 46. As may be seen, the Negro and colored students, both boys and girls, express the desire for moral and religious training of children with much higher frequency than either the East Indian or white students. While this represents a cultural norm for colored students, it is apparently emphasized as an essential requisite of approved middle-class behavior and in order to maintain social distance from the lower class, which is considered to be of low morality. For the lower-class Negro students, it is undoubtedly another indication of anticipatory socialization for mobility. White students presumably do not have to stress these normative expectations for status maintenance, and there is practically no mention of them in the essays. East Indians do not express these preoccupations of the Negro and colored students with the same frequency. This may also be a cultural "given" for East Indian children, but there may be less stress on this facet since they have had less access to urban, middle-class, Europeanized models of behavior.

Undoubtedly there has been for all the less socially advantaged groups what has been described as "a tendency for outsiders to develop unrealistic images of non-membership groups which, if they are positive reference groups, lead toward

Table 46. Mention of the Need for Moral and Religious Training for Children, by Sex and Ethnicity (First Survey Essays)

Colored		East Indian		Negro		White	
Boys (55)(a)	Girls (42)	Boys (149)	Girls (48)	Boys (100)	Girls (92)	Boys (24)	Girls (13)
38%	41%	13%	28%	40%	41%	1%	–

a. Number who spontaneously mention children in their essays.

unqualified idealization"(41). West Indian sociologists have underscored the compulsion to maintain "proper behavior" as a social class index:

> ...the black middle class person if he or she is to maintain the respectability which is the theoretical ideal of the middle and upper classes must maintain a rigid moral attitude as any deviation is treated as typical black behavior by the upper classes(42).

The need to maintain social class distance is also indicated by Braithwaite, who observes that the colored middle class stresses morality in order to distinguish itself from the lower class(43). Social mobility is thus correlated with adaptation to the perceived image of the norms and values of the middle class. This is especially clear in the emphasis on socialization of children for good manners and courtesy. As one Negro boy writes:

> If I have any boys I would try to get them to attend St. Mary's because he can learn whatever manners he did not pick up at home.

The discussions of future family life in the essays bring together many themes of desired life-styles and personal and cultural proclivities:

> I would have to get a job (and buy a car). I would then become more of a ladies gentleman and my restrictions would not be limited. I would like to be a proper ladies gentleman, suave and yet a daredevil, clairvoyant, reckless and yet with finesse, to have a rollicking good time up to about the age of 33, then I would think about settling down with a wife who would be just about 21. Then raise a family and take on the responsibilities of married life, take the utmost care in bringing up children and teach them the real values of life from an early age. (Colored)

And the son of a Hindu laborer combines all the elements in his fantasy of future life:

> Then my plan is to go to Paris, see the beauty of the city and return home with a scientific profession together with a beautiful wife. She must be so full of exquisite and matchless beauty that I shall be proud to represent her to my poor mother and father with great humility.
>
> After I had pleased my parents I shall move away to a fine house of my own. During the time of the erection of my building I would allow my wife to stay at my parents' home. There she will assist my mother and take

41. Merton, p. 351.

42. Fernando Henriques, *Family and Colour in Jamaica* (London: Eyre & Spottiswoode, 1953), p. 92.

43. See Braithwaite, "Social Stratification in Trinidad."

care of her. But by that time my father would be mean with age and he will be looking forward for my help. To be sincere, I would not neglect them – I would strain every muscle to comfort them, because, in my boyhood there were no others to take care of me; and now I am old enough, I would take care of them in turn. Oh! how would they feel; they will feel very happy to know that the only son of their offsprings is not lost in the cares of too much riches.

IX

The Ethos of Mobility and the Consumer Culture

It has been said that "a quiet revolution" is taking place in the Caribbean. As in other developing countries, political and economic change has brought in its wake social and psychological change, particularly in the attitudes and normative values of populations for whom the possibility of achieving a better way of life becomes a reality rather than a dream. The promise of individual and social progress is inherent both in the political fact of Independence and in the technological revolution of the times.

The primary concern of the mobile students is for "recognition"; one student elevates this drive to that of a "biological urge":

> Man's primary needs are food, shelter and protection, with those foregoing needs man would be able to exist in the fundamental sense of the word that is to be physiologically fit, but in this modern world a third need seems to be gradually arising: the biological urge for recognition where he could be secure, where he could be recognized in other words to attain a high social standard, and whether it is a merit or a demerit to my character this urge seems to possess a prominent place in my expectations, plans and hopes for the future. (Negro)

The drive for recognition is certainly a deeply rooted psychological urge among these boys, and is generally indivisible from the urge to attain the style of life commensurate with being respected:

> I want to be a respected man in my town. [Then, after having completed my professional studies,] I will buy shares in some business and be a gentleman in my own way. . . . I would live a life of luxury. (East Indian)

Social mobility in modern societies presupposes material improvement as part

149

of change in status, and the students are quite articulate about anticipated standards in life-style. As one student writes:

What I want out of life is not only security and position, but a way of relaxation and pleasure. (Colored)

The image of the consumer culture has been diffusing rapidly from industrial societies and provides a potent motivation for individual mobility and social change in the new nations. The consumer goods "message" heightens aspirations sparked by widening of the opportunity structure.

In 1957, when the first survey was undertaken, annual per capita income in Trinidad was $612(B.W.I.), the highest in the British West Indies(1); however, there was a high rate of both unemployment and underemployment. By 1961 the economic picture had changed somewhat(2), but the national economy was still considerably behind that of the industrially developed countries. Nevertheless, even in 1957, the imagination of the population as a whole had undoubtedly been gripped by the possibilities of social and economic change to be introduced with Independence. A number of differences by ethnicity and social class have been pointed out in examination of the students' concerns. It is significant, however, that the values of the contemporary consumer culture are shared by all groups.

The desire for fulfillment of consumer aspirations is strikingly reflected in the essays of the students. Intensity of aspiration is greater among the emergent elite whose status had previously been conditioned by both color and class and who had been furthest removed from the ideal life-style. "I want to be a recognized person in my future life" is a leitmotif in the essays of lower-class students, and there is frequently an equally compelling drive to achieve new styles of life: "I wish to accomplish culture and to have all the comforts of life." It is important, then, to examine to what extent the consumer culture has become internalized as part of the "ethos of mobility" and what changes, if any, have occurred in presumably traditional values relating to life-styles. Keeping status and personal fulfillment in mind, how do the mobile youth view their future in terms of consumer aspirations?

For one thing, by definition of being socially mobile, they aspire to a different style of life from that of their parents, both quantitatively and qualitatively:

We live in a very solitary and unconfortable shack with two rooms, so the

1. The West Indies, Federal Statistical Office, *National Income Statistics,* No. 1, 1960.

2. The CIAP Subcommittee report on Trinidad and Tobago indicates that per capita income was $812 (in T & T dollars) in 1960, Table SA-1, in Inter-American Committee on the Alliance for Progress (CIAP), *Domestic Efforts and the Needs for External Financing for the Development of Trinidad and Tobago* (Washington, D.C.: Pan American Union, 1967), hereafter cited as CIAP.

first ambition is to erect a major building and put all the necessary accommodations and necessities therein. Secondly, I will have a business installed in the same building for my family to run. By this time all my family should be at ease and comfort. (Negro boy)

The desire for material improvement is particularly characteristic of the upwardly mobile students, regardless of ethnic background:

At the very first moment that I have accumulated enough money, I would buy my own car. As all other boys today, a car is the foremost thing I think of. The life my father leads is a shade too slow for me and I would tend to step on mine a bit. I would want to lead a life that would be comfortable provided with lots of entertainment and the necessary varieties that make up a good life. (East Indian boy)

The careful frugality and parsimonious style of life which characterized generations of East Indian immigrants has given way to ideas of "the good life" which had characterized other groups in the society. East Indian students write about the expectation of enjoying life "in good old West Indian style."

The study of a plantation in British Guiana indicates that at present "style of life is a more definitive criterion" of social status than "colour or ethnic affiliation"(3). Furthermore, the "creolization" of styles in the development of consumer tastes among East Indians in British Guiana has recently been noted(4). For East Indian students in Trinidad there has also been an evident "creolization" of values concerning standards of living — from the thrift values which characterized the period of indenture and small peasant holdings to the consumer values of the contemporary period. These students' descriptions of their anticipated future life-styles range from relatively modest expectations, given the anticipation of higher status, to visions of comparative luxury, as in the following excerpts:

We will enjoy a reasonable income, so that we could afford a modern house in one of the residential areas of the islands of Trinidad. All modern facilities would be ours for the asking.

As far as my home is concerned, I hope to offer my family a very confortable and convenient one. I would fail miserably if I offer my wife and children a home lacking in the several useful amenities of life. The very atmosphere of the home would be reflected in the personality of my offsprings. I want my children to possess an impressive personality therefore I would provide them with a home confortable in as many aspects as possible.

3. Chandra Jayawardena, *Conflict and Solidarity in a Guianese Plantation*, p. 38.

4. See Jayawardena, and R. T. Smith, "People and Change," *New World, Guyana Independence Issue*, 1966, pp. 49–54.

I also hope to have a large house furnished with the latest set of furniture including a television set, to have a large kitchen garden in my backyard, the place being well fenced and all conveniences in the yard . . . pipes, bathrooms, etc. I hope to have a large car so that my wife and family could go out for drives. . . . I hope to live in the village where the place is more silence and one enjoys the fresh breezes and the beautiful songs of the birds in the wild bushes.

Although one boy can only go as far as to hope for "the ownering of a house," the home of the future is often described in detail, as though it has been clearly envisaged in dreams:

My home I can also picture. It is a moderate size house in the country district. It is made of brick and has an open gallery in the front. On leaving the darkly lighted gallery you step into a spacious drawing-room with carpeted floor and wood furniture . . . on the other side of the house is the bed-room and library. Around the house there is ample space for garden.

Here again there is a notable denominational difference in expectations. Hindu and Moslem boys tend to express greater and grander visions of their future styles of life than Christian East Indian students. One description, by the son of a Moslem vegetable vendor, is written retrospectively:

I myself began making plans for one of the greatest modern houses in Trinidad, architects from America and India came to design it and build it, the cost amounting to one and a half million dollars. The name of the house was given as "Paradise". It was situated on a high hill overlooking the valley below, the lawn seem like an endless carpet. The gardens grew with lush and yellow fruits in abundance together with the sweet smelling roses and the ivy on the wall. The melodious songs of the birds on the tree tops seemed never to end. Am I dreaming, no, this is my house for the future.

The automobile, especially, and consumer "gadgets," generally, figure heavily in East Indian students' expectations of their future life:

I am a person who admires and enjoys a luxurious life, and I would like to have a well furnished house in the quiet country side with a car for my family's private use.

I will like to be the owner of a very large automatic motorcar and wherever I go I will always carry my favorite musical instrument. . . . I will build a very large and a very modern building valued at about forty five thousand dollars and well furnished with the necessary requirements of the family.

The pleasures I would desire also are: a large automobile, a beautiful house, a house by the sea and a speedboat. Also I would like to have a well equipped office and nursing home to carry on my medical studies. . . . During or after my forties I would like to travel.

Whenever I do graduate and return to Trinidad as a Doctor of medicine, the future ahead of me will be a straight path lined with huge portals of success. When I shall have already traversed the fiftieth [year], I most likely would have already gathered together a fortune in money. This fortune I would withdraw from the bank and together with my wife and children (about a dozen of them) I would make a complete tour of the whole world . . . when I return I would like to bring back with me the latest model Cadillac convertible from the U.S.A.

Perhaps the "ultimate" in automobiles is the expectation of the East Indian boy who writes: "my car will be atom-powered"; others will settle for petrol and a Mercedes-Benz.

Material culture is seen as an essential part of high status by East Indian students; conspicuous consumption is a prerequisite of being "important" and "respected" (corresponding to the observations about style of life as a criterion of social status among East Indians in British Guiana), as in this excerpt from the essay of the son of a laborer:

I am 16 years of age and I live in a country area where there are few educated people. However, I attend a college and I am very ambitious. I want to be a recognized person in my future life. I am studying very hard to pass my CSC [Cambridge School Certificate] exam. I want to become a teacher. After teaching for many years I will buy a car. I will then marry and have children whom I hope will be educated and recognized. My wife and I will work together, and when we have collected enough money I will leave the island to study law in one of the best Universities in the world. When I am ready to return to Trinidad I will inform my friends and family so that they will come to receive me at the airport. I will ask to be driven home in a very large and luxurious car. Now I'll be a real rich man and will employ carpenters to build me one of the latest model houses. I will stock it with furniture of the latest design and buy a new car. I will open a business place and employ workmen to sell in it. I will employ servants to clean my house and car and to serve my wife and my children and I. But I will still be very friendly with everyone and respect them. I will visit my school and tell my pupils that I will not be teaching again and give every one of them a present that will be of much value to them. I will send my wife to study medicine. When I am a lawyer and my wife is a doctor, we will then be in a higher position than before. We will have our own offices and we will be kind to everyone and try to help all those who are in need. We will then buy a new car for my wife and we will send our children to colleges, then to Universities. Then we will have a feast and invite all our friends and family. This will continue for one week. During another week we will give the poor people money with which they will be able to buy food and clothes for many years. After working as a lawyer for many years I will study and become a magistrate. I will then be partial. I am an East Indian, but that does not mean that if an East Indian is found guilty I will ease him up. What I want to make clear is that I am a non-racialist.

Although I want to be a great man when I am dead I want to be buried in a simple way according to the Hindu rites.

Status achievement is the *sine qua non* of personal fulfillment, and material culture is frequently equated with happiness by the students. With the expanding vision of consumption, "luxuries" tend to become "necessities":

I will like the later part of my life to be a happy one. In my home I would like to have most of the luxuries and necessities of the world. I will like to possess two houses: one as a home and the other as a holiday resort. (East Indian)

In fact, the term "luxury" seems to have become part of the standard vocabulary of mobility: "I am a person who admires and enjoys luxurious life," writes a student with high aspirations.

White students in the sample come from backgrounds where middle-class or upper-class style of life and status have already been achieved, and there is less intensity expressed in their description of future life-styles. Status maintenance can be the goal where it implies no regression of life-style; even comparatively modest expectations are predicated on a "comfortable" middle-class style of life:

It is at this time I would be able to amass a little money, not to become wealthy but to get enough to give my family a fairly confortable life, a house of our own with a nice garden. In general a home where our children can grow up pleasantly without ever being insecure, a home where we can entertain modestly.

Although their life chances differ, prosperity for some of the white students as well as for those in other ethnic groups will depend on individual effort. Combining the consumer ethos with the values of the "Protestant Ethic," they foresee material well-being based on work and accumulation:

When my wife and I have accumulated (she will have a beautician shop at home) enough money we will like to pack up our belongings and head for either Canada, Australia or New Zealand. Although I went only to Tobago and Venezuela I like to encounter new places. From early in my life I always wanted to live in either of these places as these places hold in store prosperous futures for qualified men.

The white students do not come from families that are equal in wealth or property ownership. As the level of "status maintenance" varies within a social class range, there are variations in anticipated styles of life. For some of the white students, the concept of "necessity" may be replaced by the expectation of luxury:

I would like all the common luxuries of life – I want to be well off – without being rich – you know what I mean. The day I want a new car to be able to get one without having to scrimp and save unduly.

"Aspirations" need to be measured from the point of departure, and for some upper-class boys two houses, two cars, even a yacht, are not uncommon expectations and may well be within the realm of reality:

I will like to have two cars, one for myself and another for my wife, a beautiful two-story house equipped with a swimming pool and other facilities. I will have parties every week-end, entertaining my friends and relatives.

Moreover, for many of these boys, expectations of future luxury follow well-established leisure-class patterns:

When I have established a fair savings account, I will build myself another good house. This house will be lavishly decorated and have the most modern accommodations for my wife and I and by that time, together with my house I will buy a yacht and go cruising the West Indian islands with my children. As these islands present the most favorable conditions for cruising, I plan to spend much time doing this.

Colored students share the values of the consumer culture of both the mobile elite and traditional elite groups, and they tend to stress the pleasurable aspects of status achievement. "Civilization" and its consumer contentments are correlated in the aspirations of a boy in this group:

I would lead a completely civilized life, that are consisting of all pleasures and entertainment.

The ethos of mobility and the consumer culture is characterized by new concepts of the nature of "necessity" among the colored students as well as among the white. The contemporary nature of "necessities" is spelled out in these excerpts:

Another thing I intend to do is to enjoy life to its utmost. I would like to have every necessity for this purpose around my home. A car, and aeroplane together with appropriate dresses and friends immediately appeals to me.

Before my marriage I must make sure that I have a nice and confortable house with all the necessities of a home within. I also want to have a lovely garden, two cars, both Mercedes-Benz, and a swimming pool in my backyard. . . . Something else that I must have is a speed boat, large enough to hold eight persons.

Negro and East Indian students avidly anticipate the promises of the consumer culture and its assurance of a style of life befitting high status. Dreams about future standards of living usually revolve around marriage (following career attainment) and the styles of life befitting the family of procreation. One student describes his dream house in technicolor:

> I shall have in front of the house a nice lawn with flower beds and garden chairs and a table which is beautifully painted. If there is room, most likely would be another flower garden with beautiful roses, carnations and zenias. . . . on week-ends we would go up to the beach where we would have our own private house with a complete furniture set. All we have to carry up is the food. . . . A driver and a servant will be hired so that everything will be neatly arranged. The car will always be kept clean and also the house so that the servant and the chauffeur will always be paid enough without any complaint. . . . my children will be given cricket implements to entertain their friends with. . . . I shall join one of my favorite clubs. . . . I shall buy a nice radio, a pickup, a refrigerator and many household articles. (East Indian)

"A modern home with all modern appliances" is a minimal expectation of students in all the groups. And the other most prevalent symbol of status for all groups is the automobile. Extensive travel abroad is also an aspiration frequently mentioned in the essays of many students:

> After my studies and marriage I will like to travel around the world so as to get a first hand knowledge of the type of lives people live in comparison to others, also the way they think in comparison to others. (Negro)

For some, travel spells the opportunity to enjoy material culture as well as adventure:

> I would like to be a lecturer in a University in the United States. My reason for this is that as far as I have heard life in these parts is very luxurious. I will come to my native land to visit my family and relatives very seldom. If they are in need of anything I will try my best to obtain it for them, especially my brothers. I will see to it that they obtain a high standard of education. When I have reached the age of 58 I will stop work and live on my life savings. I will tour many places, especially a pilgrimage to Mecca.

Other Moslem students also express the desire to pay a pilgrimage to Mecca. East Indian and Negro students may combine their travel aspirations with the desire to see the land of origin of their ancestors:

> During my lifetime I would like to travel to some of the countries of the world, seeing the places and people in other lands and know how they live and what they enjoy. The country I would like to see most is Africa,

because it is the birth place of my ancestors and nowdays is no longer the Dark Continent but a very rapid developing place.

I hope to go to India to see the land where my father's father came from.

For most students, travel represents the expansion of horizons, and it is also often associated with status mobility, as travel has been an aspect of elite status. The desire to travel may also be correlated with occupational aspirations:

If I become a great sportsman my first desire to tour the world will have been fulfilled. (Negro)

I should like very much to go abroad to study aviation, for my life's ambition is to become a pilot, to see the world. (Negro)

Some students equate the desire to travel with expressed interest in comparing political and social systems, but especially in trying to understand the position of Trinidad or the West Indies in the world scene:

After my studies and marriage I will like to travel around the world. In America and England and if possible Russia because I feel these countries hold the life of the world in their hands. I will like to find out why it is that the West Indies haven't such a responsibility. (Negro)

The desire to travel, linked with high aspirations, broadens the arena of anticipated leadership roles to the international scene:

I want to be a West Indian diplomat. There is a need for men to go to foreign countries and represent the youth while there is an inter-bickering of leaders. (Negro)

The two themes of travel to seek solutions for the problems of Trinidad and of eventually providing the world with models of leadership may be combined:

In my small country of Trinidad I hear much of the outside world. I intend to travel. In this way I can find the solution to many problems which beset us and which they have already mastered. Thus in this way the development of our nation will be speeded up. In later years I would content myself to see the youths for whom I have helped in my little way follow the paths created and go to greater heights. This would be my supreme compensation, to see our nation debating with any great world power and not to be referred to as a cluster of little islands in the West Indies. (Colored)

The majority of students express, with varying degrees of fervor, their intention of traveling, either for university studies or later in life to "see the

Table 47. Mention of Desire for Extensive Travel, by Sex and Ethnicity
(First Survey Essays)

Colored		East Indian		Negro		White	
Boys (83)	Girls (52)	Boys (207)	Girls (72)	Boys (139)	Girls (115)	Boys (40)	Girls (17)
26%	41%	28%	43%	22%	52%	25%	56%

world" with their families. The percentage of those who spontaneously mention in their essays the desire to travel extensively is given in Table 47. As may be seen, the girls express a considerably higher frequency than the boys of desire to travel extensively; this may be because the girls feel free to express their fantasies in this area, or it may be a function of the woman's role in supporting elite styles of life (see Chapter VIII).

Dreams of travel are no longer simply terrestrial for youth in the second half of the twentieth century. For most adults, outer space was primarily a matter of cosmology before the dramatic events of the space age. Thus the frequency of mention of space travel in the 1957 survey surprised the research team, but some of the students were apparently avid readers of science fiction, and some incorporated vivid pictures of interplanetary travel into their projected auto-biographies. As one boy wrote:

> . . . of course, I expect by that time [the year 2000] the world will be quite different from what it is now. I may even take a trip to the moon. (Negro)

In a predictive vein, he went on to say:

> I would not be surprised to learn that Americans succeeded in putting a man in space.

In some of the essays, high aspirations are linked with fantasies of space technology, and the desire to achieve fame may be transferred to outer space, as in the following imaginative excerpts:

> I would like to have a laboratory of my own and want to accomplish things that no other scientist of the age has done. I would like to discover a drug to combat cancer germs. Then I want to build a space ship with all modern accessories and modern luxuries. Most important of all, my laboratory must be able to fit in a spaceship. I will set out with my wife to the planet Venus, and there I would prove to the men of the earth that Venus and the other planets can be reached and settled. . . . [A scientific adventure tale follows.] After 5 years of perilous hard struggle, I finally landed on a planet. I went out and dwell among the natives. I built schools and taught the young boys and girls the English language, and in the space

of three years I was the most popular man in the whole of Venus. On my departure my wife and I were given a glorious sendoff. (East Indian)

Another boy writes that he intends to "save money, then go abroad to study space travel":

As I am very desirous of traveling in the air, I feel that I should not have been sitting on my desk now. I feel that I should be flying through the air in the fastest space ship that's ever been built. I want to go to see the moon and the stars and how they are made. I want to see if there are people existing there; how big they are, how they travel, what they eat; whether there is sea as there is on the earth. I always wonder that if there are people living on the moon why they do not wish to come down and see us as it is easier to come down than to go up. As it is a fact that the moon and the earth and the stars are all planets, then they must resemble one another. If I should succeed in reaching the moon, then I will inhabit it. I will carry up people and machinery to work and cultivate the land, if conditions seem favorable. Then I will travel to the stars and do the same. I want to make travel in the air very easy, and find places for increasing populations to live. The world would then be a happy place to live in. Carry animals up there, . . . build institutions . . . good education. Encourage stock raising there on a large scale. India and China could send people there. . . . I would like to travel in a space ship during the night, high up among the stars and see how they appear. If I am successful, then it would be not only to my benefit, but to the benefit of the entire world. Everyone will find happiness and joy to live, and moreover to travel to a new land. Above would be the utmost wonder and excitement. (East Indian)

Another boy, whose ambition is to be an engineer, writes that in the future he and his family

. . . will probably be spending a vacation on Venus and possibly setting up radio transmitters on Mars as part of a contract from some government. (Negro)

Travel is no longer limited to the old elites' "grand tour" of the world. Venus, Mars, and the moon have become part of the technological culture, and what were Jules Verne's fantasies to an earlier generation are now incorporated into the envisioned style of life of the upwardly mobile youth. Fantasy and reality readily merge in the boys' sanguine expectations of the technological achievements of the future:

In the middle ages, about 1970 to 1985, I will be wandering about the universe with my family. For then space travel will be perfected. (Negro)

In ten years or more I would be buying a return ticket to the moon. (Colored)

Only one boy takes a dour view of space technology, but he will accommodate to the times and set up a travel bureau to sell "return tickets to the moon":

The world to me is a boiling mass of unrest. Nobody wants to be ruled and nobody is fit to rule. People do not follow the ten commandments. . . . [He mentions competition over space.] We have known for a century or more that man would go into space. What we did not know was that man would spend so much time, money and energy in trying to get there, and leave the world starving for a good life. Imagine – spend millions to shoot a man into the sky, leaving tens of millions of paupers to die. . . . [He suggests an international force to police space.] I myself do not expect to fly any further than London, but for all those interested they can buy return tickets to the moon from my travel bureau. (Negro)

By the time of the 1961 survey, the advancing technological culture had given a further spurt to the imagination of the students about the limitless extraterrestrial possibilities ahead:

The bonds of space and time have been broken. The Russians having accomplished such a daring feat as sending a man into space and bring him back to earth alive. (White)

The "feat of Gagarin" was specifically mentioned in a number of essays, and one boy wrote: "to me Gagarin's flight is the most wonderful historical enterprise since Columbus." "By the year 2000," another boy wrote, "a man has most probably landed on the moon."

Technology, which opens the frontiers of space, also opens new avenues of projected experience which the students quickly incorporate into their visions of the future. Some see the prospect of "cricket matches in space." Others foresee supersonic airlines that can travel for long periods without refueling and atom-powered cars and ocean liners. And why not for every man? "The future belongs to the common man," a lower-class Negro boy writes, and the consumer culture of the future is spelled out in all its science fiction visions and possibilities.

Psychological hypotheses about the function of fantasies in youth need to be placed in a social perspective. Space technology is a reality, and the consumer culture presses its charms through all the media of communication. Visions of two houses and two cars, of "every modern comfort and necessity," may be fantasy for lower-class boys, but acquiring such status symbols may no longer be impossible. The boys are not dreaming about magical intervention but hoping to achieve the material rewards of the consumer society through their own efforts. Whether or not the economy of the society can provide such high rewards, the psychological function of fantasy appears to be to provide incentives for mobility. Sociologically, it undoubtedly provides a stimulus for participation in the developing society. Moreover, these students are not alienated from the greater society, and, as will be seen, there is a strong element of altruism which interlaces their high expectations of status achievement and affluence. Their personal aspirations reflect a strong anticipatory drive to participate in and contribute to the development of the greater society.

X

Social Orientation, Personal Aspirations, and Social Goals

What do you most hope to accomplish in the course of your life? the students were asked on the questionnaire. The question stimulated intense responses, embracing multiple themes. "To do something for my country which will give me a place in its history," one student replied. Another student hopes:

> Firstly to reach a high standard of education and from there on use it to the good of my country, if not the world. (Negro)

Educational and professional attainments are for the patria as well as the persona:

> Freed from the yoke of colonialism, Trinidad can now place things in the hands of their own able leaders who know its problems and how to make best use of resources. (Negro)

Students oriented to new professions frequently express the relationship of achievement and altruism as mutual life goals:

> I am taking science to be able to help my fellow countrymen which I will need to be successful. (East Indian)

Whether traditionally or technologically oriented, many students express variants of this theme in their replies to the question concerning what they hope to accomplish.

In their pioneer study comparing the values of students in developed and developing countries, Gillespie and Allport found that the youth of the emergent societies shared a strong sense of social commitment and that their personal and social motivations tended to coincide(1). Both quantitative and qualitative findings of the present study confirm this pattern of commitment and show the convergence of personal aspirations with the perception of social requirements. Replies to multiple-choice questions, as noted in Chapter VI, indicate the frequency of an altruistic orientation. Excerpts from the 1957 essays illustrate this pattern:

> At present Trinidad is in great need of its own doctors, engineers, lawyers, priests and other professional persons, and I think that I will be of some service to Trinidad as an engineer. (Negro)

Students frequently spell out at length their views of the needs of the nation to put their "talents to use":

> Trinidad is experiencing a great change in political, social and economic life. The island will need men of integrity, knowledge and capability. Great emphasis is being laid and will be laid in the industrial expansion of the colony. The men needed to direct, control and supervise in such expansion, will be local men with knowledge and capability and I hope to fill a place in that field. By doing so, I hope to help in the uplifting of the social and economical standard of the community. I hope to fill a place especially in the oil industry for this is playing and will continue to play an important part in the Island economy. (Colored)

Preoccupation with the development needs of the nation may involve the ideal of raising the level of Trinidad among the nations of the world:

> As to money and security, which seem to be all that interest the modern world, I am partial. I am quite able to live frugally alone, and put my talents to good use. This can be done in many ways. We need sports facilities, housing, bridges and irrigation systems, to develop our backward island. Then the people must be taught economical ways of dealing with mechanical problems. I hope to see my talents put to the use of my country, the fruits of which are enough compensation to me. (Colored)

The convergence of social needs and personal ambition is most frequently put in an altruistic framework, especially among lower-class students. The universe of service may be the village, the ethnic group, the nation, or, in some cases, it may extend to all mankind. The particular focus of social commitment is structurally linked to various factors that reflect the situational context of the students' background. For example, East Indian students from backward rural areas are particularly motivated, at this stage of their lives, to work toward village improvement. The following excerpts are not unusual:

> As a youth of 17 I have made one unflinching resolution and that is to foster and promote all that is good for the love and welfare of the community in which I live.

1. Gillespie and Allport, pp. 20, 38.

I am living in a little village. For the past year the people of the village have made very little improvement in the economic and social standards of life. My great grandparents have come here as indentured laborers. I felt that my duty is to the people. How could I help my people, I had to ask myself. I must improve the education of myself. My parents know very little. They have a vague idea even of their religion and do certain things without questioning whether it is right or wrong, because they say their parents and family have done that.

My family has a little plot of sugar cane which does not yield as before because the strength of the land is failing and the scientific methods which they have is too expensive, because he has a very little holding. I can then try to help my village as a whole, for it is a little one, but it has much potential and future. I can try and see that any factories or plants be opened up in my little village where the younger men would be able to get good jobs, and the little village could be made a very good one for any one to live in. If I become an influential man I can try to have any colleges or institutes not far from my area, so that it would be cheaper for the poor village peasants to get in their children without much trouble and expense.

East Indian students frequently link their personal aspirations with a sense of social commitment stemming from their perception of the exclusion of their ethnic group from the privileges of the society. Many of the essays give lengthy descriptions of village problems which they hope to overcome through personal achievements, as in the following excerpt:

It is now 18 years of my life spent on this God forsaken land, and by this time it is hard for me to cipher my future life. My family is large. . . . I still live in hope, praying that one day our little community will . . . be remembered, this humble countryside of Chaguanas. Our community hasn't even a good recreation ground or a library. I have thought of this . . . but what can a voice that can hardly be heard, do for this countryside? . . . Our house is one I cannot boast of. . . . the surrounding is of moderate sanitation. The people are ignorant and would not even try to help themselves. How can they when they can hardly even write? Yes, this is my daily life, as I spend my dismal years getting older and older. . . . my hopes burn ever more of leaving the wretched community of Chaguanas one day and come back as a father to the humble and ignorant. Hope and more hope burns brightly in my heart as I go through this reign of terror, fighting to be a great one so that I could help my community to be better citizens of Trinidad, and as a whole, the whole wide world. Oh how cruel they have been to us and our poor majority. My brothers and sisters are also like myself in trying to make this community much better and respected. [He then dreams of the time when his little community is recognized by all the world.] This little community which was like an outcast is now at the top of the Caribbean, and serves as an example to future generations that theirs also would be like ours.

Such lengthy accounts of concern with social problems appear in the autobiographies of lower-class students whose aspirations embrace the desire to improve the conditions of "my people," "my community," or "my country." In their essays, rural East Indian students, especially, frequently reveal a strong commitment to improving the lot of the "cultivators" of the country.

> I have concentrated on studying so much that I do not wish to play nor go to the cinema, but continue studying so that one day I might be working in some sort of government institution where I can do something to improve myself and my country.... There must be someone constantly urging the government and I think that if no one does it I would be the first to do so to see that my country's people can emerge from their period of depression into one of prosperity. If I can obtain the necessary qualifications from agriculture I will be able to improve Trinidad on the whole and thus relieve the cultivators of their burden of depression which they were not relieved of since the times of abolition of slavery in the 19th century.

As an expressed concern, this social commitment is more prevalent among East Indian and Negro students than among colored and white students. While approximately one out of four of the East Indian and Negro students in the first survey spontaneously mention such concerns in their essays, about one out of ten of the white and colored students express these concerns (Table 48). Among the girls, there is less frequent spontaneous mention of social commitment than among the boys (17 per cent of the Negro girls, 13 per cent of the East Indian, and 11 per cent of the colored girls); mention of social commitment is completely absent in the essays of the white girls. This may be partly a corollary of rural-urban residence, with colored and white students underrepresented in rural schools. Data from the questionnaire, however, provide additional support for the finding on group differences in expressed social commitment. Again, Negro and East Indian students rank higher than the other groups in their manifest concern with social affairs. Also, both in 1957 and in 1961, in reply to a multiple-choice question listing six possible sources of satisfaction, these students more often than either the colored or white students selected participation in community affairs as one of the three most gratifying life activities (Table 49). Negro and East Indian girls indicate concern about community affairs almost as frequently as the boys in these groups; while none of the white boys express any interest in this choice, 20 per cent of the white

Table 48. Mention of Desire to Help "My People," "My Community," "My Country" (First Survey Essays)

Colored		East Indian		Negro		White	
Boys (83)	Girls (52)	Boys (207)	Girls (72)	Boys (139)	Girls (115)	Boys (40)	Girls (17)
11%	11%	23%	13%	24%	17%	10%	–

Table 49. Community – National-International Orientation
(First Survey Questionnaires)
(in percentage)

	Colored		East Indian		Negro		White	
	Boys (83)	Girls (52)	Boys (207)	Girls (72)	Boys (139)	Girls (115)	Boys (40)	Girls (17)
a) Rank community affairs as one of the 3 most important of 6 life sectors	16	15	32	30	34	26	–	20
b) Rank national-international sector as one of the 3 most important of 6 life sectors	15	13	26	10	22	10	17	7

Table 49a. Community – National-International Orientation
(Second Survey Questionnaires)(a)
(in percentage)

	Colored (21)	East Indian (104)	Negro (82)	White (28)
a) Rank community affairs as one of the 3 most important of 6 life sectors	15	31	24	8
b) Rank national-international sector as one of the 3 most important of 6 life sectors	25	31	14	20

a. No girls were included in the second survey.

girls do. This may be a reflection of the greater interest of these girls in club and welfare activities. Although East Indian boys rank higher than other groups on the national-international dimension in both surveys, the differences are not as striking as those concerning community affairs. An interesting difference is that between community orientation and national-international orientation among white students.

In order to measure these differences in the saliency of attitudes more extensively, an index was developed to include all possible references to the social dimension in a single score. Every student who indicated a sense of social commitment at least once, either in the essay or the questionnaire, has been given a positive score on the Index of Social Orientation. This increases the possibility of evaluating the range of social commitment, regardless of style of expression. As Table 50 indicates, Negro and East Indian students, who are the emergent elites, rank highest on this Index, followed by the colored and then the white students, who are lowest on this dimension. Use of the Index technique

Table 50. Index of Social Orientation, by Sex and Ethnicity(a)
(Essays and Questionnaires)
(in percentage)

	Colored	East Indian	Negro	White
First Survey				
Boys	(73)	(196)	(122)	(40)
	44	65	68	26
Girls	(52)	(65)	(115)	(14)
	35	46	44	29
Second Survey(b)				
Boys	(21)	(104)	(82)	(28)
	52	69	54	29

a. The Index of Social Orientation was constructed on the basis of the presence of at least one of the following indicators in the protocols: Selection of either (1) participation as a citizen in the affairs of my community or (2) participation in activities directed toward national or international betterment as one of the three activities from which the student expects to derive the most satisfaction. (3) The answer, "for my people" or "for my country," to the question, *For what end will you be willing to make the greatest sacrifice?* (4) The answers, "help one's country" and "a political career," to the question, *What two things could you conceivably accomplish during your lifetime of which you would be most proud?* (5) A spontaneous statement of desire to help one's country, one's people, or one's community in the autobiography.

b. Comparison of responses in the second survey, by school, shows that East Indian students at Presentation College, which has more rural students, are more socially oriented (79 per cent) than East Indian students (57 per cent) at St. Mary's College in Port of Spain.

markedly increases the percentage of students in all groups who indicate social concerns. Among middle-class colored students, apparently, spontaneity of expression tends to be more restrained, and direct questioning is required to elicit expression of social concerns and high personal aspirations. When the students are ranked into high, medium, and low socioeconomic status groups according to father's occupation, Negro, East Indian, and colored students in the low socioeconomic category tend to score higher on social orientation within their own ethnic group. Social status reinforces ethnicity on this dimension (see Appendix H). Although the girls, on the whole, express somewhat less social orientation than the boys, they demonstrate the same rank order by ethnicity. Differences by social class also reveal some tendency for the lower occupational strata in each ethnic group to express greater social orientation, especially among East Indian girls. The second survey reveals both the same high incidence of social orientation among East Indian students (69 per cent) and the same low incidence among white students (29 per cent). There is less consistency in the responses of Negro and colored students in the two surveys. More colored students express social awareness in the second survey; however, given the small size of the second sample, it is not certain whether this indicates a new trend or whether it may be due to sample bias.

Political orientation is a significant factor in the general social outlook of the students. Even before Independence the Peoples National Movement (PNM) had awakened a sense of political commitment and participation in national affairs, particularly in the government party which was elected in 1956. Participation in opposition parties was also activated as the process of democratization spread through the society. The change in composition of government leadership provided new national role models for the students to emulate, and the widening opportunity structure created realistic political and civil service goals to which the students could aspire. The new government introduced a series of social and economic changes and was committed to a long-range development program for the island; consequently, it is not surprising that these changes are reflected in the political interests and aspirations of the students. A sense of elation over the changes and their promise of new opportunities is manifest in many of the essays as the students identify their aspirations with the new national goals:

It rests on us . . . even more so now that we stand on the threshold of Independence, to further the fame of our country, to lead on our emerging nation in the different fields of our endeavor. (Negro)

As everybody else, I intend to be a success. I want to feel my place in the community is of vital importance to the improvement of the nation. (Negro)

The period of the West Indies Federation, albeit short-lived, also evoked a sense of wider commitment:

The cri de coeur of Trinidad at present is for higher education. This cry I suppose echoes through the world today, especially in those countries like Trinidad which were formerly under imperial rule and are now on the threshold of Independence, and it is now quite true that Trinidad youths of today are to be its leaders of tomorrow. Ours is the responsibility. In our hands is the future of our new Federation. We are entrusted, to bring to fruition that which our forefathers long and painfully have fought for. (Negro)

The "forefathers" who had "long and painfully fought for" Federation were mostly of the colored middle class, and the sense of commitment to this goal is continued by colored students who see in its achievement the fulfillment of both personal and political aspirations for a "democratic government":

I will also like to take my place in society. With the approach of an independent Federation of the West Indies there will be needed many capable leaders to steer such a young nation to attain the political and economic status which is enjoyed by such countries as the US and the UK. In the West Indies there is much latent talent which needs to be developed, and I feel that the respective governments are not doing sufficient to cultivate these potentialities. The West Indies although only a few dots on the map, has produced men in every field of activity on a par with the greatest. There is much hope for the West Indies if we the people strive for the best, and not to be satisfied with mediocre conditions. The fact that the West Indies is one of the most cosmopolitan places in the world will be an ideal place for the functioning of a democratic government.

A number of the students link their personal ambitions with emulation of Dr. Eric Williams, the new political role model for the aspiring elites:

After settling down, I shall seriously consider entering the political ring, because I feel that with my extensive knowledge of the world, its peoples and ideals, I shall be well equipped to serve my country well. I shall endeavor to put on the boots of our illustrious Premier, Dr. Eric Williams, when the time is ripe and to make as great or greater strides toward the prosperity and wellbeing of Trinidad and the Federation as a whole. (Negro)

Political as well as social themes are spontaneously and fervently discussed in the essays. While the rationale for participation or nonparticipation in political affairs, for commitment or noncommitment to national goals, varies structurally rather than idiosyncratically, the majority of students are deeply involved with the personal meaning of political change. Students from disadvantaged groups express their feelings passionately. Among East Indian students, for example, the aspiration of service to the community is frequently linked to equally fervent aspirations for political achievement, as in the following excerpt from the essay of a student in County Caroni:

In my country, there is a lack of schools and about 75% of the people are illiterate. Later I would like to be a member of the Legco [Legislative Council], because I would like to try and improve the conditions of the people in the rural areas. In places like County Caroni and the eastern counties, there are great needs for industries. The past and present governments have neglected these two areas in special, and have concentrated only on improving the urban areas. If the party to which I belong gets into power, then I would have no difficulty in improving these areas. First I would try and get the government to construct schools and get them to reclaim the large tracts of swampy areas. These swamp areas lie idle, and no move is being made to improve these wastelands. I would like the government to set up industries in these areas – a milk industry in Caroni and a coconut oil industry in the eastern counties. I would like to construct houses in these rural districts, and improve the communications facilities. If I get on the Council I would subsidize every farmer with large sums of money to cultivate the crops.

In the same vein, another East Indian student writes:

This county is altogether neglected. When, however, I enter the legislature as a prominent member, I will see to it that my country and most of all my village, gets the necessary boon of modern civilization.

For rural East Indian students particularly, status mobility is correlated with both a sense of community service and high political aspirations:

> I want to become a politician. I want to become a historian so that I can be a very good politician. I will like to be the Premier of Trinidad and Tobago some day, to become as the Hon. Dr. Eric Williams. Also to be one of the leading statesmen of tomorrow. My party, my government, should be one of the best our island has ever produced. I should also like to represent my government at all conferences in the future. I know as leader of the party one should have a very quick brain to answer very quickly. . . . I will become one of the leading historians in the world if possible. I have great confidence that I will be one. My intention is to be one of the leading statesmen in the world, as Mr. Nehru. . . . My county, Caroni, it has plenty of sugar cane, but the poor suffers very much in working the plantations. They have to work very hard. The estates takes advantage on them. All these things as a leader I would improve, these peoples' working conditions so that they can live as the wealthier ones. They are the ones I know will put me up again. All my ministers will work in unity, so that my government will not crumble. My government program will be to improve the working conditions of the laborers, fine roads, good government, not oppressive as others. My career in office should be at least for four terms. At this stage my name will be put into history, having a record in office, and also how I control my people. To show I love my people I will put heavy income tax on rum and cigarettes. Rum and cigarettes decreases a nation, while without this it builds up a nation. My last term I will try to help the poor cane farmers in giving them free tractors to plow their land, free medicines to keep away diseases which destroy them very much, so they can produce more sugar cane. My office should be from the age of about 29 to 60 years. Many men will think of me and especially the cane farmers.

The high political aspirations of lower-class East Indian students may turn in fantasy to outer space; at least in fantasy life there may be more possibility of fulfillment than in real life:

> Then I would have a world for myself and I will do as I wish. I will try to get all conveniences up there and so develop the place as the earth has been. My wish then would be that there should be no slavery.

> Up there I will rule the place as I have done in my birthplace. I would like to be as great potentate as the Romans. I would divide the land to certain lords and carry on the feudal system. Churches would be built but I would like to see only one religion carried on in the place, which would be the prevention of corruption in the churches. Priests would have to be elected by the people in the different countries. I would like the people to speak one language, and when I left the place, there must be no corruption. At the age of 55 I would give up the kingdom and divide the land to my faithful ministers. Education and development would be my most cared subjects.

Imagine now that I have passed all my exams and I am now a scientist, superior to other scientists. The great longing has finally terminated from my mind, and now I am what I always wanted to be, a great scientist. My first job is to invent a rocket to land safely on Mars. All my eagerness now awaits my invention to dominate Mars. With this great spectacle, the invention of the rocket, I have made my name in history. At last I am a great man. What I have always wanted to be. I am looked upon by the world as a great man, superior to other men. This feeling cannot stop me from exploring Mars, but arouse me to carry on my expedition. Only one thing now awaits the world . . . if my rocket could reach Mars. I was the first person to reach Mars and dominate it. When I landed back on earth safely I was a hero, and also held the greatest reputation that any man ever lived. I was now the greatest man who ever lived. I instantly made world news, and my name repeated itself daily on the headlines of newspapers. I was now sure that I will make history and remain as the greatest personage ever lived. All I have narrated are my plans, expectations and aspirations for the future. The main idea that I can base my plans for the future is I want to be a great person, and to be remembered in the minds of the next generation.

As previously indicated, 13 per cent of the East Indian students aspired to become famous political figures, while none of the white students expressed such an ambition (see Table 31). It is interesting to contrast the East Indians' expressed high political aspirations with the polar position of the white students, who specifically deny any political aspirations: "I don't want to be Prime Minister of the West Indies." Or, "One thing that has never appealed to me is participation in politics." Political achievement is expressly ruled out of daydreaming: "I do not picture myself as a dashing noisy politician." Some indicate interest in political parties, but "would not contest an election."

Insofar as social orientation is linked with political activity in the students' perception of national needs, it may be contrasted with "privatism," which has been defined as greater concern with private, as opposed to social, values(2). For the members of a group still high in status and prestige, personal motives and group goals are not necessarily interrelated. Privatist orientation implies the predominance of individual and familistic over political and broad social concerns. As far as the white students in the sample are concerned, however, this does not imply the absence of social values or of altruism, and the presence of private values should not obscure the concern with humanitarian values that characterizes students in all groups. This is especially marked among the white students who plan to study medicine or to become missionaires, as in the following excerpts:

I hope to become some day a fine surgeon who can help in some way to alleviate the sufferings of humanity.

2. Gillespie and Allport, p. 16.

I hope some day to bring fame to my country with an achievement in some professional field. I want to be a medical doctor to achieve something in the service of my people and my country.

With the desire to do my little share towards the betterment of our nation, I would see my life unfolding before me as that of a teacher.

I think I would like to go to BG [Guyana] either as a priest or a doctor to work there for the benefit of young boys, to teach them how to live properly with each other, because sir, I really do love these boys and I want to do something for them.

Missionary aspirations (including those of East Indian students who wish to work in India and Negro students who express an inclination to work in Africa) account for some of the students who profess an intention to emigrate. Attending a university abroad of necessity also involves at least temporary migration from the island. About the same number of boys in all the socioeconomic and ethnic groups state that they would like to either study, travel, or live abroad. The period and character of anticipated emigration varies, however. For some it is temporary to fulfill professional requirements; for some it is anticipated as a permanent step. As may be seen in Table 51, on the first survey, in response to a direct question, the percentage of white students, both boys and girls, who express the desire to spend the majority of their life abroad is very high. They are also more likely than other students to express spontaneously in their essays the desire to emigrate. East Indian and Negro students are less likely than students in the other groups to contemplate permanent separation from their homeland.

In the second survey, the percentage of white boys who respond in the same way to this question remains exactly the same, 50 per cent; similar responses of East Indian and colored students increase somewhat. What is most striking is the drop in the percentage of Negro students who respond that they would like to live abroad, from 31 per cent in 1957 to 7 per cent in 1961, which may be due

Table 51. Desire to Live the Majority of One's Life Abroad, by Ethnicity (in percentage)

	Colored	East Indian	Negro	White
First Survey				
Boys	(83)	(207)	(139)	(40)
	33	25	31	50
Girls	(52)	(72)	(115)	(17)
	35	21	30	60
Second Survey				
Boys	(21)	(104)	(82)	(28)
	38	52	7	50

to the limited nature of the second sample or may reflect increased optimism regarding the political situation at home. The centrifugal tendencies of white students are further confirmed by the frequency with which they express greater interest in the problems of the world than in national or regional problems, in contrast with students in other groups (see Appendix I).

The atmosphere of social change in the country, which fosters personal aspirations and links them with a sense of wider commitment, also influences the students' decisions about whether to return to Trinidad after their university studies abroad. Traditionally, many of the middle-class elite had found it either necessary or preferable to remain abroad for personal and professional reasons. The colony did not provide the social or economic scope for achievement by many of the most highly trained professionals. With the changing political situation in 1957, questions of emigration and patriotism preoccupied many of the students; one student wrote at length that "patriotism breeds from an age old tradition":

> My theory that patriotism does not as yet dominate the mind and will of West Indians is I believe borne out by the emigration en masse that annually now runs up into the thousands. (Negro)

The tide of exodus was evidently a matter of concern to many of the students. One wrote:

> Many trained men are now leaving the country. If this trend continues, it would definitely affect the growth of our nation. These men are not willing to sacrifice enough to put our nation on its feet. They are unable to get the high salary that suits their profession, due to the lean bank account of the government, and would not content themselves with a sufficient salary. Therefore they leave and we are short of properly trained men. (Colored)

This student accuses the emigrés of "dormant patriotism," and by contrast, explains his own patriotic intention to return to Trinidad:

> At this moment the nation to which I belong is on the verge of Independence and we are about to open a door behind which there remains uncertainty. It is . . . my duty as a citizen of this new-born nation to use my talents of building, to mold the foundation of our nation. I intend to let the urge to build in me blossom on my country. I am set on the study of civil engineering as I feel in this way I can do my part to build our nation.

For some students the question of return is a major decision. As one puts it:

> To return or not to return to your homeland, it is in the hands of fate, but for now I prefer to be patriotic and take the view that I will return. (Negro)

The sense of nationalism, however, supersedes concern with "fate," and for many students the decision to return is related to expressions of instilled "national spirit":

> I must make a name for myself and bring it back to this country which has given me everything I have. I have an extremely strong sense of West Indian national spirit and have always had it as long as I remember. (Colored)

Most of the students who write of their intention to return do not debate the matter but give a straightforward statement: "It is my wish to come back home here to Trinidad and live and work here with my people" (Negro). "Home" is frequently invested with a sense of deep emotional attachment:

> The bigger countries offer more scope for success, but I have always had a burning love and loyalty for my small country, even to the house I am growing up in. (Negro)

Another Negro student writes, "I defy any country in the world to produce a sunrise to equal Trinidad's," and gives a poetic description of his country.

Factor analysis of the first survey reveals a cluster of variables that may be termed "communal rootedness":

Factor H: Communal Rootedness	Factor Loading
Would like to live the main part of his life in his native country	.47
Expects to be more interested in local affairs than in national or international affairs	.37
Does not desire to settle abroad	.30
Is interested in local political and social affairs	.22
Would be willing to make the greatest sacrifice of personal time, comfort, and money to help the nation, ethnic group, or community	.20

The analysis of variance indicates significant (at .01) ethnic group differences on this factor which reflect affective attachment to the country and its people. Negro students rank first on this factor, closely followed by the East Indians, then by the colored students, with the white students last. (See Appendix F.)

The sense of nationalism, territorial or West Indian, has traditionally been the hallmark of the colored middle class who were also most concerned with the development of political parties and the spread of political participation. Mass political apathy, which was the heritage of the Crown Colony government, was pricked by the disturbances of the 1930's and the emergence of popular political leaders and the trade union movement. With the granting of a universal franchise in 1945 and the growth of political parties during the post-World War II period, interest in political participation spread through all the sections of the country, culminating in the election in 1956 of the PNM government, which was strongly committed to nationalist goals. The rapid change from political apathy to the new nationalism reflects the shift of power from one segment of the population to another. In the first wave of change, the actual or potential loss of political power and social privileges fell most heavily on the white population, which searched for new modes of accommodation. The ethnic groups which had been neither socially nor politically integrated during the colonial period had to make political choices and decisions affecting their future position in the nation. As in other world areas, the process of democratization and the spread of political participation accentuated submerged rivalries between the traditionally under-privileged groups for the protection of sectional interests in the building of the new nation. Allegiance to the two major political parties had reflected basic ethnic and class divisions in the society. The essays reflect the hopes and concerns related to the new political situation in the light of the structurally determined definition of the situation. The students freely discuss political assurances concerning nondiscrimination in community development, employment, and sectional social progress generally(3).

Several questions were added to the second survey to get further data on perception of the political situation. Factor analysis of all the data in the survey indicates a cluster of variables which reveals differences in political perception by social class and ethnic group. (See Factor I.) Analysis of variance reveals a significant difference (at .01) between ethnic groups on this factor. East Indian students rank highest on pessimism concerning the greater society and Negro students lowest on this factor; colored and white students are in intermediate positions(4).

These findings confirm findings of the first survey that the world is seen as threatening by lower-class East Indians and that this attitude is correlated with the desire for personal leadership. The strong social commitment of East Indian students tends to fall within a pessimistic framework in relation to the external environment. The social commitment of Negro students, on the other hand, is linked with a very optimistic perception of the future development of the country.

Rural East Indian students were most articulate in their concerns about the

3. See Rubin, "Culture, Politics and Race Relations."

4. Equally significant differences (at .01) are found by socioeconomic status: An inverse relationship exists between high social class position and the factor of pessimism. (Class III, the lowest socioeconomic group, is highest on the pessimism factor, and Class I, the highest socioeconomic group, is least pessimistic.) Since East Indians are highest on this factor, and Negroes, the other major low socioeconomic status group, are lowest on this factor, it is apparent that pessimism as indicated on this factor characterizes lower-class East Indians.

Factor I: Pessimism about National Affairs (Second Survey)	Factor Loading
Thinks that Trinidad has more to lose than to gain by Independence	.43
Would like to live the main part of his life in another country	.39
Considers religious beliefs and activities as an important source of satisfaction in life	.37
Thinks that Trinidad has more to lose than to gain by Federation	.29
The occupational future is perceived as marked by severe competition for good jobs	.26
Desire for personal leadership is very important	.23
Family relationships are not an important source of satisfaction in life	.21
Expects that the future standard of living will be the same as the present	.17

solution of community problems as expressed in the essays and tended to view the future with distrust in regard to the possibility of impartial support for local betterment. They did not expect to be passive observers of social change, however, but to participate actively in political as well as community affairs. For rural East Indian students the community tends to be the most powerful focus of loyalty, while among Negro youth it is the island as a whole. As has been seen, both Negro and East Indian students tend to associate individual goals with community goals; both are alert to sociopolitical problems and reveal strong group orientation. As further confirmation of this point, it is the Negro and East Indian students of the Trinidad sample who rank in the high percentage groups in international comparisons of youth who desire to participate in community affairs (Table 52).

Whether as a result of the impact of technology on change, or the impact of international politics on the Caribbean and the future course of the world, many of the students place their personal and social concerns in a larger framework. Students in the urban schools, particularly, are quite familiar with international affairs; their outlook tends to be less parochial than that of students in the rural schools, and the roles they envision are sometimes related to the world scene.

Some students express a sense of role ambiguity in the realization of confrontation with an uncertain future, with the world characterized by "unrest and insecurity."

In this very eventful era of the twentieth century we face more problems than has ever confronted children of similar ages in previous centuries. All the advantages of the modern world and also more difficulties. (Negro)

Table 52. Cross-National Comparisons of Community Orientation(a)

Low Percentage (0-30%)		High Percentage (30% up)	
United States	.20	Bantu	.45
New Zealand	.20	Egypt	.48
South Africa: English	.21	Mexico	.32
Afrikaner	.18	Trinidad: Negro	.34
France	.5	East Indian	.48
Italy	.20		
Germany	.3		
Japan	.16		
Israel	.24		
Trinidad: White	.0		
Colored	.16		

a. Based on Gillespie and Allport, *Youth's Outlook on the Future: A Cross National Study*, and Trinidad data presented in Table 48.

For some students, the chaos of the world is a source of personal confusion:

> To a boy at eighteen life has been very confusing. All his plans may be a dream, as the world is in chaos. Atomic danger of annihilation of most of the world. Religion and strong moral foundation is needed. I stare at the stars on bright nights and wonder at my maker and what he has made us for, for I am very fearful for everyone on earth. (Colored)

For students in the urban schools especially, a good deal of the uncertainty about the future stems from concern with international affairs:

> I have bright prospects for the future, but I do not even know if I would live another day, due to the difficulties there are in the world. The *Guardian* is full of reports of revolutions and rumors of war. If I live to be a man I would like to get married at the age of 30 to a girl of 20, and to live happily ever after. Instead of the big powers talking about wars, why don't they talk about drawing up a plan for man to progress and have a happy and peaceful life. Why don't they take all that wasteful money they are spending for all that sort of rubbish and put it to some useful purpose for man on earth. Can a man cultivate the stars and the moon? Can a man live by himself on the moon and be happy? No. Man must live in society if he wants to be anything of a success. Instead of fighting in the open the big powers test their power by intervening in other countries that have their private hardships. Only the UN can solve the problems in the Congo and Cuba and Laos. A third World War is building up gradually. (Colored)

A few students describe events that lead to the onset of "the third world war" in which "mankind is destroyed." One student writes he "would like a trip around the world if the Russians and Americans have not blown it up with their nuclear weapons."

For the most part, however, these are remote concerns for the students and do not constitute perceived obstacles to their goals. Some describe Wellsian interplanetary wars, but most take an optimistic view of terrestrial affairs:

> The modern world is very turbulent but I think that a war between the West and the East is impossible because of nuclear weapons. (Colored)

And some see a future in which "nuclear warfare is abolished."

Students in Catholic schools, particularly, express great concern about "world communism," "revolution," "juvenile delinquency," and the spread of "sin." They hope to "help to convert Soviet Russia and Cuba" ("Our Lady has promised that Russia would be converted"), to control "hooliganism" and "gangsterism," and to "preach the word of God to pagans in Africa."

High self-confidence, however, generally is accompanied by high hopes for their personal contribution to social advancement:

> Why am I in the world? This question should be asked by everyone. To improve and help our fellow men. . . . I wish to qualify in medicine, which takes about five years. . . . I will then return to my homeland where I will diligently teach the people of my community. I will plan and control the affairs of my church and my district. It will then be my duty to bring the people to life. At the age of 40 everything in my district will be under control. It will then be an earthly paradise if there can be any. My job will be a difficult one, but where there is a will there is a way. I will bring the hearts of my people to me. I will help my people in every possible way that I can and I will also share what I have to those who are in need. Thus, at the end of the 20th century my district will be an influence to the others, and so the whole island will be changed into a happy and joyous one. Everyone will live in harmony. At the end of the 20th century when my last few days will be at hand, I will be able to lie back in my chair and thank God for placing me in this world which will be profited by my presence. My name will also be long remembered in my community. (East Indian)

The high spirit of optimism about the future among colored as well as Negro students is nourished by political changes with the inherent promise of social progress in the country and the technological promise of the era:

> By the year 1979 the world around me would be quite different. Even games such as soccer and basketball, games that I love, are modified. In 2000 AD space travel is prevalent. Air travel would decline since gadgets for individual travel would be invented, just strap it on your back, press a button, and off you go. Quarreling between nations would cease, for they would be conquered and the race between the US and Russia would come to an end. The 21st century would be the greatest century in the glory of man. (Colored)

Confidence in technology underlies the belief in progress (as it did in the post-World War I period for an American generation). Students see a future in which there will be increased agricultural and industrial production and better utilization of resources, "doing away with famine and disease." Children will have a better education and will "play with space toys." Within a decade:

> ... the shape of cars and dress will change and houses and accessories would be revolutionized. Cities would be face-lifted and traffic modes would change. Most of all the standards of education would change and illiteracy would soon be wiped out. (Colored)

One "could go to Australia and back in a day." The technological advances anticipated are described in detail as are the social advances they are expected to bring for the eradication of poverty, illiteracy, and disease. Life expectancy will be increased and there will be more leisure. Finally, the world scene will also change; there will be "peace and international harmony and the world will be united."

> The nations of the world will be so friendly with each other that there will hardly be any need for developments of war. Conflicts between churches will come to an end and they will be united under one true religion. Color questions will be settled and the poor shall not be as they are now, but will have sufficient on which they will live. Should all these things be accomplished, the world in forty years hence will be very peaceful and happy to live in. (Negro)

Whatever may be the psychological implications of fantasy, in many cases the visions expressed are socially useful. Whatever specific political party may be seen as the channel to progress and to "righting" historical wrongs, the fact is that change is sought through political party channels, that is, through constitutional means. The aspirations in themselves are revolutionary in the history of the society, but the political ideology stems from British concepts of constitutional democracy. Unlike many of their counterparts of the same age in Latin America, the secondary school students were apparently not imbued with the ideologies of either the "new" or the "old" left; perhaps aspiring for high political office is revolutionary enough.

To what extent can these personal and social aspirations be realized? Will they lead to future alienation if they fall far from fulfillment? Can these students find Utopia?

XI

Retrospect and Prospect

Independence marks a social as well as a political change of tremendous significance in former colonial countries. In some new nations sociopolitical change has primarily involved the shift of power and decision-making from old to new elite groups, with reliance on foreign technical advisors; in other nations change has involved placing technical and managerial as well as administrative matters under national, rather than expatriate, control. Political control is considered the decisive factor in these new nations, and technical competence may or may not be viewed as immediately essential in the post-independence situation(1).

Although decision-making was a metropolitan prerogative during the colonial period, political and administrative competence were not exclusively European traits; however, restrictions on education and on role participation substantially circumscribed both training for and actual experience in nation-building roles. In heterogeneous societies such restrictions also severely limited the integration of subordinate ethnic and social-class sectors of the population. The "two nations," Disraeli's characterization of the working and ruling classes of Victorian England, had their counterpart in the plantation society, the planters and the labor force, both slave and free.

Educational opportunities and life chances were rigidly circumscribed by the social structure, which also conditioned the development of educational institutions. Expatriate elites, themselves "often of humble or socially marginal origin," formed the colonial aristocracy(2). With the acquisition of wealth in the

1. See Elizabeth Colson, "Competence and Incompetence in Context of Independence," *Current Anthropology, 8* (1967), 92–100.

2. See Richard M. Morse, "The Heritage of Latin America," in Louis Hartz, *The Founding of New Societies* (New York: Harcourt, Brace & World, 1964), pp. 123–177.

colonies, sons of the colonists were sent to metropolitan universities for a "classical education," and became prototypes for a new professional middle class. Missionary movements provided basic education as a corollary of the spread of Christianity.

In the sugar colony of Trinidad, for the mass of the population – landless rural and urban proletariat – after Emancipation there was little opportunity for the development on an extensive scale of either literacy or artisanship. The educational system was largely in the hands of two major religious denominations – Catholic and Protestant – whose initial missionary interests did not extend beyond primary grade education for the newly emancipated population. The duality of the social structure was reflected in the duality of the educational system, in terms both of denominational controls and of the larger question of who should be educated. Debates over the development of educational institutions and the national extension of education reflected the social and cultural division of interests in the society. Secondary education remained for a century the prerogative of the white upper classes, with a trickle of colored middle-class students who were able to gain admission to the exclusive schools. Education became the main channel of mobility, a goal toward which many aspired, but which few could attain. The highly competitive system of Island Scholarships "contributed to shaping the educational system towards the University and towards the metropolitan country" and "to twist the whole educational system and the orientation of the educated away from the island"(3). Processes of differential acculturation, ethnic exclusiveness, group economic competition conditioned by the plantation system, and lack of a policy of national integration reinforced cultural divergences among the major sectors of the population. The depression period after World War I saw the rise of trade unionism and the emergence of mass-based, though small-scale, political movements. Slowly, but surely, the worldwide "winds of change" in the old colonial order began to be sensed. Absorption of all the subgroups into the greater society was still dependent upon increased educational and economic opportunity and more extensive political participation.

The coming of the new political order in the post-World War II period was linked with the rise of nationalism. The decade of the 1950's, especially, saw the surge of middle-class groups toward participation in national affairs and the swelling of hitherto suppressed aspirations among lower-class groups. Latent desires for education, for occupational and status advancement, and for new national identity came to the fore, kindled by international as well as national events. In 1957, when the first study was undertaken, such hopes were still emergent. The Peoples National Movement, a new political party which was swept into power under the leadership of Dr. Eric Williams, had carried out an intensive campaign of public education, largely in the urban areas, symbolically at the "University" of Woodford Square, a park area in the center of Port of

3. Braithwaite, "The Development of Higher Education in the West Indies," pp. 54–55.

Spain. The promise of fulfillment was in the air, but actual Independence was still a matter for the future, and economic and social advancement were still a matter of privilege in a paternalistic society.

The study was undertaken to examine intra- and inter-ethnic group and social class differences in value systems and the impact of the changing social order on individual attitudes and aspirations. The upper form secondary school population, despite its selectivity, provided a feasible sample reflecting the wide range of rural-urban, social class, ethnic and denominational heterogeneity characteristic of the society. Private schools, as well as government and government-assisted denominational schools, were included in the survey. A second survey was conducted in 1961, in a smaller sample of schools, to further examine some of the conclusions which had been reached in the first survey and to evaluate the impact of new trends of social change on the aspirations of youth. A brief summary of the findings, and a discussion of their implications, are presented in this chapter.

The students who participated in the survey come from all sections of the population; they represent the heterogeneous ethnic fabric and social structure of Trinidad. They are, nonetheless, a select group for their age grades in a society where the number receiving a secondary school education has been severely limited(4). Having attained the higher forms of secondary school, the students in the sample constitute an elite group(5). This is especially true of lower-class students since enrollment in the upper forms is in preparation for examinations to qualify them for university admission. Given the history and social structure of Trinidad, they represent a new rather than a traditional elite group(6). Where secondary school education previously had been severely circumscribed by class and color, the "winds of change," first gently, then strongly sweeping colonial societies after World War II, began to modify the composition of the school population. Some students from groups previously disadvantaged with regard to educational opportunities, still underprivileged economically, could not only reach the higher forms of secondary schools, but could aspire to a university education. Consequently, students from the less privileged groups of the

4. G. W. Roberts indicates that only about one-third of all children attend secondary schools ("A Note on School Enrolment in Trinidad and Tobago," *Social and Economic Studies, 16* [1967], 2).

5. A recent study of school enrollment, based on the 1960 census, indicates that the average male child can expect to spend about 11.2 years at school, including 1.8 years after primary school. Female students spend 10.8 years at school, with 1.7 years at secondary school, leaving at a somewhat younger age than the male students. See Roberts, "A Note on School Enrolment in Trinidad and Tobago," p. 115.

6. Julian Steward points out: "The political power of the traditional elite is weakened only when the middle and lower classes have reached a threshold of economic security, national consciousness and sophistication" ("Prediction and Planning in Culture Change," *Human Organization, 18* [1959], 6).

population are an elite group for their social class. For the society as a whole they represent a "mobile elite." Whether they will in due course take their place as "strategic elites"(7), meeting the administrative, technical, and professional manpower needs of the country, whether they will leave for foreign posts, or fail to fulfill their major goals, their views and aspirations are important for the planner as well as for comparative social science.

We have analyzed in some detail the extremely high goals of the students with regard to university education. The highest aspirations, in fact, are found among the groups formerly least privileged – lower-class Negro and East Indian students, both male and female. We have tried to assess these aspirations in terms of their realism or lack of realism based on available information about actual university attendance abroad (prior to the opening of the University of the West Indies campus at St. Augustine). Disparity between aspirations and reality is most apparent among private school students, where the level of passes generally attained on qualifying examinations is too low for university admission. Even for students in government and government-supported denominational schools, where examination performance is generally higher, aspirations for attaining a university education are consistently discordant with the probabilities for students in these cohorts(8).

The students, highly aware of their conditional chances of survival in the educational hierarchy, are highly motivated to attain this most cherished goal and perceive passing the examinations as the "green light" to the future. The examination has become a *rite de passage* about which there is universal concern; it is described as "a sort of visa for entry into this imaginary journey" into the future. Again, the greatest intensity and sense of urgency is evident among lower-class East Indian and Negro students, and some anticipate they may have to repeat the examination several times in order to secure an adequate "pass," since "these days when one has a low grade he is not thought of as a person who got through the examinations." Preoccupation with passing examinations as a prelude to university admission is, then, the primary and immediate concern of these students.

The "green light" however, only opens the gate; it does not assure passage through "the golden door" of the university. Lower-class students, especially, aside from the statistically remote probability of securing an Island Scholarship, are also urgently preoccupied with the problem of financing higher studies. They discuss quite realistically the period of work that will be required in order to accumulate savings for university studies. It is interesting to see here the differences in time schedules which students from the various socio-ethnic groups project. White students, for whom higher education is a normative expectation, may decide to postpone university entrance, but this is projected as

7. See Suzanne Keller, *Beyond the Ruling Class* (New York: Random House, 1963).

8. See Roberts, "A Note on School Enrolment in Trinidad and Tobago."

a temporary hiatus in the total educational experience – for occupational apprenticeship, travel, and the like. For other students the moratorium on education is based entirely on financial necessity: the need to support themselves during the lengthy period envisaged to attain professional status, and, in many cases, the need to help support parents and younger siblings. Group differences in this respect are striking both statistically and qualitatively. Social class differentials in educational life chances are spelled out in the content of the autobiographies and, in this regard, there is no mistaking the fervency of the university aspirations of a lower-class boy who wrote: "No more will I be considered the son of a poor peasant."

Linkages between university aspirations and occupational choice fall into several categories, also along a reality-unreality continuum. Many of the boys describe their immediate as well as long-range occupational goals. The immediate goals tend to be teaching or civil service posts which are seen as intermediate to their final professional goals. While for most of the white boys the desired and expected final occupational goals tend to coincide, many of the other boys, in a realistic vein, indicate that the intermediate job may, in fact, be their life-long occupation(9). While seeming resigned to this reality, they may compensate by exalting the nature of the less desired occupational role, especially that of the teacher, imbuing it with messianic qualities. Those students who envisage the possibility of not achieving their most desired goal may attribute nonattainment to one of two reasons – failure of the self or failure of the environment.

While East Indian students tend to project the possibility of failure onto external problems – fate, perceived discrimination, environmental barriers – white students who express concern about attainment tend to attribute their problems to perceived personal shortcomings. Historical and existential factors in ethnic group and social class opportunities for achievement are undoubtedly involved in these variations in attitude. Whether the environment or the self is given primary emphasis as the determining factor in achievement, the possibility of failure is a matter for deep personal concern, especially for lower-class students.

The drive for achievement, once unleashed, lends itself to the fancy for multiple role accomplishments. Multiple occupational roles are not unusual in the West Indies; for the lower class they are in fact a necessity, as seasonal employment in agriculture and low paying semiskilled jobs necessitate supplementary income from other sources(10). Multiple occupations in this category

9. Government employment accounted for 15 per cent of the total employed labor force in 1966 (CIAP, p. II.11). In 1957 there were 17,015 employed in the civil service (Trinidad and Tobago, Central Statistical Office, *Annual Statistical Digest, 1958,* No. 8 [Port of Spain: Government Printing Office, 1959], p. 53, Table 40).

10. See George Edward Cumper, "The Differentiation of Economic Groups in the West Indies," 319–332.

are the rule rather than the exception, and for lower-class individuals it may be difficult to determine the primary occupation for census purposes(11).

For the colored middle class as well, multiple occupations are not unusual due to the pressing requirements for skilled administrative personnel in a society with a limited pool of elite manpower. As is the case with elites in Latin American countries, political party leaders and leading government officials in the West Indies generally have come from the ranks of doctors and lawyers. In addition, some have even achieved eminence in cricket. Given existing role models, then, it is not remarkable for a student to aspire to be a doctor or lawyer and a political leader and cricketer. The expectation, however, of achieving eminence in all fields – of being a world-renowned cricketer, discoverer of a cure for cancer, and Prime Minister, of having the communications media reverberate with one's achievements – we have unhesitatingly classified as fantasy. More frequently, however, there are expressions of aspirations for world renown in specified roles modeled on famous people: to be a scientist like Einstein, a leader like Churchill, and so on. Expressed expectations of such great achievements follow ethnic regularities; the essays of colored and white boys are consistently devoid of "dreams of glory," while the essays of lower-class East Indian and Negro boys express such aspirations with fairly high frequency and intensity.

A number of studies have reported consistent findings of national and ethnic differences in aspirations of youth. Youth in new nations have been found more likely to express lofty goals than Western youth; similar patterns have been reported to characterize aspirations of nonwhite as compared to white youth in several multi-ethnic societies (see Chapter VII). The implications of such cross-cultural findings for understanding adolescent thinking and self-concepts remain to be explored.

The present findings indicate that there is a cumulative effect of demographic variables on expressed aspirations: ethnicity, sex, socioeconomic status, and religious affiliation are factors that additively condition levels of aspiration. Girls, on the whole, tend to be less ambitious than boys in the sample; however, the rank order of aspirations by ethnicity is maintained: East Indian girls are the most ambitious, followed by Negro, colored, and white students, in that order. For both sexes, lower-class students among the Negro and East Indian respondents show the highest levels of aspiration, with Hindu and Moslem students more likely than Christian East Indian students to express lofty ambitions.

We have examined various possible determinants, including cultural differences conditioning overt expression of fantasy goals. White students and colored students, who have historically been closest to European models, possibly have a

11. See Lambros Comitas, "Occupational Multiplicity in Rural Jamaica," *Proceedings of the 1963 Annual Spring Meeting of the American Ethnological Society, Symposium on Community Studies in Anthropology,* pp. 41–50.

tendency toward understatement, while lower-class students are presumably more "spontaneous" and, consequently, less restricted in expressing such idealized self-images. This, however, also raises the question of whether fantasy goals may function as a spur to achievement for socially mobile youth. As one student wrote, "The main idea that I can base my plans for the future is I want to be a great person and to be remembered in the minds of the next generation." For those who envisage the possibility of frustration or failure of high goals, the aura of great expectations may be transferred to lesser goals, or vicariously projected to the roles of teachers or parents who prepare the succeeding generation of youth to achieve high goals.

Psychological imperatives of status mobility are inherently different from those of status maintenance. As the students are differentiated along these dimensions, differences in levels of aspiration and intensity of motivation for achievement must be examined within the social framework. Fantasy is functional for the cane-cutter's son aspiring to professional levels; dreaming of becoming world-renowned is an added incentive to passing the examinations and to enduring the long period of work, sacrifice, and study essential to achieving even the more limited goals. As has been seen, even the more limited goals may need to be invested with messianic qualities to be acceptable to an idealized self-image. The possibility must be borne in mind that it is the most ambitious individuals in each group who actually attain the upper forms of the secondary schools, and that ambition is a strong incentive to fantasy. Nevertheless, there are clear-cut group differences in the frequency and intensity of idealized expectations. For the "have" students we may surmise that there is little need to fantasize about assured life chances. Private fantasies certainly exist, but they are not expressed as occupational role aspirations. The patterning of such responses is too consistent to be idiosyncratic. White students who plan to be doctors may stress the humanitarian Schweitzer-like qualities of the medical role, but they do not express aspirations for role glorification. Negro students tend to express the expectation of satisfaction in occupational performance dimensions as part of their goal aspirations, while lower-class East Indian students tend to express the glorification of role performance per se more frequently than others. To a certain extent this is consonant with their position in the social structure, which would further bear out the hypothesis of fantasy as a function of social mobility and perceived social frustration. The pervasive theme among lower-class students, "We wish to be looked upon," may thus have components of anticipated fulfillment in performance or in fame as separately perceived dimensions of the self-image. Both orientations are linked to status achievement and serve to stimulate motivation: "Let the name of my family be raised, so that they can without doubt go to the upper class."

The capacity for fantasy is certainly not foreign to the youth of Trinidad, who witness and participate in the fascinating pageantry of Carnival. Carnival provides an annual platform for the acting out of fantasy roles from the pasquinade to the heroic. At various levels of society, Carnival provides a psychological catharsis; for some it has a substitutive function which makes bearable a humdrum existence during the rest of the year and is sufficiently compelling to stimulate considerable expenditures of time and energy, as well as money. Playing 'mas(12), even for a day, undoubtedly fulfills many psychological needs, but, except for prizewinners, it does not bestow social status.

Many boys in the society must have high aspirations, but aspirations alone do not guarantee achievement. It was necessary to examine whether there was a correspondence between high levels of aspiration and actual commitment to achieve goals. The findings indicate that the desire of East Indian and Negro students to reach high goals is accompanied by a strong sense of goal commitment. It is relevant to the understanding of social change to recognize that when opportunity is available, a reservoir of striving can be uncovered among different ethnic groups, regardless of previous "cultural" differences in orientation.

Among the strivers, preoccupation with career aspirations takes primacy over family orientation. Among the youth who are "established" in terms of social class, that is, white students, family life is forecast as the greatest source of life satisfaction. All the students, however, are concerned with future plans for marriage and family life. For lower-class students, delay of marriage is seen as a necessary requisite to status mobility. Some of the girls evince ambivalence or actual conflict about perceived incompatibility between marriage and career aspirations, and struggle for a personally and culturally viable solution. Romanticizing and fear of traumatic premarital or extramarital experiences is especially salient among lower-class Negro girls, for whom *de jure* marriage is an essential concomitant of mobility.

West Indian society has provided a fertile environment for variation in the forms of mating and family life; the various forms of mating constitute available social class alternatives. Non-marriage has to be psychologically supportable to the persons involved, especially if the norm of legal marriage cannot be attained easily. However, aspirations for legal marriage and conventional family life are closely correlated with mobility striving. The young people in the study come from apparently stable two-parent families, and they perceive the correlation between marriage and status in the greater society. Their projections about marriage and the family of procreation are an important facet of the ethos of mobility.

One of the striking "universals" in the students' aspirations is the expectation of high levels of material consumption. For the economically advantaged students, this is generally a concomitant of normative expectations of status maintenance; "you know, normal middle class" may subsume luxury levels of living. Moreover, emphasis on security rather than on status mobility, consonant with cross-national findings for white students, accentuates pleasure as a leisure

12. *'Mas* is Creole for mask or Carnival.

class indice rather than prosperity per se as a status symbol. Colored students also tend to emphasize the pleasurable aspects of status achievement, while lower-class East Indian and Negro students tend to stress affluent consumer styles of life in terms of status symbols. Whatever may be the subtle class or cultural differences in the finding of universal aspiration for high levels of consumption, it is very striking, and some of the implications will be discussed below.

High standards of consumer expectations may be problem-provoking for planners but are not unexpected in an era of instant communication, when styles of affluence are diffused from centers which produce vast quantities of consumer goods. The one-time apocryphal United States campaign promise of "a chicken in every pot and a car in every garage" can be expanded to include a whole repertory of new science fiction fantasies which the technological revolution potentially can turn into consumer realities. Atom-powered automobiles may still be distant, but there are immediate material goods, whether symbols of affluence or artifacts of the "good life," which the students feel should be within their reach. For "haves," again, this is frequently a concomitant of inherited status and life-style; for the "have-nots," it is undoubtedly as much a spur to achievement as the anticipation of status-associated fame and glory. Higher status is associated with affluence, not with austerity.

Cross-cutting the materialistic elements of the "ethos of mobility" is a very forceful theme of social commitment. Most clearly and forcibly expressed by lower-class Negro and East Indian boys, seldom explicitly mentioned by colored students, and sometimes frankly rejected by white students, a strong theme which signals the convergence of personal and social goals emerges. Personal goals are conceived in the light of social needs; for the East Indian student this may be expressed in terms of "uplifting" the community or "my people," while Negro students tend to express social commitment at the national level. Again, this is undoubtedly historically and experientially conditioned, and is also correlative with urban-rural residence. The rural East Indian student is absorbed by the historical depths of social deprivation of the East Indians as a group and the contemporary problems of the village; Negro students, who outnumber East Indian students in the urban areas, perceive their group emergence as a national force. Perception of the replacement of expatriates by new elites is doubly meaningful: "Our nation" will need new people to fill the jobs "vacated by the English." Opening of the opportunity structure thus embraces service to the nation(13). This sense of strong commitment of lower-class boys to "my people," "my community," "my nation" cannot be overemphasized. Some of

13. Melford Spiro has also noted the convergence of social and personal functions in role performance where high personal and high social motivation coincide. See Spiro, "Social Systems, Personality, and Functional Analysis," in Bert Kaplan (ed.), *Studying Personality Cross-Culturally* (Evanston, Ill.: Row, Peterson, 1961) pp. 106 ff.

the white students also express this view, but most who spontaneously state broad social goals tend to be oriented to the international, rather than the national, scene (the United Nations, world peace aims, and so forth). Attitudes of the white students in the sample who emphasize personal interests more than national interests parallel the Gillespie and Allport findings on "privatism" as a characteristic of students in Western industrial societies in comparison with youth in new nations(14). While the colored group shows concern about political and social change, this interest tends to be expressed in terms of self-reference rather than of nationalism. Colored students, also, even those who have political ambitions, tend to be "cool" about social commitments; however, this may be a seeming detachment due to style of expression.

The social structure has changed most radically for lower-class students; they perceive the relationship between national development and the possibility for personal achievement, and they internalize the goals of social development in striving for personal achievement. Moreover, they perceive social commitment as a significant element in personal fulfillment. Such youth are a potent resource for a "budding" nation. Can their sense of commitment both produce personal fulfillment and contribute to social development? The essential poignant theme of "we wish to be looked upon" merges with the theme of social need and of service to the greater community. Self-orientation and family status orientation are dependent upon and may be superseded by a new aspect of the self-image – national identity.

In affluent societies, it may be considered a mark of sophistication to be cynical about the professed idealism of youth in developing societies: "They say they would like to, but they don't really do anything." For those "realists" who believe that self-seeking is the prime motive for achievement, it is especially interesting that in new nations a participation syndrome has emerged and identification with social goals may become thoroughly interwoven with "particularistic" goals; emergent nationalism can capture the imagination of youth(15). The problem lies in the need for social awareness of the congruency between personal and national requirements, for programming for appropriate utilization of the untapped resource of youth for orientation to projected manpower needs.

Given the proclivity of lower-class boys, who are the most ambitious and the most socially oriented, to aspire to the traditional status-conferring occupations of medicine and law, it is necessary to look at the probabilities for higher education as well as manpower requirements. Given the limited opportunities for university enrollment, it is highly improbable that all the boys with high

14. Gillespie and Allport, *Youth's Outlook on the Future.*

15. "Massa Day Done connotes a political awakening and a social revolution" (Dr. Eric Williams, Address, March 22, 1961).

aspirations can actually reach university levels(16). There has been considerable controversy in the literature about the relative benefits of inputs for higher education in regard to economic growth in developing countries. It has been asserted that a highly educated population per se is not sufficient to produce rapid economic growth: "The people have got to want to achieve, to care about putting their knowledge to productive uses"(17). A gloomier point of view, based on the problem of unemployed intellectuals in India, asserts that secondary education in poor nations should be curtailed to avoid overproduction of elites who become personally frustrated and a "festering source of anomie"(18). Without entering into the maze of economic theorizing(19) which may or may not be of predictive value for educational planning with regard to rapid economic growth, it should be considered whether the problem of higher education for developing nations may be one of underutilization rather than of overproduction.

For one thing, the problem of "overproduction" of educational elites may be more theoretical than actual. The youth of Trinidad and Tobago today (those under twenty-five years of age) are estimated to be about 50 per cent of the total population, and the proportion of youth will be increasing with population expansion. Although the government has been extremely concerned about the expansion of educational facilities, and a comparatively high percentage of the budget is devoted to educational development providing free education both at the secondary and primary levels(20), the construction of secondary schools and the teacher training program still lag behind the needs of a rapidly growing

16. Roberts' analysis of school enrollment in 1960 leads him to estimate that "about seven per cent of the males aged 17–18 in secondary schools move on to universities," in contrast with about 35 per cent of male students in the United States who enter universities ("A Note on School Enrolment in Trinidad and Tobago," p. 118). He quotes Chandler's study of educational output by levels, which reports 69 per cent of the male population in the U.S. aged 17–18 in secondary schools, half of whom enter universities. See Appendix E.

17. David C. McClelland, "Does Education Accelerate Economic Growth?" *Economic Development and Cultural Change, 14* (1966), 269.

18. Edward A. Tiryakian, "Educational Changes in Underdeveloped Areas and Consequences for the Social Structure." Paper presented to the Annual Meeting of the American Sociological Association, August, 1960. Mimeographed.

19. See Sir W. Arthur Lewis, "Education and Economic Development," *Social and Economic Studies, 10* (1961), 113–127.

20. See the Draft Plan, and Trinidad and Tobago, National Planning Commission, *Draft Second Five-Year Plan, 1964–1968* (Port of Spain: Government Printery, 1963). About 91 per cent of the population between five and twelve years were in primary schools by 1966, and the percentage of those from fifteen to seventeen in secondary schools was: age 15, 14 per cent; age 16, 12 per cent; age 17, 8 per cent (CIAP, p. IV.11, 13).

population(21). The expansion of faculties at St. Augustine (University of the West Indies) has brought higher education within the reach of more students, although, again, university resources are not as yet sufficient to provide even for the potential pool of qualified students(22).

Aside from the problem of providing adequate school places for a population with increasing educational aspirations, there is the problem of education to meet the needs of the society. Except for the great interest in teaching, which, however, is often projected as an intermediate occupation, the orientation toward routine civil service and traditional occupations may be anachronistic in a developing nation which needs agronomists, technicians, engineers, managerial and administrative personnel, and entrepreneurs. The Draft Plan for educational development for the 1968–1983 period states: "the key to [economic] growth is the rate at which the educational investment of a country progresses or regresses"(23). Dr. Williams has referred to the need to develop "essential qualifications for the professional, technical and administrative staff of highest quality that would be required for an independent country"(24). For developing countries in general, Theobald, considering the problem of education for new roles, forsees the redundancy of "those whose education and training has been slanted almost entirely toward conformity in order to enable them to perform tasks which no longer will be needed by the socio-economic system"(25). In Trinidad and Tobago, even for the present, although underemployment is a persistent factor at lower occupational levels, there is a continuing need for skilled personnel and professional workers to meet new manpower requirements(26). In these new capacities, there is "room at the top," but the boys who are aspiring to reach it are products of a traditional educational system and a traditional milieu of mobility. As has been noted, rural boys, especially, are too distant from modern role models (even sometimes from the traditional

21. Jack Harewood estimates that, in Trinidad and Tobago, "with a rate of growth among the world's highest," if the present rate of growth is maintained, the population "would have reached two and one-half million" by the year 2000 ("Population Growth in Trinidad and Tobago in the Twentieth Century," *Social and Economic Studies, 12* [1963], 1). See also CIAP, p. IV.8.

22. See CIAP, and Roberts, "Reproductive Performance and Reproductive Capacity in Less Industrialized Societies."

23. Draft Plan, p. 6.

24. Eric Williams, *Three Speeches: Reorganisation of the Public Service* (Port of Spain: PNM Publishing Co., 1965), p. 77.

25. Robert Theobald, "Technological Change: Threat or Promise?" *American Journal of Orthopsychiatry, 37* (1967), 136.

26. The CIAP report cites the 1966 unemployment figure of 14 per cent, with a shortage of trained and experienced technicians and executives in the civil service (p. II.4).

ones) to internalize new role identifications and prepare for them. Lower-class boys in urban areas as well tend to gravitate toward traditional occupations, perhaps in precautionary orientation to status mobility. Doctors and lawyers are "looked upon," and it is to be expected that the first wave of new status aspirants will move in this direction(27). Of the sample population in this study, the colored students — in both the 1957 and 1961 surveys — were exceptional in selecting "modern" occupations. We speculated that this resulted from longer group experience in social and occupational mobility, and adjustment to changing role requirements.

Various measures have been adopted to incorporate more science teaching at the secondary school level, and vocational and technical schools are being established. The most recent Draft Plan for education calls for a major reorientation: "The dynamic circumstances of education in a developing country today have created in Trinidad and Tobago a need for educational planning such as has never before been experienced. The constantly evolving economic, social and cultural needs of the nation contrast sharply with the almost static conditions of the past. National objectives in education today are both more ambitious and more diverse"(28).

This approach may be instrumental in stimulating new occupational role identifications. For modern development, however, a broad technical-scientific orientation in education, rather than the addition of courses in physics, chemistry, and vocational training per se should be considered. Rural school children lack experience with technical and mechanical practice and principles. Although the products of mass production — automobiles, radios, and television sets — are readily available throughout most of the country, children do not generally have the common learning experience of children in industrial countries of taking apart and putting together motor parts to see "what makes them run." In addition, agriculture, whether farming or work in the cane fields, is seen in terms of necessary but highly undesirable labor, and is seldom related to principles of agronomy, or even to modern farming practices. Historical "aversion to manual labor" is the classic reason given for the orientation to "white collar" and "white glove" occupations(29).

27. The CIAP report notes that although health levels are exceptionally high in Trinidad and Tobago, the ratio of doctor to population is unfavorable, especially in the rural areas. Nevertheless, the ratio is very high as compared with other Latin American countries, except for Argentina (p. IV.5). The report notes that "the main challenge in the health factor is to make better use of existing facilities and manpower" (p. IV.6).

28. Draft Plan, p. 79.

29. Williams, *Three Speeches: Reorganisation of the Public Service.* The CIAP report states that in the decade 1951–1961 population growth was outstripping food production for domestic consumption. Uneconomic small peasant farms and farming practices and cultural attitudes are cited as problems in increasing productivity (p. II.4). In this regard,

It is perhaps not sufficiently recognized in developed as well as developing societies that "today's children will reach maturity in a totally new world"(30). While it has been proposed that poor countries should directly "move . . . from the agricultural era to the cybernetics era"(31), they still need to program for immediate industrial and managerial skills as well as for the long-range development of technically and scientifically oriented manpower, if, indeed, cybernetic development is to be feasible. Scientific and technical education needs to start at the primary school level with simple demonstrations and experiments to inculcate early orientation to scientific principles and methods. It has been stressed that "the teaching of science should be introduced into all levels of the educational system. . . . Education in the sciences is not enough; a parallel program must be instituted to train the 'foot soldiers of the army' — the technicians, instrument makers, and their like"(32). These changes can only be made if they are judged worthwhile by society(33), and if the structural conditions for their realization exist. The level of expenditures feasible for a "poor society"(34) can achieve their optimum with recognition of the need for "a social framework to provide the skills and knowledge necessary for living in a technologically advanced world"(35).

Orientation to entrepreneurship as a possible career interest is noticeable by its relative infrequency in the survey. Historically, as was pointed out, capitalist entrepreneurial skills were not encouraged among either the "free people of color" or the newly emancipated Negro population. The colonial society needed local artisans and professionals, but the ownership or management of large-scale enterprises was the prerogative of the planters and expatriate business interests.

Arthur Lewis observes that "Farmers, workers, and entrepreneurs must find it worth their while to improve their skills or change their jobs or take new risks (*Politics in West Africa* [New York: Oxford University Press, 1965], p. 42).

30. Theobald, p. 129.

31. *Ibid.,* p. 136.

32. George Basalla, "The Spread of Western Science," *Science, 156* (1967), 618.

33. Ralph Romain points out the need for "the attitudinal infrastructure without which change cannot take place" ("The Character of West Indian Society and Its Implications for Teacher Training," Appendix 4, in UNESCO/UWI Seminar on Curriculum and Teacher Training, University of the West Indies, Trinidad, 1967, *Report* [St. Augustine, Trinidad: The University of the West Indies, 1968], p. 6).

34. The Draft Plan stresses the problems of financing education by "the poor society" (p. 5).

35. David Apter, *Politics of Modernization* (Chicago: University of Chicago Press, 1965), p. 67.

Even middle-scale enterprises were developed largely by Middle Eastern and Chinese, rather than by Negro and colored, entrepreneurs. East Indians, as has been noted, eventually also became middle- and large-scale business owners, principally of service enterprises (transport, cinemas, merchandising). However, the drive to achievement of the sons of rural lower-class East Indians as seen in the surveys is toward the normative status image of the society – the professions. Development of managerial and entrepreneurial skills is obviously essential to society whether under traditional or new forms of social, political, and financial control.

It has been postulated that certain structural regularities may be expected to follow in the wake of culture change from traditional to emergent industrial societies(36). These include the rise of new middle classes with new roles in the society. In a theoretical formulation of "the processes of culture change which originate in an emerging world industrial culture," Steward states that "one does not have to indoctrinate entrepreneurship. The drive appears when basic conditions of change are fulfilled"(37). Provided that the course of change is essentially determined by greater social forces, the problem for planners remains how to "accelerate trends" and establish guidelines for directed change, even for short-range programs. The motivation and commitment of the youth needs to be matched by an education geared to modern needs, relevant career guidance, and meaningful opportunities for fulfillment.

One of the pervasive themes which the first survey revealed (both in the essays and in the group discussions that followed) was the trend to urban and suburban residence and styles of life. The problem of "urban drift" which confronts most societies can probably be countered in the long run by bringing urban amenities to rural centers, introducing "agro-industries," and the like. The pace of such socioeconomic transformations of rural life must obviously depend on budgetary needs and developmental priorities. The government of Trinidad and Tobago has been very much concerned with social disparities in rural-urban levels of development. An agricultural development program to encourage small farming and to increase food production(38) and various community "betterment" programs have also been devised. Community centers have been established and folk arts programs fostered through national competitions. The competitions encourage both local interest in folk arts and the development of the national symbols of culture.

The rise of nationhood in Trinidad was accompanied by a florescence of the

36. Julian H. Steward, "Prediction and Planning in Culture Change," pp. 5–7.

37. *Ibid.*, p. 6.

38. The "Crown Lands Scheme," initiated in 1966 utilizes reserve lands belonging to the government. Twenty thousand acres of land have been set aside to create approximately 1800 farms of varying acreage for crops, cattle, pigs, and poultry. (See CIAP, p. A.6).

arts – painting, sculpture, dance, music (with the proliferation of steel bands), and a generally renewed interest in "folk arts". This dynamic creative expression can serve as a basis for the evolution of integrated rurban(39) communities, as well as for national integration. Recognition of the need for a "cultural policy" in the 1968 Draft Plan may help to maintain the enthusiasm initially generated by the community programs and encourage youth and adult leadership to initiate as well as continue these projects(40).

The instrumental role of education in nation building is being increasingly stressed by economists: the "creation of human capital by investment in education is now recognized as an important element in economic growth," and "educational planning should be linked with general development planning. . . . It has to be treated as an investment good, not only a consumption good"(41). This point of view is well-known to planners and has been extensively applied in Trinidad and Tobago. The need for reorientation of the educational system and recognition that "educational content and methods also demand attention in relating education to development"(42) are emphasized in the development plans(43). We should like to examine another dimension which emerged in the background study on the historical development of a pluralistic education system and the function of education in a developing society. The social class and ethnic divisions of the colonial society were reinforced by the educational system which developed as a structural consequence of the social system. The children of both ex-slaves and indentured servants received an elementary education in the course of being Christianized, but instruction was given along denominational lines that served to further isolate them from each other. The complex denominational system tended to reinforce identity within a religious, ethnic, or social class, rather than within a national framework, and the consequent problems for nation-building have been recognized:

> The situation becomes socially a cause for concern when a racial analysis is made of some of the Christian and non-Christian primary schools, where both types of schools are found in certain rather mixed and populous areas, and where in spite of the great mixture of the population one observes, to quote the case of some schools in such mixed racial areas as

39. "Rurban" implies a mixture of rural and urban ways of living. See Vera Rubin, "Fifty Years in Rootville," doctoral dissertation, Columbia University, 1951, p. 19.

40. See the Draft Plan, p. 68. The Draft Plan states: "A nation is identified by its culture. Its development is governed by its cultural assumptions and behavior and attitudes. Its survival is directly related to the survival of its culture."

41. Eugene Staley, "Education's Role in Nation Building," *Science, 153* (1966), 47.

42. *Ibid.*, p. 48.

43. See the Draft Plan.

San Fernando, Tunapuna, and Couva, among others, that the schools appear to be racially divided, in that we find ninety-seven out of every hundred pupils in the same school to be of one race(44).

During this period of reexamination of national institutions, an outside observer noted that the parochial and ethnic concept embodied in the dual system of education "must give way to national aims and purposes"(45) and that this was the main task facing the new government. More recently, with increased government assistance to schools, enrollment at denominational schools tends to transcend ethnic and denominational affiliations. Discussing the religious affiliation of the school population, Dr. Williams concluded that "the principal agency for the integration of the population of Trinidad and Tobago is today the Government secondary school"(46).

Cultural diversity in a heterogeneous society serves as a continuing source of cross-fertilization which can best be sustained through contact between groups. Without obstructing religious values, the spread of government-assisted denominational schools and secular government schools may integrate rather than separate children and assure the developmental function of education in a society where status is increasingly determined by objective criteria of achievement rather than by ethnic origin. Education for participation in the national decision-making process is as essential as education appropriate for the new technological era.

The complex society of Trinidad, shaped by multi-ethnic strands and external as well as internal forces, needs to be viewed in historical perspective. The "culture-historical" viewpoint of the social scientist, however, often tends to be oriented toward cultural persistence rather than cultural change. Just as the "Africanist" school has traced (or attempted to trace) contemporary cultural phenomena to "Africanisms," the persistence of traditional elements of East Indian culture has been emphasized(47). There have been divergent views on this position, ranging from studies of acculturation to assertions of complete assimilation, and the literature on the subject is growing(48). There have also

44. Maurice Committee Report, pp. 50, 51.

45. Nathaniel M. Gooding, "Education in Trinidad, Past and Present," doctoral dissertation, University of Connecticut, 1961, p. 253.

46. Williams, *Three Speeches: Reorganisation of the Public Service*, p. 3.

47. See Morton Klass, *East Indians in Trinidad: A Study in Cultural Persistence* (New York: Columbia University Press, 1961).

48. See Crowley; Niehoff and Niehoff; Jayawardena; Schwartz; R. T. Smith, *The Negro Family in British Guiana*, and "People and Change"; and Elliot Skinner, "Group Dynamics and Social Stratification in British Guiana," in Vera Rubin (ed.), *Social and Cultural Pluralism in the Caribbean, Annals of the New York Academy of Sciences, 83*, 5 (1960), 904–912.

been a few culture and personality studies involving comparisons of national character traits of Negroes and East Indians(49). The most recent one reaches conclusions similar to a study previously undertaken by Mischel (1961); based on a study of twelve-year old children in primary schools, the author concludes:

> Negroes are oriented to the present, whereas East Indians are oriented toward the past by their religion and caste heritage, and toward the future by their interest in material security and accumulation(50).

The findings of the present study do not substantiate deductions about the "apparent and well-known disparity" in motivations and aspirations "between these two sub-cultures"(51). To the contrary, the findings reveal an "ethos of mobility" which cross-cuts posited ethnic differences in future orientation, and disclose cross-ethnic motivation to defer present gratifications and to undergo deprivation for the attainment of future goals and the commitment to work toward long-range goals. Culture and personality do not exist in a social vacuum(52); the differences in the historical as well as cultural backgrounds of the Negro and East Indian subsystems in Trinidad underlie differences in their ways of life. Cultural contact and the changing social structure, however, continue to modify both subsystems and to produce convergence in significant areas of behavior, particularly with regard to motivation for achievement, perception of the means to achievement, and new identity roles. This is not a unique historical phenomenon, and it may be especially marked in new nations in a technological era(53).

49. For a recent discussion of national character theory and studies, see "National Character in the Perspective of the Social Sciences," *The Annals of the American Academy of Political and Social Science, 370* (March 1967).

50. Green, p. 209. This view is further delineated as follows: "Negro children are not as interested in possessions nor worried about long range plans, suggesting that they are focused on the 'here and now'. In contrast the East Indian youths give answers indicating that they would deprive themselves in the present for betterment in the future. These values form two different ways of life apparent today in the well-known disparity between these two sub-cultures" (p. 204).

51. Green, p. 204.

52. As previously noted, the widespread stereotype of inability of lower-class Negroes to defer gratification is being questioned in studies of the "culture of poverty" in the United States. See Liebow.

53. A cross-ethnic survey of consumption aspirations recently undertaken in rural British Honduras points out that: "Peasants who look into the future with confidence and those who prefer to see their country independent tend to have greater aspirations" (Burkhard Strumpel, "Consumption Aspirations: Incentives for Economic Change," *Social and Economic Studies, 14* [1965] 189). Furthermore, "Peasants who have greater aspirations tend to be more industrious and more mobile. They show a particularly strong readiness for change" (p. 192).

Emphasis on the primary or exclusive significance of infantile and childhood experience as behavioral determinants in culture and personality studies fails to take into account significant events of youth and adulthood and especially "the reality of the institutional integrations to which the individual must adapt if he is to succeed within the social organization"(54). Change is multidimensional; as the aspirations of lower-class East Indian and Negro boys have converged, mobility striving has merged the original differences in consumer aspirations. Boys in both groups look to similar new styles of life as well as similar new statuses. A study of consumer aspirations in British Honduras finds that "school education exercises a strong influence on the emergence of consumption aspirations"(55). Whether as a result of education or the influence of mass media or both linked to a changing social order, rising consumer aspirations are contemporary social phenomena(56).

The rapid diffusion of "the world industrial culture"(57) in recent decades and the rise of consumer aspirations have created cross-cultural regularities in the development of new nations. The emergence of such structural regularities, however, does not imply cultural homogeneity. Homogeneity is not possible in complex societies nor would it be desirable. Individual and subgroup variations of the core culture are a dynamic function of social life. Heterogeneity provides a continual source of cross-fertilization, and the recognition of cultural as well as individual differences and provision for their expression are essential to the development of a viable society.

It is possible to overstress both cross-cultural similarities and differences, and even the presumed "objectivity" of the social scientist may be clouded by the observation of neatly definable patterns of behavior, especially on homogeneous small-scale samples. Current social science categories based on a "live for

54. Yehudi A. Cohen, "On Alternative Views of the Individual in Culture-and-Personality Studies," *American Anthropologist, 68* (1966), 355.

55. Strumpel, p. 193.

56. As Strumpel points out for British Honduras: "These peasants whose outlook towards their and their children's future is 'dynamic', who are aware of living in a changing world, who have a feeling of belonging to a greater national community, appear to have particularly high consumption aspirations" (p. 193). For the social planner, Strumpel adds a positive note: "An Indian's consumption aspirations have a positive influence on his readiness to accept opportunities to change his way of life and to increase his productive contribution to the economy" (*ibid.*).

57. Steward states: "The important characteristics of this culture include pure science, applied science, mass production and distribution, commerce, communications, education and many others resulting from world technological developments" (p. 5). Steward further observes that "the increased flow of material goods, together with the desire for new kinds of services, creates new middle classes of merchants, mechanics, transport workers, clerks and professionals, and it stimulates the growth of towns and urban centers" (*ibid.*).

today—live for tomorrow" dichotomy are reminiscent of the "Dionysian-Apollonian"(58) typology of which another generation has been critical(59). Social science efforts to underemphasize cultural differences, however, may also fall short of the mark of social reality. It is difficult to capture the dynamics of the situation and to avoid a static approach. It is essential, however, to examine the profound nature of social changes which have taken place over the last two decades and to determine their impact on changing value systems.

The subordinate position of East Indians in the society reinforced tendencies to cultural conservatism, and separatist tendencies laced with pessimism with regard to equality of opportunity were strengthened(60). In this respect, we find that although East Indian students may express a sense of insecurity concerning the social environment — in that they fear external obstacles may interfere with their achievement — and some may perceive it as potentially threatening, they nevertheless apparently have sufficient confidence to cope with the situation and to aspire to higher status. The experience of successful learning, for all students, is in itself an ego-strengthening factor. They are also motivated by the new sociopolitical environment to contribute more to their society than they were called upon to contribute in the past or could have conceived as desirable. New aspirations are linked with the sense of new obligations and responsibilities in the shaping of new identities.

Substantively one may say, as the present study and other studies indicate, that participation in political parties has been correlated with ethnic membership(61). Structurally, however, it is highly important to observe that members of all ethnic groups currently participate in political parties and gain experience both in decision-making processes and in expanding social democracy, as a function of the electorate. For the emergent elites, social class is the primary factor in anticipation of future political roles, and it is the formerly disprivileged who are most concerned with assuming leadership roles in the thrust toward social development, regardless of political party vehicle.

Mobility, seen as a new social dynamic, can transcend ethnic differences in culture and group identification. High motivation to achievement and to the accompanying emoluments of the consumer culture provide an integrating mechanism in the society. Furthermore, the social commitment of youth from underprivileged ranks can be channeled to the national purpose. In this respect, the Trinidad findings parallel those of the Gillespie and Allport international

58. Ruth Benedict, *Patterns of Culture* (Boston: Houghton Mifflin, 1934).

59. See Rubin, "Fifty Years in Rootville."

60. Strumpel, p. 189, finds that people who are pessimistic about the future tend to have low aspirations.

61. See Rubin, "Culture, Politics and Race Relations."

survey showing that youth in developing countries who expressed strong emphasis on personal achievement also revealed strong group orientation. Motivation for achievement may thus be a function of the social situation rather than of particular personality structure or cultural heritage(62).

Erikson calls attention to the "unity of personal and cultural identity" which is "identical in the core of the individual and yet also identical in the core of a communal culture"(63). Communal cultures are now integrally linked to national societies, and as the life chances of the individual perceivably expand "in all parts of the world, the struggle now is for anticipatory and more inclusive identities"(64). The new identity is seen as the fulfillment of a promise "to the youth . . . of countries which must overcome . . . their colonial past"(65).

If it is not consumed by structural rivalries, the opportunity to achieve new roles in the society reinforces common denominators of culture. In Guyana the observation has been made that "the whole society shares a common cultural equipment which can serve as the basis for unity, as the foundation of creativity and future growth and as a bridge to participation in the wider communities of the Caribbean and of the world at large"(66). The foundation for growth lies in the youth who share common perspectives on the future, and who, in the words of a noted political leader, "can help to supply what the West Indian countries so sorely need today . . . people who place the national service above glorification of self"(67). It has been said that "the people of Trinidad, regardless of cultural or ethnic background, have common goals of mobility, seek the same opportunities and share a common loyalty to their new nation"(68). The problem of opportunity becomes the crucial factor in the society. As Dr. Williams pointed out in an address, "the real problem is to transfer a satellite economy, satellite of a metropolitan country, with a colonial mentality, into the economy of an independent country that doesn't have a lot of room to maneuver"(69).

62. See Talcott Parsons, *Essays in Sociological Theory* (Glencoe, Ill.: The Free Press, 1954).

63. Erik H. Erikson, "The Concept of Identity in Race Relations: Notes and Queries," *Daedalus, 95* (1966), 145–171.

64. *Ibid.*, p. 165.

65. *Ibid.*

66. R. T. Smith, *British Guiana.* (London: Oxford University Press, 1962), pp. 198–199.

67. Eric Williams, Address to the graduating class of the University of the West Indies, February 16, 1963.

68. Sherlock, "Prospects in the Caribbean," p. 751.

69. Williams, *Three Speeches: Reorganisation of the Public Service,* p. 85.

Paraphrasing McClelland's well-known thesis about the "need for achievement" and the rate of economic growth(70), it would appear that, institutional factors permitting, high levels of the "need for achievement" among young people in the society are predictive of potentially high rates of social development, provided that such individuals can play a role in social development. The development of the society will tell the story of the students' chances and achievements. One thing is certain: Having "looked upward" to the future, they will never be content with a return to the past.

> Should you
>
> shatter the door
> and walk
> in the morning
> fully aware
>
> of the future
> to come?
> There is no
> turning back(71).

70. See McClelland, "Does Education Accelerate Economic Growth?" and *The Achieving Society* (Princeton, N.J.: Van Nostrand, 1961).

71. Edward Brathwaite, *Rights of Passage* (London: Oxford University Press, 1967), p. 86.

Appendix A

Secondary School Data

SCHOOLS PARTICIPATING IN THE STUDY

Government and Government-Assisted Secondary Schools:
Bishop Anstey High School
Bishop's High School (Tobago)
College of St. Philip and St. James
Fatima College
Holy Faith Convent (Couva)
Naparima College
Naparima Girls' High School
Presentation College (San Fernando)
Queen's Royal College
St. Augustine Girls' High School
St. Joseph Convent (Port of Spain)
St. Joseph Convent (San Fernando)
St. Mary's College

Private Secondary Schools:
Burke College
Hindu College
Holy Name Convent (Port of Spain)
Ideal High School
Kenley College
Osmond High School for Boys
Osmond High School for Girls
Progressive Educational Institute (Boys)
Progressive Educational Institute (Girls)
St. Joseph Convent (Arima)
St. Thomas Aquinas High School
San Juan Secondary School

Participating Schools Not Included in the Analysis:
  Boys Industrial School (Diego Martin)
  Caribbean Union College
  Caribbean Training College
  Catholic Women's Training College for Teachers
  Government Training College for Teachers
  Naparima Teacher Training College
  Tacarigua Orphanage

CAPITAL AND OPERATING EXPENDITURES

Total capital and operating expenditures in 1960 for secondary schools were as follows: for government and government-assisted schools, $3,948,682.83 (T&T); for private schools, $973,097.31 (T&T)(1).

DATA ON ENROLLMENT IN UPPER FORMS OF GOVERNMENT AND GOVERNMENT-ASSISTED SECONDARY SCHOOLS: 1957 AND 1961

There were 20 government and government-assisted secondary schools in Trinidad and Tobago in 1957, and 30 in 1961(2). In 1957, there were 1,611 students in Form 5 of these schools (1,053 boys and 558 girls) and 519 students in Form 6 (371 boys and 148 girls). By 1961, the number of students in Form 5 had increased to 2,229 (1,382 boys and 847 girls), and there were 722 students in Form 6 (461 boys and 261 girls)(3).

DATA ON ENROLLMENT IN UPPER FORMS OF PRIVATE SECONDARY SCHOOLS

There were 21 registered private secondary schools in Trinidad and Tobago in 1957, and 27 in 1961(4). Enrollment figures for 1957 are not available for private registered secondary schools. In 1960, there were 1,342 students in Form 5 (755 boys and 587 girls) and 84 students in Form 6 (54 boys and 30 girls)(5). No figures are available on nonregistered private secondary schools.

1. Trinidad and Tobago, Central Statistical Office, *A Digest of Statistics on Education, 1961* (Port of Spain: Government Printing Office, 1964), p. 137.

2. *Ibid.*, p. 97.

3. *Ibid.*, p. 103.

4. *Ibid.*, p. 121.

5. *Ibid.*, p. 124.

Table A-1. General Education Enrollment by Level of Education and Age, Secondary Education (December 1957) (a)

Forms	Preparatory I		Preparatory II		Form I		Form II		Form III		Form IV		Form V		Form VI Higher School Certificate				Total		Grand Total
															1st Year		2nd Year				
Year of School Course	5		6		7		8		9		10		11		12		13				
Ages	M	F	M	F	M	F	M	F	M	F	M	F	M	F	M	F	M	F	M	F	
8–9	—	4	—	—	—	—	—	—	—	—	—	—	—	—	—	—	—	—	—	4	4
9–10	—	14	—	2	2	1	—	—	—	—	—	—	—	—	—	—	—	—	2	17	19
10–11	—	14	—	17	25	17	—	—	—	—	—	—	—	—	—	—	—	—	27	48	75
11–12	—	4	—	28	77	103	30	8	4	—	—	—	—	—	—	—	—	—	111	143	254
12–13	—	—	—	15	250	252	119	51	22	9	4	—	—	—	—	—	—	—	395	327	722
13–14	—	—	—	8	338	340	322	259	85	72	26	5	1	—	—	—	—	—	772	684	1,456
14–15	—	—	—	3	215	141	335	337	310	205	91	58	35	1	1	—	—	—	987	745	1,732
15–16	—	—	—	—	48	23	187	111	324	244	261	181	78	22	15	—	—	—	913	581	1,494
16–17	—	—	—	—	3	1	63	23	190	108	245	263	237	151	44	22	4	2	786	570	1,356
17–18	—	—	—	—	—	—	11	—	58	16	152	109	318	207	100	55	17	25	656	412	1,068
18–19	—	—	—	—	—	—	1	—	6	3	46	22	236	129	84	80	15	30	388	264	652
19–20	—	—	—	—	—	—	—	—	—	—	—	—	111	32	35	51	20	—	166	83	249
Total	—	36	—	73	958	878	1,070	789	999	657	825	638	1,016	542	279	208	56	57	5,203	3,878	9,081

Note: These figures are in respect of government and assisted schools only.

a. Trinidad and Tobago, *Administration Report of the Education Department, Annual Summary for 1957* (Port of Spain: Government Printing Office, 1963), p. 60

205

Table A-2. Number of Students on Roll by Age, 1954–1963,
in Government and Assisted Secondary Schools(a)

YEAR	Sex	All Ages(b)	YEAR	Sex	All Ages(b)
1954	Total	6,713	1959	Total	10,639
	Boy	3,875		Boy	5,926
	Girl	2,838		Girl	4,713
1955	Total	7,070	1960	Total	12,097
	Boy	4,097		Boy	6,523
	Girl	2,973		Girl	5,574
1956	Total	7,430	1961	Total	13,191
	Boy	4,374		Boy	6,840
	Girl	3,956		Girl	6,351
1957	Total	9,188	1962	Total	15,445
	Boy	5,348		Boy	8,039
	Girl	3,840		Girl	7,406
1958	Total	9,932	1963	Total	17,272(c)
	Boy	5,574		Boy	8,781
	Girl	4,358		Girl	8,491

a. Trinidad and Togabo, Central Statistical Office, *A Digest of Statistics on Education, 1962–63.* (Port of Spain: Government Printing Office, 1966), Table 48.

b. Age range included is from 9 to 19 years, covering post-primary education.

c. In 1963, there were 13,791 students in private secondary schools: 6,523 boys and 7,268 girls (*A Digest of Statistics on Education, 1962–63,* p. 103).

Appendix B

Population and Literacy Data

The estimated population for 1957 of the fifteen to nineteen year age group was 67,800: 34,350 males and 33,450 females(1). The estimated population for 1961 of the fifteen to nineteen year age group was 86,550: 42,350 males and 44,150 females(2). According to the 1960 census, in the total population there were approximately twice as many women as men fifteen years old and over who had received no education: 35,592 women and 18,494 men(3).

Table B-1. 1960 Population, by Census Racial Categories(a)

Ethnic Categories	Trinidad and Tobago		Trinidad Only	
	N	%	N	%
Negro	358,588	43.3	327,614	41.2
White	15,718	1.9	15,445	1.9
East Indian[b]	301,946	36.5	301,509	37.9
Chinese	8,361	1.0	8,301	1.0
Mixed	134,749	16.3	133,253	16.8
Lebanese, Syrians	1,590	.2	1,538	.2
Other	6,714	.8	6,673	.8
Not Stated	291	.0	291	.0
Total	827,957	100.0	794,624	99.8

a. Trinidad and Tobago, Central Statistical Office, Population Census Division, *Eastern Caribbean Population Census, 1960: Series A, Trinidad and Tobago, Bulletin No. 1, Population by Sex, Age-Group and Race* (Port of Spain: Government Printing Office, 1961).

b. East Indian population is listed by religious denomination as follows: Hindu, 63.0 per cent; Moslem, 16.5 per cent; Christian, 20.5 per cent.

1. Trinidad and Tobago, Central Statistical Office, *Annual Statistical Digest,* 1962, p. 18.

2. *Ibid.,* 1965, p. 16.

3. Trinidad and Tobago, Central Statistical Office, *Eastern Caribbean Population Census, 1960: Trinidad and Tobago,* Vol. II, Part A, pp. 8B-1 and 8B-2.

Table B-2. Population Analysis by Racial Group and Literacy, 1946 Census(a)

	White	Black	East Indian	Syrian	Chinese	Mixed or Colored	Race not stated	All races
Total persons in racial group	15,283	261,485	195,747	889	5,641	78,775	150	557,970
Percentage of total population	2.7%	46.9%	35.1%	0.2%	1.0%	14.1%		100%
Population 10 years and over	12,467	201,353	132,363	608	4,514	55,431	139	406,875
Literate persons(b) 10 years and over	12,030	181,494	65,153	520	3,834	50,351	89	313,471
Illiterate persons(c) 10 years and over	385	18,932	66,153	83	654	4,710	24	91,563
Illiterate persons as % of total persons 10 years and over	3.1%	9.4%	50.4%	13.6%	14.5%	8.5%	17.1%	22.5%

a. Trinidad and Tobago, Central Statistical Office, *Annual Statistical Digest, 1955* (Port of Spain: Government Printing Office, 1956), Table 12.
b. Literate persons are defined as those who declared themselves as (a) able to read and write, or (b) able to read only.
c. Illiterate persons are defined as those who declared themselves as (a) unable to read and write, or (b) unable to read.

Appendix C

Socioeconomic Index

To determine the socioeconomic ratings each student was asked to state the occupation of his or her father (or head of household), and to specify the degree of his father's managerial responsibility, the size of business or farm, and the monthly income of the family. In some cases, the teachers supplemented or amended the information given by the students. To establish the rank order of the occupational groups obtained, the Central Statistical Office of Trinidad and Tobago was consulted. Originally, six occupational groups, or socioeconomic classes, were established on the basis of census categories. In the present study, the six groups have been reduced to three main groups in order to facilitate statistical computation.

The upper socioeconomic group (Class I) roughly corresponds to the upper-middle class; it comprises such occupations as physician, dentist, lawyer, principal of secondary school, head of department in the civil service (but not including principal officers), and farmers owning more than 100 acres.

The middle socioeconomic group (Class II) comprises principal officers to second-class clerks in the civil service group, small business owners, merchants, private secondary school teachers, inspectors, sergeants of police, junior executives and managers of local stores, bookkeepers, farmers owning 21 to 100 acres, semiprofessionals, and primary school teachers.

The lower socioeconomic group (Class III) is composed of the following: store clerks, barbers, farmers owning less than 20 acres, artisans, taxi drivers, and semiskilled and unskilled laborers.

Appendix D

Essay Form and Questionnaires

AUTOBIOGRAPHY FROM NOW TO 2000 A.D.

In this assignment you are asked to cooperate in a worldwide study which is being conducted among students of your own age in many different countries. We will appreciate your cooperation in this study.

We would like to know the thoughts that come to your mind spontaneously. If you do not wish to write about yourself, you may take as your subject any imaginery young person of your own age and write from his or her point of view.

Instructions:

1. Begin at the present and write about your expectations, plans, and hopes for the future. You may write from 50 to 60 minutes on this subject.

2. You need not write about the future year by year or decade by decade; it would be well to write first of the near future as you see it and then of your expectations for middle age and later life.

3. In this study, it is not necessary for you to give your name unless you choose to do so. The study is in two parts; the autobiography which you are now being asked to write, and a simple questionnaire which you will be asked to answer later on. We would like to put the two sections together without anyone knowing your name, therefore this instruction sheet has a special code number on it. Please write this number on your autobiography and remember it so that you can put it on the questionnaire which you get later. Thank you for your cooperation.

Code Number   Age   Sex

Name (optional)   Religious affiliation

FIRST SURVEY QUESTIONNAIRE

This is not an examination. Some of the questions which follow may be answered simply by making a check mark. Others you are asked to answer with a phrase or two in your own words.

Please answer every question. Thank you for your cooperation.

1. What two things would you most like to know about the future up to 2000 A.D.?

   (1)_____

   _____

   (2)_____

   _____

2. Please indicate your sex, age, and present marital status:

   Sex: _____ Male   Age _____

   _____ Female

   Present marital status:_____ Single, not betrothed

   _____ Single

   _____ Married

3. To what socioeconomic class would you say that the family in which you were reared belonged?

   _____ Upper Class

   _____ Middle Class

   _____ Working Class

   _____ Lower Class

4. What two things would you most like to have that you don't now have?

   (1)_____

   (2)_____

5. What three situations or events in your past life, up to the present, do you consider to have been most important or significant? That is, what three events in your past have had the greatest effect upon your present life?

   (1)_____

   (2)_____

   (3)_____

   _____

6. a. What is your father's principal occupation? (If he is retired or not living, what was his occupation? Or if you were brought up by some relative or guardian, what is or was his principal occupation?)

7. Do you expect to enter –
   The same occupation as your father or guardian?
   The same occupation as your mother?
   A closely related occupation?
   A different occupation?

8. Do you expect to marry some time or other? (In this as in other questions, you may have no definite expectation, but even so, you are asked to make a guess).
   _____Yes
   _____No

9. If so, at what age do you expect to marry?

10. If you marry, how many children do you *expect* to have?
    _____None   _____Three   _____More than five
    _____One   _____Four
    _____Two   _____Five

11. If you marry, how many children would you like to have?
    _____None   _____Three   _____More than five
    _____One   _____Four
    _____Two   _____Five

12. How old do you expect to be when your first child is born?_____

13. As a parent, what two specific lessons will you try hardest to teach your children?
    (1)_____
    _____
    (2)_____
    _____

14. What two things would you like your child most to have that you yourself did not have?
    (1)_____
    (2)_____

15. Which one of the following qualities do you regard as most important in a good wife or husband?

_____Shares my own opinions and beliefs

_____Intelligence — common sense

_____Pleasant disposition — a good companion

16. If you get married and have a family, who do you expect will be more influential in the direction and control of the affairs of the family?

_____Myself

_____My wife (or husband)

_____Both equally

17. What is your present state of health?

_____Excellent

_____Good

_____Fair

_____Poor

18. Would you like to live the main part of your life in

_____ your native country?

_____ some other country? (please specify_____)

19. Do you expect to be able to travel (at some time during your life) as extensively as you would like to?

_____Yes

_____No

20. If you were able to travel, what three foreign countries would you like most to visit?

(1)_____

(2)_____

(3)_____

21. For what end would you be willing to make the greatest sacrifice of personal comfort, time, and money?

_____

22. What do you think is likely to be the cause of your death?

_____

23. If you had a personal problem that worried you (for example, a difficult decision to make), whom would you *prefer* to talk it over with?

_____Members of your immediate family

_____Relatives outside your immediate family

_____Some trained person (e.g., doctor or psychologist)

_____Other (please specify_____)

24. Would you like to have more friends than you now have?

_____Yes

_____No

Would you like to have some friend more intimate than you now have (i.e., in whom you can confide, on whom you can rely)?

_____Yes

_____No

25. Concerning your personal future, would you say that in general you feel

_____enthusiastic?

_____hopeful?

_____indifferent?

_____resigned?

_____embittered?

26. What three things or activities in your life do you expect to give you the most satisfaction? (Please mark the most important source of satisfaction with the number 1, the next most important with a 2, and the third with a 3.)

_____Your career or occupation

_____Family relationships

_____Leisure-time, recreational activities

_____Participation as a citizen in the affairs of your community

_____Participation in activities directed toward national or international betterment

_____Religious beliefs and activities

27. Looking ahead to 2000 A.D., which of the five 10-year periods between now and then do you expect to give you the greatest satisfaction in living?

_____1950–1960

_____1960–1970

_____1970–1980

_____1980–1990

_____1990–2000

28. When you become a man (woman) do you expect your own standard of living to be the same, higher, or lower than your family now?

    _____Higher standard

    _____About the same

    _____Lower standard

29. Looking ahead to 2000 A.D., which of the five 10-year periods between now and then seems clearest to you in your imagination as you think about them? Which seems least clear? Number the clearest decade with a 1, and the least clear with a 5.

    _____1950–1960

    _____1960–1970

    _____1970–1980

    _____1980–1990

    _____1990–2000

30. In general, what will help you most to get ahead, ability or "pull" (that is, personal contacts or influence, through your family or friends)?

    _____Ability

    _____Pull

31. What are the two worst things that could *conceivably* happen to you during your lifetime?

(1)_____

(2)_____

32. What are the two worst things that are *likely* to happen to you during your lifetime?

(1)_____

(2)_____

33. To what extent would you agree with the following proposition?

"The world is a hazardous place, in which men are basically evil and dangerous."

    _____Agree

    _____Slightly agree

    _____Slightly disagree

    _____Disagree

34. Do you expect to be more interested in
_____ problems of Trinidad?
_____ problems of the West Indies?
_____ problems of the world?

35. Do you expect to be more successful as a leader in your field than the average person in your field who has the same amount of education?
_____ More successful
_____ About the same
_____ Less successful

36. To what extent do you expect your relatives (i.e., members of your present family and your future in-laws) to be of assistance to you in your lifetime?
_____ Constantly available and almost indispensable
_____ Available, whenever needed, for helpful advice and assistance, both personal and financial
_____ Emergency economic assistance only
_____ Of no assistance at all

37. If you should get a large sum of money five years from now, what would you do with it?

_____

_____

38. What two things could you conceivably accomplish during your lifetime that you would be most proud of?
(1) _____

(2) _____

39. What are the two worst things that could justifiably be said about you during your lifetime?
(1) _____

(2) _____

40. Do you expect your destiny to be
_____ determined largely by what you yourself make of it?
_____ determined largely by external circumstances over which you have little control?

41. Will there be another world war between 1957 and 2000 A.D.?
_____Yes, within 5 years
_____Yes, within 15 years
_____Yes, within 30 years
_____Yes, within 50 years
_____No

42. If there should be another world war, what would be its effect on the world as we now know it?
_____Much or most of civilization would be destroyed.
_____Destruction would not be permanent, but world progress would be very seriously retarded.
_____Things would go on much as before.

43. By the year 1975, for what purposes do you expect atomic energy to be more widely used?
_____Constructive (e.g., industrial) purposes
_____Destructive (e.g., wartime, belligerent) purposes

44. War is
_____a needless and preventable occurrence.
_____a necessary evil.
_____sometimes a good thing.

45. As a solution to the problem of international relations, four principal possibilities have been suggested. Please check the one you yourself favor, and the one you think most likely to come about in your lifetime

	Would like	Expect
(1) A situation of strong nationalism, where each country retains its full sovereignty, much as in the recent past	_____	_____
(2) Development of regionalism, for example, Pan-American Union, a United States of Western Europe, etc.	_____	_____
(3) Federal union of most noncommunist countries, with door open to Russia and other nations not at first participating	_____	_____
(4) A world government, worked out perhaps through an extension of the United Nations	_____	_____

46. Would you like to see greater equality between white and colored races within your lifetime?
_____Yes
_____No

47. Do you *expect* to see greater equality between white and colored races within your lifetime?

_____ Yes

_____ No

48. Democracy is often defined in the words of Abraham Lincoln as "government of the people, by the people, and for the people." If you were forced to do so, would you personally give greater emphasis to the conception

_____ by the people?

   or

_____ for the people?

49. Do you feel that you require some form of religious orientation or belief in order to achieve a fully mature philosophy of life?

_____ Yes

_____ No

_____ Doubtful

QUESTIONS ADDED TO THE QUESTIONNAIRE
IN THE SECOND SURVEY

1. Please indicate your age and number of brothers and sisters.

   _____Age

   _____Number of brothers and sisters

2. Consider to what extent a job or career would have to satisfy *each* of these requirements. For each of the following ten statements indicate with a check whether it is very important, somewhat important, or of little importance to you.

	Very Important	Somewhat Important	Of Little Importance
1. Provide an opportunity to use my special abilities	_____	_____	_____
2. Enable me to look forward to a stable, secure future	_____	_____	_____
3. Permit me to be creative and original	_____	_____	_____
4. Give me an opportunity to be helpful to others	_____	_____	_____
5. Provide me with a chance to earn a good deal of money	_____	_____	_____
6. Give me an opportunity to work with people rather than things	_____	_____	_____
7. Give me a chance to exercise leadership	_____	_____	_____
8. Leave me relatively free of supervision	_____	_____	_____
9. Give me social status and prestige	_____	_____	_____
10. Provide me with adventure	_____	_____	_____

   Which *one* of the ten preceding requirements is the most important of all? Write number_____

3. What do you most hope to accomplish in the course of your life?

   _____

   _____

   _____

   _____

4. Which one of the following comes nearest to being your goal in life? (Check only one.)

_____To hold high political office?

_____To achieve financial security through your own work?

_____ To become wealthy through hard work?

_____To live for the day without worrying about the future?

_____To achieve fame by doing something outstanding?

_____ To devote oneself to helping others?

_____Doing the kind of work you like without worrying about money or fame?

5. State frankly how often you experience these feelings.

I feel doubtful that I have sufficient ability to achieve my career goal.

_____Never

_____Sometimes

_____Often

I feel that external circumstances will prevent the realization of my career.

_____Never

_____Sometimes

_____Often

I feel that my determination is not strong enough to sustain me until my career goal is achieved.

_____Never

_____Sometimes

_____Often

6. Which of the following statements concerning women working do you come closest to agreeing with? (Choose only one.)

_____In general, I don't approve of women having careers.

_____I approve of a woman having a career if she wants one, providing she is not married.

_____I approve of a married woman having a career if she wants one, providing she has no children.

I approve of a married woman having a career if she wants one, providing her children are older than:

_____ Infancy to preschool (up to 5 years)

_____ Grade school (6–10 years)

_____ Junior high (11–14 years)

_____High school (15–17 years)

_____Eighteen or older

_____I approve of a married woman having a career if she wants one, regardless of the age of her children.

7. How do you expect the future standard of living (economic income) in Trinidad will compare with the present standard of living?

_____Higher standard

_____Lower standard

_____About the same

8. Which of these statements comes closest to what you think is an adequate description of the occupational situation in Trinidad? (Check only one.)

_____There will be many well-paying, secure positions available ten years from now for a person with my future qualifications.

_____There will be competition for good jobs for a person of my qualifications since there will be more people seeking work than positions available.

_____There will be severe competition for good jobs for a person of my qualifications since there will only be a few openings available and many people seeking employment.

9. Trinidad now has a greater measure of political independence from Great Britain. Do you think Trinidad will have more to gain or to lose by this situation? (Check only one.)

_____Trinidad has more to gain.

_____Being politically independent makes no difference one way or the other.

_____Trinidad has more to lose.

Please explain your answer. _____

_____

_____

10. Does Trinidad have more to gain or to lose by being a member of the Federation? (Check only one.)

_____Trinidad has more to gain.

_____Being a member of the Federation makes no difference one way or the other.

_____Trinidad has more to lose.

Please explain your answer. _____

_____

_____

11. Check the statement that most closely corresponds to your expectations. (Check only one.)

_____I do not expect to participate actively in politics.

_____I expect to take an active part in the political party of my choice.

_____I expect to devote myself entirely to a political career.

12. What is the political party of your preference?

_____DLP

_____PNM

_____Other (please specify _____)

_____None

Appendix E

Data on Higher Education

SECONDARY SCHOOL ENROLLMENT AND QUALIFICATIONS FOR UNIVERSITY ENTRANCE

Statistical analysis of school enrollment in Trinidad and Tobago for the year 1960 has recently been carried out by Roberts(1). He emphasizes the significance of obtaining census data on educational attainment at the secondary school level, especially with regard to the successful completion of the School Certificate or its equivalent as a qualification for university admission. Table E-1, taken from Roberts' study, gives the percentage of all children with School Certificates in the fifteen to nineteen year age group.

Table E-1. Proportion (%) with School Certificate among Children in School and Children Who Have Left School(a)

Age	Children in School		Children Who Have Left School		All Children Who Have Ever Been to School	
	Male	Female	Male	Female	Male	Female
15	1.55	1.15	2.29	2.07	1.82	1.63
16	4.07	3.00	2.46	3.18	3.12	3.12
17	10.39	7.33	3.98	4.66	5.93	5.30
18	15.67	11.19	3.20	3.55	5.56	4.59
19	20.63	9.55	3.66	2.51	6.52	3.32

Note: It is assumed that the age distribution of children with school certificate who have left school is the same as those with school certificate who remain in school.

a. Roberts, "A Note on School Enrolment in Trinidad and Tobago, 1960," p. 117.

1. G. W. Roberts, "A Note on School Enrolment in Trinidad and Tobago, 1960" *Social and Economic Studies, 16* (1967), 113–126.

Table E-2. Trinidadian Students in the United States,
Canada, and the United Kingdom

Country	Year	Number of Students
United States	1956–57	173(a)
	1957–58	183
	1958–59	198
	1959–60	255
	1960–61	253
	1961–62	317
	1962–63	395
	1963–64	480
	1964–65	594
	1965–66	572
Canada	1962–63	619(b)
United Kingdom	1963–64	227(c)

a. *Open Doors* (Institute of International Education, 1948-49 through 1965-66).
b. *UNESCO Statistical Yearbook for 1964* (UNESCO, 1966), p. 274.
c. *Ibid.*, p. 275.

Table E-3. West Indian Students in the United States(a)

Year	Number of Students
1948–49	750(b)
1949–50	703
1950–51	676
1951–52	619
1952–53	696
1953–54	854
1954–55	924
1955–56	831
1956–57	1,248
1957–58	1,274
1958–59	1,444
1959–60	1,563
1960–61	1,644
1961–62	1,594
1962–63	1,788
1963–64	2,091
1964–65	2,465
1965–66	2,432
Total	23,596

a. Statistics for students in other countries have been collected only since 1963, and only for fifteen sample countries.
b. *Open Doors* (Institute of International Education, 1948–49 through 1965–66).

As Roberts indicates, however, a detailed analysis would have to be undertaken of the subjects and level of passes to determine which students, in fact, are qualified to enter universities. Inferring from existing census data, Roberts estimates that there are about 550 male students and about 510 female students, at age seventeen, who hold a school certificate or its equivalent(2). Based on these estimates, Roberts calculates "very roughly" that 2.5 per cent of the male cohort and 1.4 per cent of the female cohort qualify for entry into universities(3). He concludes that "about 175 of the male and 58 of the female cohorts pass through Universities," although there may be about 2,600 males and 1,100 females in the age range of twenty to thirty-four "available for higher education in 1960(4)."

2. Of these, Roberts estimates that 250 boys are in school and 300 are out of school and that 140 of the girls are in school and 370 are out.

3. Roberts, p. 118.

4. *Ibid.*

Appendix F

Factor Analysis of the Data

In addition to standard frequencies and index construction for both surveys, factor analyses and analyses of variance were carried out. In the first survey, each category obtained from the data was arranged into either scalar or dichotomous form, as indicated. A set of seventy-five variables representing all the responses to the questionnaires and essays was obtained. The variables were intercorrelated via the Pearson Product Moment Correlation technique(1). The 75 X 75 correlation matrix was subjected to a centroid extraction process(2). The retained centroid factors were rotated orthogonally via the varimax method; scores were then computed to represent the rotated factors. Computation was made using the factor loadings as multipliers for the prospective variable. The factor scores were analyzed by the analysis of variance technique to test differences between the following variables: age, ethnicity, religion, SES, and school. No statistically significant differences in the analysis of variance by age were obtained; consequently results by age were not included.

Separate factor analyses were carried out for the male and female samples. Data from the second survey were handled in the same manner as data from the first survey, except that only twenty-seven selected variables were included. The 1961 analysis of variance tested differences on only two variables, ethnicity and SES.

1. A. L. Edwards, *Experimental Design in Psychological Research* (New York: Holt, Rinehart & Winston, 1962).

2. Harry H. Harman, *Modern Factor Analysis* (Chicago: University of Chicago Press, 1960).

Ethnic affiliation

The difference between ethnic group means is significant (.01) on this factor. East Indian and Negro subjects are more likely to perceive obstacles to achievement than white subjects. The colored subjects fall between these groups.

Ethnicity	Mean	S.D.
East Indian	2,110	6,180
Negro	2,075	6,924
Colored	1,803	6,894
White	1,516	6,787

Socioeconomic status

The difference between groups of different socioeconomic status is significant (at .01); the mean scores indicate that the degree of feelings of deprivation decreases with higher socioeconomic status.

SES	Mean	S.D.
III (Lower)	2,288	5,557
II (Middle)	1,835	6,770
I (Upper)	1,580	6,692

The analysis of variance in regard to religious affiliation, type of school attended, and age shows no significant differences.

Independent Variables	Source of Variation	S.S.	D.F.	M.S.	F	P
Ethnicity	Between	167.053	4	41.763	9.236	.01
	Within	2382.982	527	4.522		
SES	Between	533.097	3	177.699	43.617	.01
	Within	2216.260	544	4.074		
Religion						N.S.(a)
School						N.S.
Age						N.S.

a. Not significant.

FACTOR B: PESSIMISTIC OUTLOOK AMONG GIRLS

Ethnic Affiliation

Analysis of variance shows a significant difference (0.01) between ethnic groups on this factor. The means indicate the white girls tend to be less pessimistic as compared to the other groups. East Indian and Negro respondents are more likely to be pessimistic. The rank order of means is the following:

Ethnicity	Mean	S.D.
East Indian	1,192	3,189
Negro	1,115	3,344
Colored	1,056	3,690
White	0,897	2,773

Socioeconomic status

The results show a significant difference (.01) between different socioeconomic status groups. The examination of means shows that pessimistic orientation decreases as socioeconomic status increases. The rank order is the following:

SES	Mean	S.D.
III	1,204	3,619
II	1,029	2,868
I	1,055	3,726

Type of school attended

The difference between groups in the different types of schools is significant (.01). The means obtained indicate that the girls at private schools are more likely to be pessimistic than the girls at government schools. The rank order is the following:

School	Mean	S.D.
Private Form 5	1,160	3,167
Government and Government-Assisted Form 5	1,077	3,421
Government and Government-Assisted Form 6	1,038	3,305

The analysis of variance in regard to religion and age is not significant.

Independent Variables	Source of Variation	S.S.	D.F.	M.S.	F	P
Ethnicity	Between	16.679	4	4.168	3.573	.01
	Within	327.760	281	1.166		
SES	Between	20.893	3	6.964	6.038	.01
	Within	342.542	297	1.153		
School	Between	47.515	3	15.838	14.095	.01
	Within	333.713	297	1.124		
Religion						N.S.(a)
Age						N.S.

a. Not significant.

FACTOR C: FEAR OF FAILURE

Socioeconomic status

The difference between various status groups on this factor is significant (.05). The mean score of the lower class, signifying anxiety about achievement, is higher than the mean scores of the other SES groups. Group III is followed by Group I. The rank order is as follows:

SES	Mean	S.D.
III	0,188	2,472
I	0,181	2,599
II	0,158	2,319

The analysis of variance in regard to ethnic and religious affiliation, type of school attended, and age does not show significant differences.

Independent Variables	Source of Variation	S.S.	D.F.	M.S.	F	P
SES	Between	4.800	3	1.600	2.737	.05
	Within	317.890	544	.584		
Ethnicity						N.S.(a)
Religion						N.S.
School						N.S.
Age						N.S.

a. Not significant.

FACTOR D: STRIVING ORIENTATION

Ethnic Affiliation

The difference between ethnic groups on this factor is significant (.01). The group means indicate that East Indian students are more likely to have a striving orientation than students in other groups. The white group has the lowest mean, demonstrating the least striving orientation.

Ethnicity	Mean	S.D.
East Indian	9,576	4,607
Negro	7,594	5,127
Colored	7,161	5,043
White	6,130	4,884

Religious affiliation

The difference between groups is significant (.01). The means indicate a greater striving tendency among the Hindu-Moslem group than among Protestant and Catholic students.

Religion	Mean	S.D.
Hindu-Moslem	1,034	4,350
Protestant	0,765	4,738
Catholic	0,733	5,015

The analysis of variance in regard to socioeconomic status, type of school attended, and age shows no significant differences.

Independent Variables	Source of Variation	S.S.	D.F.	M.S.	F	P
Ethnicity	Between	45.441	4	11.360	4.798	.01
	Within	1247.718	527	2.368		
Religion	Between	54.707	3	18.236	7.722	.01
	Within	1221.644	544	2.361		
SES						N.S.(a)
School						N.S.
Age						N.S.

a. Not significant.

FACTOR E: "GREAT EXPECTATIONS"

Ethnic affiliation

There are significant differences (.05) between ethnic groups in means shown in the following table. The means of the various groups are presented in their rank order — the higher score signifies a low incidence of "great expectations," the lower score a high incidence of such expectations.

Ethnicity	Mean	S.D.
Colored	1,501	4,789
White	1,493	4,130
Negro	1,388	4,464
East Indian	1,367	4,653

Religious affiliation

The results show a significant difference (.05) between religious groups. The analysis of means obtained by the various religious groups shows that the Hindu-Moslem group (lower score) is more likely to have "great expectations" when compared to the other religious groups (Catholic and Protestant). The rank order is the following:

Religion	Mean	S.D.
Catholic	1,447	4,437
Protestant	1,441	4,776
Hindu-Moslem	1,320	4,544

The analysis of variance in regard to socioeconomic status, type of school attended, and age does not show significant differences on this factor.

Independent Variables	Source of Variation	S.S.	D.F.	M.S.	F	P
Ethnicity	Between	21.240	4	5.310	2.517	.05
	Within	1111.445	527	2.109		
Religion	Between	23.996	3	7.999	3.759	.05
	Within	1157.439	544	2.128		
SES						N.S.(a)
School						N.S.
Age						N.S.

a. Not significant.

FACTOR F: NON-ACHIEVEMENT ORIENTATION (SECOND SURVEY)

Ethnic affiliation

The results show a significant difference (.05) between ethnic groups. Comparing the means obtained by the groups, the colored and white students generally show lack of ambition more frequently than the other groups. East Indian students show the least lack of ambition. The rank order is the following:

Ethnicity	Mean	S.D.
Colored	3,973	4,678
White	1,685	4,540
Negro	0,828	5,097
East Indian	0,230	5,191

Socioeconomic status

There is a significant difference (.01) between the groups. The means obtained by the groups indicate that the lower-class students are considerably less likely to express lack of ambition than students in the other groups. The rank order is the following:

SES	Mean	S.D.
II	1,985	5,085
I	1,756	5,066
III	0,561	4,835

Independent Variables	Source of Variation	S.S.	D.F.	M.S.	F	P
Ethnicity	Between	26.961	3	8.987	3.478	.05
	Within	591.698	229	2.584		
SES	Between	33.360	2	16.680	6.615	.01
	Within	574.833	228	2.521		

FACTOR G: PRIVATISM

Ethnic affilation

The difference between ethnic groups is significant (at .05) on this factor. The means obtained by the various groups show that the white students are more likely to be privatistic as compared to the other groups. The Negroes and the East Indians have the lowest scores on this factor.

Ethnicity	Mean	S.D.
White	9,350	1,673
Colored	8,571	1,902
East Indian	8,472	1,771
Negro	8,449	1,857

Type of school attended

The difference between the groups attending various types of schools is significant (.05). The students in Form 6 of government and government-assisted schools are most likely to score high on this factor; those in Form 5 of such schools are less likely to do so; and those at private schools show the least degree of privatistic orientation.

School	Mean	S.D.
Government and Government-Assisted Form 6	9,113	1,690
Government and Government-Assisted Form 5	8,558	1,843
Private	8,218	1,692

The analysis of variance in regard to socioeconomic status, religious affiliation, and age shows no significant differences.

Independent Variables	Source of Variation	S.S.	D.F.	M.S.	F	P
Ethnicity	Between	404.374	4	101.094	3.078	.05
	Within	17306.544	527	32.840		
School	Between	349.409	3	116.470	3.609	.05
	Within	17553.006	544	32.260		
SES						N.S.(a)
Religion						N.S.
Age						N.S.

a. Not significant.

FACTOR H: COMMUNAL ROOTEDNESS

Ethnic affiliation

There are significant differences (.01) between ethnic groups. The lower the score, the higher the communal rootedness.

Ethnicity	Mean	S.D.
White	1,012	4,796
Colored	0,805	4,839
East Indian	0,706	4,262
Negro	0,778	4,347

The analysis of variance in regard to socioeconomic status, religious affiliation, type of school attended, and age shows no significant differences on this factor.

Independent Variables	Source of Variation	S.S.	D.F.	M.S.	F	P
Ethnicity	Between	39.375	4	9.844	4.980	.01
	Within	1041.557	527	1.976		
Religion						N.S.(a)
SES						N.S.
School						N.S.
Age						N.S.

a. Not significant.

FACTOR I: PESSIMISM ABOUT NATIONAL AFFAIRS
(SECOND SURVEY)

Ethnic affiliation

There is a significant difference (.01) between ethnic groups on this factor. According to the means obtained by the various groups, the East Indian students rank highest, followed by the colored and white, and the Negro students rank lowest on this factor. The rank order is the following:

Ethnicity	Mean	S.D.
East Indian	2,102	7,486
Colored	1,815	6,898
White	1,790	8,482
Negro	1,489	5,456

Socioeconomic status

The difference between socioeconomic groups is significant at .01. Comparing the means obtained, the lower-class students are more likely to score high on this dimension than the two other groups. The rank order is the following:

SES	Mean	S.D.
III	2,092	7,909
II	1,673	5,766
I	1,628	8,274

Independent Variables	Source of Variation	S.S.	D.F.	M.S.	F	P
Ethnicity	Between	170.984	3	56.995	11.708	.01
	Within	1114.742	229	4.868		
SES	Between	102.577	2	51.289	9.897	.01
	Within	1181.500	228	5.182		

Appendix G: Achievement Orientation

Table G-1. Profile of Achievement Orientation, by Sex and Ethnicity (First Survey)
(in percentages)

	BOYS				GIRLS			
	White	Negro	East Indian	Colored	White	Negro	East Indian	Colored
	(40)	(139)	(207)	(83)	(17)	(115)	(72)	(52)
Mentions occupation, education and/or money as one of two things he would most like to have that he does not now have.	52	58	74	39	20	56	62	49
Mentions occupation, education and/or money as one of two things he would most like his child to have that he himself did not have.	17	45	48	35	27	44	37	32
Mentions career or occupation as the most important source of satisfaction in life.	36	51	57	35	47	47	57	41
Expects to be more successful as a leader in his field than the average person with the same amount of education.	48	56	56	47	13	39	49	28
Would be willing to make the greatest sacrifice of personal comfort, time, and money for education.	5	12	16	13	—	8	15	4
Expects to achieve world fame, power, and/or riches as final goal (in essay).	26	39	46	17	—	—	4	—
As a parent will try hardest to teach his children value of education, striving, and hard work.	33	42	45	23	20	26	34	19
Mentions university education for his children (in essay).	25	37	45	27	25	37	45	22
Mentions obtaining profession, achieving goal, as life accomplishment of which he would be proudest.	68	73	67	69	14	59	54	49

Table G-2. Profile of Achievement Orientation
by Ethnicity (Second Survey)(a)
(in percentage)

	Colored (21)	East Indian (104)	Negro (82)	White (28)
Mentions occupation, education and/or money as one of two things he would most like to have that he does not now have	33	69	39	36
Mentions occupation, education and/or money as one of two things he would most like his child to have that he himself did not have	48	57	48	18
Mentions career or occupation as the most important source of satisfaction in life	19	47	46	36
Expects to be more successful as a leader in his field than the average person in his field who has the same amount of education	48	52	45	57
As a parent will try hardest to teach his children the value of education, striving, and hard work	27	57	33	32

a.The number of items included in the second survey is smaller than in the first. Only the items common to both are enumerated here.

Appendix H

Social Orientation

Table H. Index of Social Orientation,
by Ethnicity and Socioeconomic Class(a) (First Survey)
(in percentage)

Socioeconomic Class	Colored	East Indian	Negro	White(b)
Boys				
Class I	(22)	(30)	(12)	—
	36	57	60	
Class II	(23)	(63)	(20)	—
	47	60	69	
Class III	(28)	(103)	(50)	—
	13	69	69	
Girls				
Class I	(14)	(19)	(10)	—
	36	37	30	
Class II	(15)	(14)	(24)	—
	33	29	46	
Class III	(22)	(30)	(79)	—
	36	60	47	

a. SES is based on father's occupation.
b. SES breakdown of white sample was not possible due to their homogeneity.

Appendix I

Students' Interest in National, Regional, and World Problems

Table I. Percentages of Students Most Interested in Problems
of Trinidad, the West Indies and the World, by Sex and Ethnicity

	Colored	East Indian	Negro	White
First Survey				
Boys	(83)	(207)	(139)	(40)
Problems of Trinidad	29	25	23	21
Problems of West Indies	20	20	31	12
Problems of World	47	53	42	64
No Answer	4	2	4	3
Girls	(52)	(72)	(115)	(17)
Problems of Trinidad	43	47	24	13
Problems of West Indies	14	9	31	13
Problems of World	43	42	41	73
No Answer	—	2	4	1
Second Survey	(21)	(104)	(82)	(28)
Problems of Trinidad	34	33	27	25
Problems of West Indies	14	3	18	14
Problems of World	52	64	55	61
No Answer	—	—	—	—

Appendix J

Expectations of Marriage

Table J. Expectations of Marriage, by Ethnicity and
Socioeconomic Class(a)

	Colored			East Indian			Negro		
	N	%	No Answer	N	%	No Answer	N	%	No Answer
Boys									
Class I	(22)	91	9	(30)	87	13	(21)	90	10
Class II	(24)	96	4	(63)	88	12	(30)	93	7
Class III	(29)	86	14	(105)	93	7	(73)	92	8
Girls									
Class I	(14)	100	–	(25)	97	3	(11)	100	–
Class II	(15)	100	–	(17)	100	–	(24)	100	–
Class III	(22)	87	13	(34)	97	3	(81)	95	5

a. Percentage answering *yes* to the question: *Do you expect to marry some time or other?*

Bibliography

Antonovsky, A., and Lerner, M. "Occupational Aspirations of Lower Class Negro and White Youth," *Social Problems, 7* (1959), 132–138.

Apter, David. *Politics of Modernization.* Chicago: University of Chicago Press, 1965.

Atreya, B. L. "Indian Culture: Its Spiritual, Moral and Social Aspects," in United Nations Educational, Scientific and Cultural Organization, *Inter-relations of Cultures.* Paris: UNESCO, 1953. Pp. 123–157.

Ausubel, David P. *Maori Youth.* Wellington, New Zealand: Price Milburn, 1961.

Basalla, George. "The Spread of Western Science," *Science, 156* (1967), 611–622.

Benedict, Ruth, *Patterns of Culture.* Boston: Houghton Mifflin, 1934.

Blake, Judith. *Family Structure in Jamaica.* New York: Free Press of Glencoe, 1961.

Bloom, L. "Self-Concepts and Social Status in South Africa: A Preliminary Cross-Cultural Analysis," *The Journal of Social Psychology, 51* (1960), 103–112.

Braithwaite, Lloyd. "The Development of Higher Education in the West Indies," *Social and Economic Studies, 7* (1958), 1–64.

———. "The Role of the University in the Developing Society of the West Indies," *Social and Economic Studies, 14* (1965), 76–87.

———. "Social Stratification in Trinidad," *Social and Economic Studies, 2, 2–3* (1953), 5–175.

———, and Roberts, G. W. "Mating Patterns and Prospects in Trinidad," in Trinidad and Tobago, Central Statistical Office, *Research Papers, No. 4.* Port of Spain: Government Printing Office, 1967. Pp. 120–127.

Brathwaite, Edward. *Rights of Passage.* London: Oxford University Press, 1967.

Brenner, Charles. *An Elementary Textbook of Psychoanalysis.* Garden City, N.Y.: Doubleday, 1955.

Burns, Sir Alan Cuthbert. *History of the British West Indies.* London: Allen & Unwin, 1954.

Carmichael, Gertrude. *The History of the West Indian Islands of Trinidad and Tobago, 1498–1900.* London: Redman, 1961.

Carr, Andrew. "The Rada Community in Trinidad," *Caribbean Quarterly, 3* (1953), 36–54.

Carrington, Edwin. "The Post-War Political Economy of Trinidad and Tobago–I," *New World Quarterly, 4, 1* (1967), 45–67.

Clarke, Colin. "Caste among Hindus in a Town in Trinidad: San Fernando," in Barton M. Schwartz, ed., *Caste in Overseas Indian Communities.* San Francisco: Chandler, 1967. Pp. 165–199.

Cohen, Yehudi A. "On Alternative Views of the Individual in Culture-and-Personality Studies," *American Anthropologist, 68* (1966), 355–361.

Colson, Elizabeth. "Competence and Incompetence in Context of Independence," *Current Anthropology, 8* (1967), 92–100.

Comitas, Lambros. *Caribbeana 1900–1965: A Topical Bibliography*. Seattle: University of Washington Press, for Research Institute for the Study of Man, 1968.

———. "Occupational Multiplicity in Rural Jamaica," in *Proceedings of the 1963 Annual Spring Meeting of the American Ethnological Society, Symposium on Community Studies in Anthropology*, pp. 41–50.

Crowley, Daniel J. "Plural and Differential Acculturation in Trinidad," *American Anthropologist, 59* (1957), 817–824.

Cumper, George Edward. "The Differentiation of Economic Groups in the West Indies," *Social and Economic Studies, 11* (1962), 319–332.

Curtin, Philip D. "Epidemiology and the Slave Trade," *Political Science Quarterly, 83* (1968), 190–216.

———. *The Image of Africa*. Madison: University of Wisconsin Press, 1964.

Danziger, Kurt. "Psychological Future of an Oppressed Group," *Social Forces, 42* (1963), 31–40.

De Verteuil, L. A. *Trinidad: Its Geography, Natural Resources, Administration, Present Conditions and Future Prospects*, 2nd ed. London: Cassell, 1884.

Edwards, A. L. *Experimental Design in Psychological Research*. New York: Holt, Rinehart & Winston, 1962.

Elkins, Stanley. *Slavery: A Problem in American Institutional and Intellectual Life*. Chicago: University of Chicago Press, 1959.

Erikson, Erik H. *Childhood and Society*. New York, Norton, 1950.

———. "The Concept of Identity in Race Relations: Notes and Queries," *Daedalus, Proceedings of the American Academy of Arts and Sciences, 95* (1966), 145–171.

Figueroa, John. *Staffing and Examinations in the British Caribbean Secondary Schools: A Report of Conference of Caribbean Heads, July, 1961*. London: Evans Bros., 1964.

Frazier, E. Franklin. *The Negro Family in the United States*, rev. and abridged ed. New York: Dryden Press, 1951.

Freud, Anna. *The Ego and the Mechanisms of Defense*. New York: International Universities Press, 1946.

Freud, Sigmund. *Collected Papers*, Vol. IV. London: Hogarth Press, 1956.

Freyre, Gilberto. *The Masters and the Slaves: A Study in the Development of Brazilian Civilization*. New York: Knopf, 1956.

Gillespie, James M., and Allport, Gordon W. *Youth's Outlook on the Future: A Cross National Study*. New York: Doubleday, 1955.

Gist, N. P., and Bennett, W. S. "Aspirations of Negro and White Students," *Social Forces, 42* (1963), 40–48.

Glock, Charles Y., ed. *Survey Research in the Social Sciences*. New York: Russell Sage Foundation, 1967.

Goldsen, Rose K.; Rosenberg, Morris; Williams, Robin M., Jr.; and Suchman, Edward A. *What College Students Think*. Princeton, N.J.: Van Nostrand, 1960.

Goode, William J. "Illegitimacy in the Caribbean Social Structure," *American Sociological Review, 25* (1960), 21–30.

Gooding, Nathaniel M. "Education in Trinidad, Past and Present," Doctoral dissertation, University of Connecticut, 1961.

Gordon, Shirley C. *A Century of West Indian Education*. London: Longmans, 1963.

Goveia, Elsa V. *Slave Society in the British Leeward Islands at the End of the Eighteenth Century*. New Haven: Yale University Press, 1965.

Gray, S. "The Vocational Preferences of Negro School Children in Trinidad," *Journal of Genetic Psychology, 64* (1944), 239–247.

Great Britain, Central Office of Information. *Education in the United Kingdom Dependencies.* Reference Pamphlet No. 4. London: H.M.S.O., 1955.

Green, Helen. "Values of Negro and East Indian School Children in Trinidad," *Social and Economic Studies, 14* (1965), 204–224.

Greenfield, Sidney. *English Rustics in Black Skin.* New Haven: College and University Press, 1966.

Hanke, Lewis. "The Dawn of Conscience in America: Spanish Experiments and Experiences with Indians in the New World," *Proceedings of the American Philosophical Society, 107* (1963), 83–92.

Harewood, Jack. "Population Growth in Trinidad and Tobago in the Twentieth Century," *Social and Economic Studies, 12* (1963), 1–26.

Harman, Harry H. *Modern Factor Analysis.* Chicago: University of Chicago Press, 1960.

Henriques, Fernando. *Family and Colour in Jamaica.* London: Eyre & Spottiswoode, 1953.

Herskovits, Frances and Melville J. *Trinidad Village.* New York: Knopf, 1947.

Himmelweit, Hilde T. "Social Background, Education and Work: A Conceptual Analysis Derived from a Follow-up Study of Adolescents." Paper presented at the International Congress of Psychology, Moscow, 1966.

Hoetink, Harry. " 'Colonial Psychology' and Race," *Journal of Economic History, 21* (1961), 629–640.

Hyman, Herbert H.; Payaslioğlu, A.; and Frey, F. W. "The Values of Turkish College Youth," *Public Opinion Quarterly, 22* (1958), 275–291.

Indian Centenary Review: 100 Years of Progress, 1845–1945, Trinidad, B.W.I. Port of Spain: Indian Centenary Review Committee, no date.

Inhelder, Bärbel, and Piaget, Jean. *The Growth of Logical Thinking.* New York: Basic Books, 1958.

Inter-American Committee on the Alliance for Progress (CIAP). *Domestic Efforts and the Needs for External Financing for the Development of Trinidad and Tobago.* Washington, D.C.: Pan American Union, 1967.

Jahoda, Gustav. "Social Aspirations, Magic and Witchcraft in Ghana: A Social Psychological Interpretation," in P. C. Lloyd, ed., *New Elites of Tropical Africa.* London: Oxford University Press, 1966. Pp. 199–212.

Jayawardena, Chandra. *Conflict and Solidarity in a Guianese Plantation.* London: Athlone Press, 1963.

Kahl, Joseph A. "Educational and Occupational Aspirations of 'Common Man' Boys," *Harvard Educational Review,* No. 23 (1953), 186–203.

Keller, Suzanne. *Beyond the Ruling Class.* New York: Random House, 1963.

———, and Zavalloni, Marisa. "Ambition and Social Class: A Respecification," *Social Forces, 43* (1964), 58–70.

Klass, Morton. *East Indians in Trinidad: A Study in Cultural Persistence.* New York: Columbia University Press, 1961.

Klineberg, Otto. *Social Psychology.* New York: Holt, 1940; rev. ed., 1954.

Lamming, George. *The Pleasures of Exile.* London: Michael Joseph, 1960.

Lampl-de Groot, J. "Ego-Ideal and Super-Ego," in Ruth S. Eissler et al., eds., *The Psychoanalytic Study of the Child,* Vol. 17. New York: International Universities Press, 1962. Pp. 94–106.

Lehman, Harvey C., and Witty, Paul A. "A Study of Vocational Attitudes in Relation to Pubescence," *American Journal of Psychology, 43* (1931), 93–101.

Lerner, Daniel. *The Passing of Traditional Society.* Glencoe, Ill.: The Free Press, 1958.

Lewis, Gordon K. *The Growth of the Modern West Indies.* New York: Monthly Review Press, 1968.

Lewis, Hylan, "Culture, Class and the Behavior of Low Income Families." Paper prepared for Conference on Views of Lower Class Culture, New York, June 27–29, 1963.

Lewis, Oscar. *A Study of Slum Culture: Backgrounds for La Vida.* New York: Random House, 1968.

Lewis, Sir W. Arthur. "Education and Economic Development," *Social and Economic Studies, 10* (1961), 113–127.

———. *Politics in West Africa.* New York: Oxford University Press, 1965.

Liebow, Elliot. *Tally's Corner.* Boston: Little, Brown, 1967.

Lipschütz, Alejandro. *El Indoamericanismo y el Problema Racial en las Américas,* 2nd ed. Santiago de Chile: Nascimento, 1944.

Lipset, Seymour, and Bendix, Reinhard. *Social Mobility in Industrial Society.* Berkeley: University of California Press, 1959.

Lowenthal, David. *The West Indies Federation.* New York: Columbia University Press, 1961.

McClelland, David C. *The Achieving Society.* Princeton, N.J.: Van Nostrand, 1961.

———. "Does Education Accelerate Economic Growth?" *Economic Development and Cultural Change, 14* (1966), 257–278.

McDonald, Ellen. "Educated Women: The Last Minority?" *Columbia University Forum, 10,* 2 (1967), 30–34.

Mead, Margaret. *New Lives for Old: A Cultural Transformation, Manus, 1928–1953.* New York: Apollo Editions, 1956.

Merton, Robert K. *Social Theory and Social Structure,* rev. ed. Glencoe, Ill.: The Free Press, 1957.

Miller, D. R., and Swanson, G. E. *Inner Conflict and Defense.* New York: Holt, Rinehart & Winston, 1960.

Millette, James. "The Founding of a New Society – Trinidad, 1783–1810." Typescript, 1966.

Mischel, Walter. "Delay of Gratification, Need for Achievement and Acquiescence in Another Culture," *Journal of Abnormal and Social Psychology, 62* (1961), 543–552.

Moerman, Michael. "Ethnic Identification in a Complex Civilization: Who Are the Lue?" *American Anthropologist, 67* (1965), 1215–1230.

Mörner, Magnus. "The History of Race Relations in Latin America: Some Comments on the State of Research," *Latin American Research Review, 1,* 3 (1966), 17–44.

———. *Race Mixture in the History of Latin America.* Boston: Little, Brown, 1967.

Morse, Richard M. "The Heritage of Latin America," in Louis Hartz, *The Founding of New Societies.* New York: Harcourt, Brace & World, 1964. Pp. 123–177.

Murray, Henry A., et al. *Explorations in Personality.* New York: Oxford University Press, 1938.

Naipaul, V. S. *A House for Mr. Biswas.* London: Deutsch, 1961.

Narain, Dhirendra. "Indian National Character in the Twentieth Century," *The Annals of the American Academy of Political and Social Science, 370* (1967), 124–132.

Nath, Dwarka. *A History of Indians in British Guiana.* London: Thomas Nelson and Sons, 1950.

"National Character in the Perspective of the Social Sciences," *The Annuals of the American Academy of Political and Social Science, 370* (1967).

Niehoff, Arthur. "The Function of Caste among the Indians of the Oropuche Lagoon, Trinidad," in Barton M. Schwartz, ed., *Caste in Overseas Indian Communities.* San Francisco: Chandler, 1967. Pp. 149–163.

———, and Juanita. *East Indians in the West Indies.* Milwaukee: Milwaukee Public Museum Publications in Anthropology, 1960.

Ottley, Carlton Robert. *The Story of Port of Spain.* Port of Spain: The Author, 1962.

Parry, John Horace, and Sherlock, Philip M. *A Short History of the West Indies.* New York: St. Martin's Press, 1956.

Parsons, Talcott. *Essays in Sociological Theory.* Glencoe, Ill.: The Free Press, 1954.

Patterson, Orlando. *The Sociology of Slavery.* London: MacGibbon & Kee, 1967.

Roberts, George W. "A Note on School Enrolment in Trinidad and Tobago, 1960," *Social and Economic Studies, 16* (1967), 113–126.

———. "Populations of the Non-Spanish-Speaking Caribbean," in Pan-American Assembly on Population, Cali, Colombia, 1965, *Population Dilemma in Latin America.* Washington, D.C.: Potomac Books, 1966. Pp. 61–85.

———. "Reproductive Performance and Reproductive Capacity in Less Industrialized Societies," *The Annals of the American Academy of Political and Social Science, 369* (1967), 37–47.

———. "Some Aspects of Mating and Fertility in the West Indies," *Population Studies, 8* (1955), 199–227.

———, and Abdulah, N. "Some Observations on the Educational Position of the British Caribbean," *Social and Economic Studies, 14* (1965), 144–153.

———, and Braithwaite, Lloyd. "Fertility Differentials in Trinidad," in International Population Conference, Vienna, 1959, *Report.* Vienna: The Working Committee of the Conference, 1959.

———. "Mating among East Indian and Non-Indian Women in Trinidad," *Social and Economic Studies, 11* (1962), 203–240.

Roberts, G. W., and Byrne, J. "Summary Statistics on Indenture and Associated Migration Affecting the West Indies, 1834–1918," *Population Studies, 20* (1966), 125–134.

Rodman, Hyman. "The Lower Class Value Stretch." Revision of paper read at the Annual Meeting of the Eastern Sociological Society, April, 1961.

Roe, Anne. *The Psychology of Occupations.* New York: John Wiley, 1956.

Romain, Ralph. "The Character of West Indian Society and Its Implications for Teacher Training," in UNESCO/UWI Seminar on Curriculum and Teacher Training, University of the West Indies, 1967, *Report,* Appendix 4. St. Augustine, Trinidad: University of the West Indies, 1968.

Rosenberg, Morris. *Society and the Adolescent Self-Image.* Princeton: Princeton University Press, 1965.

Rouse, Irving. "The Arawak," in Julian H. Steward, ed., *Handbook of South American Indians,* Smithsonian Institution Bureau of American Ethnology Bulletin 143, Vol. 4. Washington, D.C.: Government Printing Office, 1948. Pp. 507–546.

Rubin, Vera. "The Adolescent: His Expectations and His Society," in *The Adolescent in the Changing Caribbean: Proceedings of the 3rd Caribbean Conference for Mental Health, University of the West Indies, Jamaica, 1961.* Pp. 56–67.

———. "Approaches to the Study of National Characteristics in a Multicultural Society," *International Journal of Social Psychiatry, 5* (1959), 20–26.

———. Caribbean Studies: A Symposium, 3rd ed. American Ethnological Society Monograph No. 34. Seattle: University of Washington Press, 1966.

———. "Colonialism, Nationalism and Parochialism in the West Indies." Paper read at American Association for the Advancement of Science Symposium on the Development of New Nations, New York, December, 1960.

———. "Culture, Politics and Race Relations," *Social and Economic Studies, 11* (1962), 433–455.

———. "Family Aspirations and Attitudes of Trinidad Youth," in *Children of the Caribbean—Their Mental Health Needs: Proceedings of the 2d Caribbean Conference for Mental Health, St. Thomas, Virgin Islands, 1959.* San Juan, Puerto Rico: Department of Health, 1961. Pp. 59–68.

———. "Fifty Years in Rootville." Doctoral dissertation, Columbia University, 1951.

———. "The West Indian Family," in *Family Relationships: 4th Caribbean Conference for Mental Health, Curacao, Netherlands Antilles, 1963.* Caribbean Federation for Mental Health, 1965. Pp. 53–65.

248

————, ed. *Plantation Systems of the New World.* Washington, D.C.: Pan American Union and Research Institute for the Study of Man, 1959.

————, and Comitas, Lambros. "The Caribbean as an Ethnographic Region: Theories and Methodologies for the Study of Complex Societies." Paper read at the VII International Congress of Anthropology and Ethnology, Moscow, 1964.

Ryan, Selwyn Douglas. "Decolonization in a Multiracial Society: A Case Study of Trinidad and Tobago." Doctoral dissertation, York University, Toronto, 1967.

Schachtel, Ernest G. *Metamorphosis.* New York: Basic Books, 1959.

Schwartz, Barton M., ed. *Caste in Overseas Indian Communities.* San Francisco: Chandler, 1967.

————. "The Failure of Caste in Trinidad," in Schwartz, ed., *Caste in Overseas Indian Communities.* San Francisco: Chandler, 1967. Pp. 117–147.

Sherlock, Philip M. "Prospects in the Caribbean," *Foreign Affairs, 41* (1963), 744–755.

————. *West Indian Folk-Tales.* London: Oxford University Press, 1966.

Sieuchand, A. C. "A Study of the Aspirations of Three Racial Groups in the Grammar Schools of Trinidad, West Indies." Thesis, Diploma in Social Psychology of Education, University of Leicester, Institute of Education, 1961.

Singer, Milton. "Religion and Social Change in India: The Max Weber Thesis, Phase Three," *Economic Development and Cultural Change,* 14 (1966), 497–505.

Skinner, Elliott P. "Group Dynamics and Social Stratification in British Guiana," in Vera Rubin, ed., *Social and Cultural Pluralism in the Caribbean, Annals of the New York Academy of Sciences, 83,* 5 (1960), 904–912.

Smith, M. G. "Historical and Cultural Conditions of Political Corruption among the Hausa," *Comparative Studies in Society and History, 6* (1964), 164–194.

————. "Social and Cultural Pluralism," in Vera Rubin, ed., *Social and Cultural Pluralism in the Caribbean, Annals of the New York Academy of Sciences, 83,* 5 (1960), 763–777.

————. "Some Aspects of Social Structure in the British Caribbean about 1820," *Social and Economic Studies, 1,* 4 (1953), 55–80.

Smith, R. T. *British Guiana.* London: Oxford University Press, 1962.

————. *The Negro Family in British Guiana.* New York: Grove Press, 1956.

————. "People and Change," *New World, Guyana Independence Issue,* 1966, pp. 49–54.

Spiro, Melford. "Social System, Personality, and Functional Analysis," in Bert Kaplan, ed., *Studying Personality Cross-Culturally.* Evanston, Ill.: Row, Peterson, 1961.

Staley, Eugene. "Education's Role in Nation Building," *Science, 153* (1966), 47–49.

Steward, Julian. *Area Research: Theory and Practice.* New York: Social Science Research Council, 1950.

————. "Prediction and Planning in Culture Change," *Human Organization, 18* (1959), 5–7.

Stoetzel, J. *Without the Chrysanthemum and the Sword.* New York: Columbia University Press and UNESCO, 1955.

Strumpel, Burkhard. "Consumption Aspirations: Incentives for Economic Change," *Social and Economic Studies, 14* (1965), 183–193.

Tannenbaum, Frank. *Slave and Citizen, the Negro in the Americas.* New York: Knopf, 1946.

Theobald, Robert. "Technological Change: Threat or Promise?" *American Journal of Orthopsychiatry, 37* (1967), 127–138.

Thibaut, J. W., and Kelly, H. H. *The Social Psychology of Groups.* New York: John Wiley, 1959.

Tiryakian, Edward A. "Educational Changes in Underdeveloped Areas and Consequences for the Social Structure." Paper presented to the Annual Meeting of the American Sociological Association, August, 1960.

Trinidad and Tobago. *Draft Plan for Educational Development in Trinidad and Tobago.* Port of Spain: Government Printery, 1968.

———, Central Statistical Office. *Annual Statistical Digest, No. 8.* Port of Spain: Government Printing Office, 1957.

———. *A Digest of Statistics on Education, 1959.* Port of Spain: Government Printing Office, 1961.

———. *A Digest of Statistics on Education, 1961.* Port of Spain: Government Printing Office, 1964.

———. *The Size and Structure of the Labour Force: Report on the Labour Force Survey, No. 2, 1956.* Port of Spain: Government Printing Office, 1957.

———, Committee on General Education. *Education Report 1959* Port of Spain: Government Printer, 1960.

———, Ministry of Labour. *Report on the Manpower Situation in Trinidad and Tobago, No. 1.* Port of Spain: Government Printing Office, 1959.

———, National Planning Commission. *Draft Second Five-Year Plan, 1964–1968.* Port of Spain: Government Printery, 1963.

———, Office of the Premier and Ministry of Finance. *Economic Survey, 1958.* Port of Spain, 1959.

———, Working Party on Education in Trinidad and Tobago. *Report.* Port of Spain: Government Printing Office, 1954.

Veness, Thelma. *School Leavers: Their Aspirations and Expectations.* London: Methuen, 1962.

Weinstein, Edwin A. Review of Lloyd H. Rogler and August B. Hollingshead, *Trapped: Families and Schizophrenia* (New York: 1965), *Caribbean Studies,* 6, 3 (1966), 56–60.

Weller, Judith Ann. "A Study of the Regulation of the East Indian Indenture System in Trinidad, 1845-1917." Doctoral dissertation, Columbia University, 1965.

White, R. W. *The Abnormal Personality,* rev. ed. New York: Ronald, 1957.

Williams, Eric. *Capitalism and Slavery.* Chapel Hill, N.C.: University of North Carolina Press, 1944.

———. *Education in the British West Indies.* Port of Spain: Guardian Commercial Printery, 1950.

———. *The Historical Background of Race Relations in the Caribbean.* Port of Spain: The Author, 1955.

———. *History of the People of Trinidad and Tobago.* London: Deutsch, 1964.

———. *Massa Day Done.* Port of Spain: PNM Publishing Company, 1961.

———. *The Negro in the Caribbean.* Bronze Booklet No. 8. Washington, D.C.: Associates in Negro Folk Education, 1942.

———. *Three Speeches: Reorganisation of the Public Service.* Port of Spain: PNM Publishing Company, 1965.

———. *The University–Symbol of Freedom.* Port of Spain: Government Printing Office, 1963.

Wolf, Eric. Review of Emerich Francis, *Ethnos und Demos: Soziologische Beiträge zur Volkstheorie* (Berlin, 1965), *American Anthropologist,* 68 (1966), 1258–1259.

Wood, Donald. *Trinidad in Transition: The Years after Slavery.* London: Oxford University Press, 1968.

Worsley, Peter. *The Third World.* Chicago: University of Chicago Press, 1964.

Wright, Richard. *Black Boy.* New York: Harper & Row, 1945.

Index

251

252